Parkinson's Disease:

Studies i~ ~~~~~~~~~~~~~~~~ ~~~~~ ~~~~

Parkinson's Disease:
Studies in Psychological and Social Care

Edited by

Ray Percival and Peter Hobson

Parkinson's
Disease Society

BPS
BOOKS

THE BRITISH
PSYCHOLOGICAL
SOCIETY

First published in 1999 by BPS Books (The British Psychological Society),
St Andrews House, 48 Princess Road East, Leicester LE1 7DR, UK; and the
Parkinson's Disease Society, 215 Vauxhall Bridge Road, London SW1V 1EJ, UK.

Transferred to Digital print 2003

A catalogue record for this book is available from the British Library.

ISBN 1 85433 299 6

Printed and bound in Great Britain by
Marston Lindsay Ross International Ltd,
Oxfordshire

Contents

Part II. Assessments and interventions

Figures

Contents

Yvonne Awenat, Clinical Nurse Practitioner, Salford NHS Trust

Margaret Boddy, Speech and Language Therapist, Community Health, Sheffield NHS Trust

Dr Colin Chandler, Reader in Social Work, Health and Education, University of Northumbria at Newcastle

Rosemary Chesson, Reader in Health Services Research, Robert Gordons University

Dr Carl E. Clarke, Reader in Clinical Neurology, University of Birmingham

Dr Anne D. M. Davies, Senior Lecturer in Psychology, University of Liverpool

Roger Grimshaw, Research Associate, Centre for Crime and Justice Studies

Caroline Haw, Speech and Language Therapist, Community Health, Sheffield NHS Trust

Peter Hobson, Senior Research Officer, University of Wales

Dr Robert Jones, General Practitioner and Senior Lecturer (retired), University of Exeter

Professor Ruth Lesser, Professor of Speech & Language, University of Newcastle-upon-Tyne

Professor Nadina B. Lincoln, Professor of Clinical Psychology, University of Nottingham

Margaret Lloyd, Senior Lecturer in Social Policy and Social Work, University of Manchester

Dr Marie Oxtoby, Social Scientist, Welfare Research Committee, Parkinson's Disease Society

Dr Brian Pentland, Consultant Neurologist, University of Edinburgh

Ray Percival, Educational Psychologist and Scottish Office Senior Adviser (retired), Welfare Research Committee, Parkinson's Disease Society

Sue Watts, Clinical Psychologist, Salford NHS Trust

Stella Yarrow, Research Fellow, University of Westminster

Foreword

Parkinson's disease is often thought of as just a medical condition, and the social aspects are sometimes overlooked. The physical effects of the condition can be very distressing and disabling themselves, but they also influence the social aspects of someone's life. The ability to perform daily living activities that many of us take for granted, like driving, shopping, eating out, and conversation, are all affected by Parkinson's.

The social effects of Parkinson's, in addition to the physical symptoms, are an abiding memory of my own personal experience of the condition. Many people remember Terry Thomas as a great comic actor, as do I, but I also remember him as my second cousin who had Parkinson's.

Sadly, the larger than life character that Terry was both on and off the screen is very different from the man I remember during the later stages of his life. At times unable to talk, walk, or move in the way he wanted to, Terry fought his own personal battle up until his death in 1990. It is a battle that thousands of others are fighting every day.

I remember a time with Terry when the two of us were alone together. I thought he might like a drink, so I asked him if he would like a glass of champagne. He didn't answer at first, he just looked at me and I looked at him. The silence carried on for a couple of minutes, and still we looked at each other. I wasn't sure what to do until, after another couple of minutes had gone by, he said: 'How about a crate?'

It wasn't that he made me wait on purpose, or that he couldn't think of anything to say, it was simply that he couldn't answer my question when he wanted to. He needed time to give his response, and to make me laugh as he always did. He found starting to talk difficult, just as people with Parkinson's find it hard to start any activity.

There are thousands of stories like Terry's, stories of people whose quality of life has been affected by Parkinson's. My own clear memories of Terry meant that I didn't hesitate when I was invited to become President of the Parkinson's Disease Society. And for the past five years I have seen at first hand how the Society provides real help and support for people with Parkinson's and their families.

Medical research into Parkinson's is vital, so that one day we can find the cause of the illness and then hopefully find a cure. However, research into the effects of Parkinson's on quality of life issues, so that we know more about what it is like to live with the condition, is also crucial.

Parkinson's Disease: Studies in Psychological and Social Care provides an insight through past research into what it is like to live with Parkinson's, both as someone with the condition and as someone caring for a family member. Carers play a very important role in the management of Parkinson's and their needs, as well as those of the person they care for, need to be considered.

This book also illustrates how therapies other than drug treatments play a key role in the management of Parkinson's. Speech and language therapy and physiotherapy, to name but two, can be of enormous benefit to people with Parkinson's.

The more that is known about Parkinson's, and the needs of people living with the condition, then the more the PDS and others can use this information to ensure that the best possible services are provided. The research projects included in *Parkinson's Disease: Studies in Psychological and Social Care* will help to achieve this aim.

Richard Briers OBE
President – Parkinson's Disease Society

Preface

The Parkinson's Disease Society was founded in 1969 and has grown to be a national UK charity with over 25,000 members, many of them attached to some 230 branches.

The Society has three basic aims:

1 to help sufferers from Parkinson's disease and the people who look after them (their carers) with problems arising out of the disease;
2 to collect and disseminate information about Parkinson's disease;
3 to encourage and provide funds for research into Parkinson's disease.

The Society is governed by an elected Council of Management. These Trustees appoint relevant committees and panels, some of which are made up of unpaid volunteers from members of the Society, and unpaid professionals from the various medical and welfare services working with Parkinsonians.

Research proposals are considered by the Medical Advisory Panel (MAP) and the Welfare Advisory Panel (WAP). The latter has a subcommittee, the Welfare Research Committee (WRC), which looks in detail at proposed research projects in the welfare field and makes recommendations in respect of funding to the WAP.

This book is not an overview of all welfare research into Parkinson's disease over the past few years or, indeed, all such work carried out by the Society and its branches, but it reviews some of the research considered for funding by the WRC, endorsed by the WAP, and approved by the Council of the Society.

The researchers concerned have willingly contributed shortened versions of their research and, for those readers who are interested, their listed references give some idea of the wider research on which their studies are based.

Dr Marie Oxtoby's report 'Parkinson's disease patients and their social needs', based on research carried out in 1979 and published in

1982, may be regarded as the key point in the development of welfare research as far as the Society is concerned. It provided detailed information on many aspects of the lives of patients and brought to light many of the issues upon which the later research projects were to focus.

In the mid-1980s, welfare research still had neither a separate budget nor its own committee. However, in the late 1980s the WRC was established and money allocated to it.

At that time there were only ten or so applications made for welfare research grants each year and most of these came from consultants in neurology and geriatric medicine who were in direct contact with the Society. In 1991, the WRC adopted a method of working which, with improvements, is in operation at the present time. Advertisements inviting applications for funding were placed in various professional journals, advice was taken from referees and projects were individually scored. Those scoring highest were recommended to the WAP and subsequently to the Council of Management to be awarded funding as appropriate.

By 1997 the demand on the Society for funding for welfare research had increased to such an extent that the WRC paused in its work for a year while one of its members carried out a review to suggest future strategy (Nanton, 1997).

The first task was to define welfare research and this was done as follows:

> Welfare research is all research relating to Parkinson's disease which does not aim to find a cause or cure for the condition or to test the efficacy of drugs or surgery in the control of symptoms. Welfare research may thus be epidemiological in focus. It may investigate the effectiveness of any non-drug or non-surgical interventions in alleviating the effects of the condition. It may involve the evaluation of a particular service provision. It also includes studies which examine different aspects of the experience of the condition for patients and carers. Correspondingly, methodologies may vary from cross-control designs and longitudinal studies using primarily standardised measurement scales and procedures through to smaller in-depth qualitative investigations.

It is money collected by members which underwrites research and the second task was to seek their views about topics of importance to them. The third main task was to consider how to set up a more systematic approach to commissioning research.

Arising from discussion with members, two topics became apparent:

1 the membership would like to see Dr Oxtoby's survey updated;
2 there was a strong interest in alternative therapies.

As a result, the Public Services Institute was commissioned to update and carry out a survey of members based on the Oxtoby report, and an extract from this new survey is included in Chapter 1.

Members of the Society were asked about their experiences of the use of alternative therapies and currently the WRC is exploring acceptable ways of conducting research into such therapies.

As a result of the third action point, a three-year rolling programme calling for grant applications was put into action in September 1997. Each year, one project evaluating a service was to be advertised, and each year in rotation applications from one of the three major accepted therapies (speech, occupational and physiotherapy) was to be invited. Limiting applications to one discipline at a time has made selection much easier.

This book is a response to the wish of the WRC to see some of the work being done recorded, so that members of the Society, those involved with the treatment of Parkinsonism, administrators, government interests responsible for providing services and the lay population in general can be made aware of the conclusions and recommendations of the welfare research. The topics are a mixture of earlier work carried out and work carried out after the review. Part I, 'Parkinson's disease in the community', after a preliminary chapter outlining the medical background to the remainder of the book, reports the results of a series of surveys which together give a good picture of the circumstances of people with the disease and their carers. Part II, 'Assessments and interventions', comprises shorter chapters detailing the methods and results of a series of studies. A final chapter provides a concluding overview.

As someone who has suffered with Parkinson's disease for the past ten years, it has been a privilege to work, as a volunteer, with the WAP and WRC and to have been able to play a leading role in editing this book.

I am sure the Parkinson's Disease Society would wish to thank the British Psychological Society, and in particular Joyce Collins, their publisher, for her help which has made this book a joint project.

Above all, thanks are due to all the Parkinsonians, their carers, and those professionals and others who work with them, who have given freely of their time to filling in questionnaires and talking with researchers. This book is dedicated to them.

Ray Percival
June 1999

References

NANTON, V. (1997) *Review of the Work of the WRC of the PDS*. London: PDS.
OXTOBY, M. (1982) *Parkinson's Disease Patients and Their Social Needs*. London: PDS.

Part I
Parkinson's disease in the community

Chapter 1

The nature and course of Parkinson's disease

Brian Pentland

James Parkinson described the disease which now bears his name in 1817. Noting the key features of tremor combined with reduction or loss of movement he used the term 'shaking palsy' or 'paralysis agitans'. Parkinson's disease, to this day, is diagnosed on the basis of the presence of the three principal disturbances of movement: tremor, rigidity and hypokinesis. It is not possible to prove that a patient has Parkinson's disease and postmortem studies have shown that experts get the diagnosis wrong in up to a quarter of cases. Although we now understand much more about what happens to the nervous system in Parkinson's disease and can often alleviate symptoms effectively, the cause remains unknown and we cannot prevent or cure the condition. Parkinson's disease is progressive and inevitably the severity and experience of the disorder varies considerably between individuals affected, so that only a general outline of its nature and course is possible here.

Incidence and prevalence

Approximately 1 in 1,000 people in the general population have Parkinson's disease. It affects an estimated 1.6 per 100 of the population over the age of 65 years but it should be noted that more than one in ten sufferers are diagnosed before the age of 50 years. In the UK around 120,000 people are currently affected (McCall, 1995).

The basis of Parkinson's disease

The central nervous system (brain, cerebellum, brain stem and spinal cord) consists of a complex arrangement of nerve cells (neurones), which transmit electrical impulses between each other and to the peripheral nerves, which in turn stimulate the muscles. These electrical messages are dependent on chemicals within the nerve cells called neurotransmitters. One such neurotransmitter chemical is dopamine and nerve cells which contain dopamine are termed dopaminergic neurones. In Parkinson's disease there is loss of certain dopaminergic neurones deep within the brain, in a part called the basal ganglia. The basal ganglia and their connections are important in controlling aspects of movement and posture. However, there are other parts of the central nervous system which are also involved in the control of movement, in particular the pyramidal system and cerebellar pathways. The basal ganglia and its connections are therefore sometimes referred to as the extrapyramidal system. Thus, to summarize, Parkinson's disease is often described as a disorder of the extrapyramidal system characterised by loss of dopaminergic neurones in the basal ganglia.

This tells us what the damage, or pathology, within the central nervous system is, but it does not tell us why it happens and the cause of Parkinson's disease is not known. Sometimes, however, the same symptoms and signs can occur in circumstances where the cause is known. In such cases the person may be described as having Parkinsonism rather than Parkinson's disease. Causes of Parkinsonism include a viral infection of the brain (encephalitis); the effects of certain medicines, particularly those used to treat mental illness; and disease of the arteries supplying the brain. These conditions are usually referred to as post-encephalitic, drug-induced and arteriosclerotic Parkinsonism, respectively, and they should not be confused with Parkinson's disease.

It is beyond the scope of this chapter to discuss theories of the cause of Parkinson's disease. There are numerous attractive hypotheses and encouraging studies postulating possible genetic, toxic, environmental and other factors which may play some role, but the answer has not yet emerged.

Key diagnostic features

The cardinal features of Parkinson's disease are hypokinesis, rigidity, tremor and impairment of postural reflexes. These disturbances underlie the major symptoms that sufferers describe and the signs found in the condition, and it is appropriate to define them in a little more detail.

Hypokinesis (literally 'reduced movement') includes a number of components: delay in initiation, poverty, imprecision and slowness of movement (bradykinesis), fatigue and impairment of sequential actions. Thus there may be hesitation in starting to do something, the size and speed of movement may be reduced and it may be done clumsily or in an uncoordinated manner. Some movements which are normally done without thinking, such as swinging the arms when walking, may be reduced or lost.

Rigidity is the term used to describe the increased resistance to passive muscle stretch found in the condition. Thus, when a doctor or therapist manipulates the person's limb, there is an abnormal degree of tightness in the muscles (or increase in muscle tone) which is present throughout the range of movement. This is classically described as 'lead pipe' or 'plastic' rigidity. If there is a tremor present in the limb being examined, the rigidity is described as of 'cog wheel' type. Rigidity is present not only in the limb muscles and is most easily detected clinically in the muscles around the shoulders and neck. It is possibly this which is largely responsible for the stooped posture characteristic of the disease and rigidity may contribute to the stiffness of muscle described by the person with Parkinson's disease.

Tremor in Parkinson's disease is usually described as a slow, coarse tremor, in contrast, for example, to the more rapid fine tremor seen in people who are anxious. The Parkinsonian tremor is, however, aggravated by stress or anxiety. It is usually most marked when the affected part of the body is at rest. Clinically, in the early stages at least, the tremor is more of a social embarrassment than anything, but, as the disease progresses, tremulous movements may interfere with everyday tasks.

Impaired postural reflexes are included by some authors under the heading of hypokinesis. If the patient is standing and his or her body is displaced by the examiner they are likely to have difficulty maintaining their stance. Thus, if pushed from in front they tend to stagger backwards (retropulsion), from behind they stumble forwards (propulsion) and a force displacing them sideways sends them off in the direction of that force (lateral propulsion). These findings of disequilibrium on examination are reflected in everyday difficulties in maintaining balance in busy streets, frequent falls and the hurrying (or 'festinating') gait which is not uncommon with advancing disease.

Onset and early features

The onset of Parkinson's disease is insidious and, in the earliest stages, the diagnosis is often difficult. While tremor is the most common presenting symptom it may be absent and some individuals present with rather vague symptoms of fatigue, diffuse aches, pains or muscle cramps or feelings of tension and restlessness. The components of hypokinesis (described above) may manifest singly so that an individual may exhibit only delay in starting a movement, which may appear simply as hesitancy, or alternatively may show only poverty of movement, which is misinterpreted as mild weakness. Slowness or clumsiness in the arms or legs can be wrongly attributed to the effects of advancing years alone. Various parts of the body may be first affected and only with the passage of time and involvement of other functions does the diagnosis become obvious.

Common symptoms and signs

Parkinson's disease can result in a wide range of symptoms and associated disabilities experienced by the person affected and signs detected by the doctor or other health professional on examination. Some features may never occur in one individual while another may have them. There is also variation in the way symptoms develop during the course of the disease in different individuals. For convenience, symptoms are grouped below according to parts of the body or particular activities rather than by frequency or time of appearance during the life of a sufferer. It is not possible to provide a comprehensive account of all symptoms that may occur during the lifetime of a person with Parkinson's disease and only the more common are given here.

Face

Several changes occur in the face, principally due to hypokinesis. Spontaneous movements of the muscles of facial expression and the eyes are reduced, as is blinking, and the eyes may develop a staring appearance. In advanced cases, the classic 'mask-like' countenance and 'reptilian gaze' may be seen. These changes may make the sufferer appear unemotional, hostile or lacking in intelligence. There is considerable social disability resulting from the reaction of others to the appearance of patients with Parkinson's disease .

Hands

Manual dexterity is reduced and may result in changes in handwriting, turning the pages of a book or newspaper, and later difficulty using door keys, fastening buttons or tying shoe laces. The handwriting abnormality is classically described as micrographia. This is not simply script which is smaller than normal but includes changes such as loss of loops on '1's and 'f's and flattening of 'm's and 'n's, resulting in a rather cramped and characterless form of writing. Alternate rotation of the hand and forearm forwards and backwards or trying to touch each finger in turn rapidly with the thumb may reveal some or all of the features of hypokinesis, such as start hesitation, poverty, clumsiness and slowness of movement.

Gait and trunk movement

Loss of arm swing on one or both sides is often an early feature. In the feet, heel strike is lost and the individual tends increasingly to walk on the balls of the feet with gradually reducing stride length, eventually leading to the short, shuffling gait. Impairment of postural reflexes is perceived by the affected person as a loss of balance with a tendency to stumble forwards, backwards or sideways if knocked into by another person or when reaching out too far. The stooped, flexed posture and impaired postural reflexes can result in a festinating gait, where individuals shuffle forward more and more quickly as if chasing their centre of gravity. Pivotal or turning movements are often impaired, the individual appearing to move the whole body en bloc. Apart from during walking, difficulty in turning may be particularly notable in bed.

Gait may also be disturbed by the phenomenon of 'freezing', where the person's progress is suddenly stopped as if the feet were stuck to the floor. This is particularly liable to occur at doorways despite the door being open. Conversely, some individuals can run quite fast although they walk slowly, particularly under stress, in episodes of 'kinesia paradoxica'. Another fluctuating phenomenon which may affect gait is foot dystonia, an involuntary twisting movement, which can occur in untreated as well as treated cases.

Communication

Although attempts have been made to describe all the speech disturbances comprehensively in a single term, this is not possible. Common features include defective enunciation and an impaired voice, but there are also changes in the distribution of stress and intonation which comprise the melody of speech, or 'prosody'. The speech changes are usually considered to be largely attributable to the hypokinesis, but rigidity and tremor can contribute to the disturbances seen. The delay in initiation of movements may result in hesitant, almost stuttering, speech; the poverty is represented in monotony of pitch and loudness; enunciation is often imprecise, words may come in short rushes and impaired breath control may give a breathy voice quality.

In addition to speech, non-verbal communication is also impaired. Loss of facial expression and its possible effects have been described above but other aspects of body language are often affected. Thus the posture may be stooped, gestures reduced or lost and body movements generally slowed.

Sensory features and pain

While sensory symptoms, in the form of numbness or pain, are not uncommon, sensory signs are absent. Cramp-like pains and diffuse aches and pains are common. These may be a secondary effect of rigidity or immobility or the result of osteoarthrosis which accompanies the disease. A number of patients do complain of severe, distressing pain either before the institution of treatment or, more commonly, when fluctuations in motor performance develop after therapy with levodopa. These pains, which may involve the trunk or limbs, often fluctuate in parallel with the variations in motor function.

Bladder and bowel function

Urinary bladder symptoms are reported in 31% to 71% of cases. These figures come from selected populations and many factors other than the effect of Parkinson's disease on the autonomic nervous system, which controls bladder function, such as cognitive impairment, physical immobility, concomitant urological conditions and the effects of medications may be responsible. Patients may report frequency, urgency, incontinence or hesitancy and retention, and investigation by a urologist is often necessary to identify the nature and so indicate the cause of the problem. Men with Parkinson's disease are sometimes submitted to unnecessary prostatectomies through failure to recognize that the disease causes bladder dysfunction.

Constipation is common and although autonomic dysfunction, with the added effect of the anticholinergic drugs used to treat the condition, may be responsible, other factors are important. Changes in diet due to feeding difficulties, lack of exercise and practical difficulties in getting to the toilet can all contribute.

Feeding and nutrition

Problems with salivation occur in about 70% of cases, most commonly drooling, which causes considerable distress and embarrassment. It may be a result of reduced rate of automatic swallowing, combined with the effects of flexed head posture and poor lip seal. There is no evidence of actual excess production of saliva. In some individuals the complaint is of a dry mouth. This is a common side-effect in those taking anticholinergic medication. Feeding is often complicated by difficulties in handling cutlery as a result of hypokinesis or tremor. Chewing can also be impaired and difficulty with swallowing occurs much more commonly than in the general population. Marked swallowing difficulties most commonly occur in the advanced stages of the disease, when other severe motor impairments are present.

Weight loss is common. Contributory factors include increased metabolic demand as a result of tremor, rigidity or dyskinesia, reduced appetite associated with feeding or swallowing difficulties, and depression, but the cause is not always apparent.

Mental state

The personality, mood state and cognitive function may all be altered in Parkinson's disease, although such changes are by no means universal and controversy exists over the frequency of such disorders. With a disease of insidious onset, which may be present for some years before the sufferer complains to a doctor, it is difficult to define 'premorbid' personality, but there is a large literature which suggests that many Parkinsonian patients exhibit emotional and attitudinal inflexibility, lack of affect (emotion), a tendency to depression and introverted, over-controlled personality traits. Depression is common in Parkinson's disease and probably affects about half of all cases, although reported frequencies of the association vary from 20% to 90%. Some of this variability is due to differences between hospital and community cases, studies of individuals at different stages of the disease and, perhaps foremost, the diagnostic criteria for depression used. The depression in Parkinson's disease is similar to that seen in arthritis, being characterised by pessimism and hopelessness, reduced drive and motivation and increased concern with health, rather than negative feelings of guilt and worthlessness. There is some evidence that it correlates with severity of illness and disability.

A vast literature exists on the incidence of dementia and cognitive impairments in the condition, with frequencies of dementia in Parkinson's disease being given as from less than 10% to over 80%. Again, variation in diagnostic criteria used and patient selection methods help to explain the differences. The presence of depression and the effects of medication also significantly influence the diagnosis of dementia. A recent estimate is that one in five Parkinsonian patients is demented. In the absence of overt dementia there is, however, considerable evidence that non-specific cognitive defects are fairly common in Parkinson's disease. Difficulties may occur in shifting from one thought to another, topics may be unnecessarily repeated in conversation and a general slowing of thought processes may be present. The term 'bradyphrenia' is sometimes used to describe the subtle cognitive slowing which occurs in Parkinson's disease.

Sleep disturbance

Sleep disorders can be categorised as insomnias, excessive daytime somnolence and parasomnias, and all occur commonly in Parkinson's
disease. Insomnia in the form of inability to get off to sleep or early
morning waking can occur as a result of anxiety or depression, respectively. The most common variety of insomnia, however, is 'sleep
fragmentation', characterised by recurrent waking. Patients often attrib-
ute this to joint pains, rigidity, tremor or the desire to urinate, but sleep
studies suggest that spontaneous arousal is the initial event. The start of
levodopa therapy may be associated with difficulty getting to sleep but
tolerance to this effect usually develops fairly quickly. Fatigue is common and sufferers may describe this as sleepiness but some individuals
have true excessive somnolence during the day which may or may not
be accompanied by nocturnal wakefulness. Parasomnias are behavioural
events such as nightmares, sleepwalking or talking during sleep and such
problems usually relate to anti-Parkinsonian medication.

Sexual function

People troubled with sexual dysfunction are often reluctant to mention
it to their doctor, who in turn may not enquire about it. The literature
on sexual difficulties in the condition is limited but reveals a high frequency of difficulties in both sexes. Apart from the adverse effects of
anxiety, depression and fatigue on libido, sexual function may be select-
ively impaired by the disease process. Certainly, improvement in libido
with levodopa or selegiline treatment is recognised. Hypokinesis and
rigidity impair body language, perhaps making the sufferer appear less
attractive to others or, indeed, themselves, with loss of self-esteem.
These physical impairments, by interfering with bodily movements, also
cause mechanical difficulties in love making such as hindering pelvic
movements or the adoption of a satisfactory sexual position. Simple
counselling and sensitive advice may help couples overcome some of
these problems. Medication can also contribute to impaired sexual performance.

Course of the disease

It is now 30 years since the discovery of levodopa and its introduction as
an effective treatment. It is rare nowadays for people to live for years
without drug treatment, and to describe the course of the condition one
must therefore also discuss the effects of treatment – both its success
and its failure. Current treatment does not offer a cure for Parkinson's

Table 1.1. *Staging of Parkinson's disease (Hoehn and Yahr, 1967)*

Stage	Features
I	Unilateral involvement; little or no functional impairment
II	Bilateral or mid-line involvement without impaired balance
III	First signs of impaired righting reflexes; some functional restriction but capable of independent living and may be able to work
IV	Fully developed, severely disabling disease; can stand and walk unaided
V	Confined to wheelchair or bed

disease. The condition is progressive, although the speed of progression varies between individuals. Thus one person may note only slow and slight deterioration over years, while another may report rapid decline in dexterity and mobility despite treatment. The most common pattern is gradual decline with increasing need of medication over a period of years.

There were few detailed descriptions of the course of the disease before the discovery of levodopa and other related treatments. One such study, by Hoehn and Yahr (1967), included a classification of the stages of the disease. The 'Hoehn and Yahr scale' (see Table 1.1) is still used today to provide a rough guide to the severity of Parkinson's disease. A range of more detailed scales are used in research trials to evaluate changes in symptoms and disabilities during the course of treatment.

Treatment

In medical texts there is a tendency to start accounts of the management of Parkinson's disease with reference to drugs. While there have been dramatic improvements in drug therapy in the last 30 years, it is essential to consider other aspects. This book contains authoritative chapters on these issues and only an overview is given here. It is vital that the person with Parkinson's disease, and their families, are informed about the disease and its prognosis and, wherever possible, actively participate in their own treatment. At the time of diagnosis, information must be delivered and subsequently reinforced, and time must be found for questions to be answered. In some centres a social worker has been effective in a counselling role, supporting the work of the physician at diagnosis and subsequently, while in other centres a similar function is performed by a specialist nurse.

The skills of many professions – nursing, physiotherapy, occupational therapy, speech and language therapy, clinical psychology, social work and others – can be invaluable in assisting the person cope with the disease. Such expertise should not be reserved for people with advanced disease but be available from early in the course of the illness. At present, many patients are not seen for regular medical review; about 15% may see a physiotherapist or occupational therapist and 3–4% a speech and language therapist. Even when resources are scarce, it should be possible to improve on this by organizing services better. The Parkinson's Disease Society does much to disseminate advice to patients and their families as well as acting as a source of support.

Drug treatment

As described above, Parkinson's disease results from the loss of certain nerve cells which use dopamine as their neurotransmitter. It is not possible to take dopamine itself as a drug, as it is destroyed in the body, but it was discovered that levodopa, which is converted into dopamine in the brain, can be taken. Levodopa is still the mainstay of drug treatment of Parkinson's disease. When it was first used, in the late 1960s/early 1970s, levodopa was hailed as a medical miracle, transforming the lives of people rendered severely immobile with Parkinson's disease. Oliver Sacks' (1973) book *Awakenings* and the subsequent film give some impression of what occurred.

Most people find their symptoms improve with the introduction of levodopa-containing drugs (e.g. Sinemet and Madopar). Indeed, failure to respond puts the diagnosis in doubt. A few individuals cannot tolerate these medications because of nausea or other side-effects, but the great majority benefit, at least initially. However, as time passes, it is usually necessary to increase the dose to maintain the improvement from the drug. In addition, unwanted effects, particularly involuntary movements, often become more frequent and severe. Gradually, the person may find the levodopa-containing medication loses its effectiveness. In some people the troublesome 'on–off' phenomenon occurs, usually after some years of treatment. In this the person swings unpredictably from 'on', when they are mobile, often with involuntary movements, to 'off', during which they are rigid and immobile. If we describe the problems of loss of effectiveness and fluctuations in control as 'late failure' of the drug, it is true to say that after a variable period of months to years most people will experience degrees of late failure.

To try to prevent late failure occurring or to overcome it once it has happened, a number of strategies have been employed. Thus, the levodopa-containing drugs have been prepared in different doses and formulations, such as controlled-release forms or in dispersible form. Also, new drugs have been developed which act like dopamine and are called 'dopamine agonists'. Other agents act by delaying the normal breakdown of dopamine. Examples of these different drugs are given in Table 1.2.

Table 1.2. *Examples of drugs used to treat Parkinson's disease*

Type of drug	Nature of action	Examples
Levodopa-containing agents	Replace dopamine	Sinemet (co-careldopa), Madopar (co-beneldopa)
Dopamine agonists	Mimic the action of dopamine	Bromocriptine, lysuride, pergolide, ropirinirole, cabergoline, apomorphine
Enzyme inhibitors	Prevent dopamine breakdown	Selegiline, entacapone
Anticholinergics	Reduce acetylcholine action	Benzhexol, benztropine, orphenadrine, procyclidine

Opinions vary as to how best to use these different medications. Thus, some experts recommend starting with dopamine agonists, while others start with a levodopa-containing drug first and add in one of the other agents later. There is still controversy about the long-term effects of beginning treatment earlier rather than later in the course of the disease. Most doctors would agree, however, that the best time to start a patient on medication is when the symptoms are resulting in disability.

People with Parkinson's disease may also benefit from medications directed at relieving symptoms, sometimes referred to as symptomatic, as opposed to specific, treatment. For example, the judicious use of hypnotics for insomnia, antidepressants for confirmed depression, simple non-steroidal agents for musculoskeletal pains and quinine for cramps should be considered.

Surgical treatment

Surgery for Parkinson's disease is probably best regarded as a research activity at the present time. Neurosurgery has been used, especially for severe tremor, since the 1950s, that is before the introduction of levodopa. The most common procedures were stereotactic pallidectomy and ventral thalamotomy, but there was significant morbidity. There has been renewed interest in stereotactic neurosurgical procedures in recent years to try to improve things for those in late failure. Techniques include both ablative (destructive) procedures and high-frequency electrical stimulation of three target areas of the brain: the thalamus, the subthalamic nucleus and the globus pallidus. All these structures lie deep inside the brain – hence the term 'deep brain stimulation'. Implantation of fetal tissue, sometimes erroneously described as 'brain transplantation', to boost brain dopamine production has attracted much recent interest but requires further evaluation.

Terminal stages

Many people with Parkinson's disease lead full lives and modern treatment has extended the life expectancy to make it about the same as for those not affected by the disease. However, when treatment approaches fail, the person may be rendered very disabled and dependent on others because of immobility. Assistance may be required in all activities of daily living and special aids and equipment may be needed. Thus, wheelchairs and hoists may be necessary, communication aids to understand the individual's wishes and changes to the home or even a move to a different home or to residential care may be necessary. Immobility carries with it a number of risks. The ability to fight off infection, particularly involving the lungs, is impaired if a person cannot move about or summon up a good cough, so that pneumonia may prove fatal. The bones require movement to maintain normal mineralization and prolonged immobility increases the risk of fracture from a fall. Circulatory problems and skin care difficulties are also more common when normal mobility is compromised. In advanced disease, adequate nutrition may be threatened by difficulty with swallowing and techniques such as gastrotomy tube feeding may be required.

Nowadays most people with Parkinson's disease die from heart disease, stroke or other common causes of death.

References and further reading

CAIRD, F.I. (Ed.) (1991) *Rehabilitation of Parkinson's Disease*. London: Chapman and Hall.

HOEHN, M.M. and YAHR, M.D. (1967) Parkinsonism: onset, progression and mortality. *Neurology, 17*, 427–442.

KOLLER, W.C. and TOLOSA, E. (1998) Current and emerging drug therapies in the management of Parkinson's disease. *Neurology, 50* (Supplement 6).

MARSDEN, C.D. (1995) Parkinson's disease. In C.M. Wiles (Ed.) *Management of Neurological Disorders*. London: BMJ Publishing Group.

McCALL, B. (1995) Coping with Parkinson's disease: the patient's and carer's experience. *British Journal of Therapy and Rehabilitation, 2*, 549–554.

PARKINSON, J. (1817) *An Essay on the Shaking Palsy*. London: Whittingham and Rowland.

PENTLAND, B. (1993) Parkinsonism and dystonia. In: R.J. Greenwood, M.P. Barnes, T.M. McMillan and C.D. Ward (Eds.) *Neurological Rehabilitation*. Edinburgh: Churchill Livingstone.

QUINN, N. (1995) Parkinsonism – recognition and differential diagnosis. *British Medical Journal, 310*, 447–452.

SACKS, O. (1973) *Awakenings*. London: Gerald Duckworth.

Chapter 2

The new community care for people with Parkinson's disease and their carers

Margaret Lloyd

Care in the community

In 1993, the process which had begun with Sir Roy Griffiths' report in 1988 to the Secretary of State, on the changes needed in the organization and delivery of health and social care services (Griffiths, 1988), culminated in the implementation of the core of the National Health Service and Community Care Act 1990 – the system of care management incorporating a multidisciplinary assessment of need and individually tailored packages of care. The principal objective stated in the White Paper *Caring for People* (Department of Health, 1989) was, through the provision of day, domiciliary and respite services, to enable people affected by ageing, disability or illness to live in their own homes for as long as they wish and are able. The National Health Service and Community Care Act (NHSCCA) embraced both health and social care provision within the system of care management, the intention being to provide an integrated system of care to people whose needs span both sectors. Thus, the laudable aim of a 'seamless service' was to be realized.

Clearly, these changes have great significance for people with Parkinson's disease (PD), whose medical, social, psychological and emotional needs are experienced as a whole. Moreover, a system which purports to provide individually tailored packages of care could, if effective, go a long way towards addressing those individualized scenarios, fraught with sensitive issues, which characterize the experience of living with a disease which is both unpredictable in the longer term and experienced in the present as a highly variable and fluctuating condition.

It seemed particularly important, therefore, to study how this group of people, who both represent those with chronic progressive illness but also demand specialist knowledge and understanding of the particular features of PD, are faring under the new arrangements. Both the pilot studies of care management undertaken by the Personal Social Services Research Unit at the University of Kent (e.g. Challis and Chessum, 1990; Challis *et al.*, 1995) and the early evaluative studies of the implementation of the NHSCCA (e.g. Lewis and Glennerster, 1996) pointed, however, to the observation that the management of PD in the community presented certain challenges to the care management system.

First, it was envisaged that the unpredictable progress of PD for each individual would make long-term planning difficult, in a system which is based on a one-off assessment to determine current need and to set up a system to monitor that provision. While, theoretically, the monitoring of the care package would trigger reassessment as needs changed, in practice a fairly intensive model of intervention would be required for people with PD, to pick up the changing needs in any one sector of the person's (and carer's) life and the knock-on effects of unmet need. Further, professional judgements concerning the point when a comprehensive assessment of need (or even the need for one specific service) is indicated might be difficult in an illness whose disabling effects are insidious. Thus, people with PD and their family and friends make minor, but incremental, adjustments, learning to cope with living with the disease and to scale down their expectations of quality of life, rather than developing expectations of outside help through a sudden and overwhelming event.

Second, the close intertwining of medical and social needs presented in PD means that there are inevitably knock-on effects in another arena, of both changes in the condition and changes in the treatment and their effect. This means that it is essential for a holistic picture to be built up and *maintained* through good interagency communication, in each individual situation. Problems in joint working between health and social services was a major contributory factor in the 1980s drive for reform (e.g. Means and Smith, 1994; Wistow *et al.*, 1994) and there has continued to be widespread acknowledgement of communication problems between health and social care agencies since the implementation of the new assessment and care management arrangements in 1993 (e.g. Wistow *et al.*, 1996). However, policy and practice guidance for improving interprofessional working (Department of Health and Social Services Inspectorate, 1991) runs counter to the realities of the way in which PD is managed. The NHSCCA gives to the local authority social services department the lead responsibility in coordinating a multidisciplinary assessment of need, whereas the starting point for people with PD is inevitably medical care. If people with PD are treated first and foremost as medical patients, social services' familiar mechanisms for uncovering need might not be activated until problems have reached a level of severity resulting, for example, in hospital admission. This problem has been recognized by Warburton (1994) in a review of research concerning admissions to residential care, where risk of admission increased when services were uncoordinated and fragmented at the point of delivery to the individual service user. Thus, a whole raft of *preventive* measures and measures to improve quality of life, fundamental to effective community care, might be being denied to people with PD.

Third, the person with PD crosses many of the organizational boundaries of health and social care services. For example, in both the health and social care sectors the specific needs arising from the disease might be ignored in older sufferers, who may be pushed instead into general older people's services and psychogeriatric medicine. Equally, the majority of day and respite services are geared to the needs of the frail and/or dementing elderly person, and it is rare for social care services designed specifically for younger physically disabled people to have available the medical and nursing expertise which is required for the management of PD. These services also lack the particular (paramedical) therapies which contribute to respite having positive treatment outcomes for the person with PD. Thus, it was possible that the system might be serving the needs of neither the older nor the younger person with PD.

Fourth, the concept of the individual 'disability career' (Oliver *et al.*, 1988) was employed to consider what would be required of a flexible, multidisciplinary service system, if it was to respond appropriately over time to the needs of individuals with PD and those informal carers supporting them. A 'career' perspective emphasizes the *relative* significance at any one point in time of physical, social, emotional and practical features, as well as the 'trigger' effect of key events and developments. For the person with PD, a whole range of personal and circumstantial features interact with the progress of the disease to produce a highly individualized and changing pathway. Meeting the needs of people with PD would test both the flexibility of the system and its ability to initiate and maintain a holistic response.

If the assessment of need and delivery of tailored packages of care through the care management system represented the 'cornerstone' of the new arrangements, as the White Paper suggested, the changes in the roles of the key players – health and social services – were the important organizational change. In the 'new world' of community care, both the local authority social services department and the health authority cease to be primarily direct providers of care and become instead enablers of the development and delivery of a mixed economy of welfare from a range of providers. Within such a system, services are contracted and purchased. Therefore the 'independent sector', made up of voluntary organizations and private businesses, is a key contributor, sometimes known as the 'third sector' in community care. Such a change provides both opportunity and challenge for voluntary organizations such as the Parkinson's Disease Society (PDS), in two main directions. First, although the local authority is charged with the responsibility for producing the annual locality community care plan – including an assessment of the needs of the locality, its actual and potential service resources and its blueprint plan to address those needs over the next 12 months – it must do so in consultation with service users and their representatives and known providers of care. Such a contribution fits neatly with the stated objectives of the PDS to provide information, raise awareness and advocate on behalf of its members. However, it requires a level of co-working with statutory organizations which has not previously taken place, except in isolated instances and geographical pockets. Second, the requirement for the local authority to spend 85% of its special transitional grant (to effect the transfer of resources into community care over the period 1993–7) in the independent sector made the latter's role, as direct provider of services, clearly significant in the evolving 'new world'. The direct provision of services has been limited within the PDS to a relatively small-scale operation – a few special holidays and the provision of welfare visitors, mostly volunteers but also some paid visitors who are PDS members (usually combining welfare visiting with some other role within the local branch). Whether, and in what way, the PDS might involve itself in influencing the type of services available to its members seemed another important question to explore.

The study reported in this chapter (Lloyd and Smith, 1998) was funded under the PDS's Welfare Research Programme and aimed to investigate the process of assessment and the provision of community care services for people with PD and their carers under the new arrangements. The fieldwork took place between June 1996 and March 1997. Some eight years had thus elapsed since the publication of the Griffiths report. It was therefore reasonable to suppose that the systems for meeting the needs and managing the care of people with a chronic progressive disease like PD were as bedded in as they were going to be without some particular reason or motivation for further action or change. The study aimed to find out to what extent, and in what ways, these new systems were 'delivering' for people with PD. Very importantly, it needed to explore how a group of patients whose medical care is located very firmly within specialist secondary health care provision, albeit whose day-to-day management of care crucially involves the general practitioner (GP) and primary health care team, were faring under a system led by the local authority social services department and contained within a generic model of social care provision.

The study

Because the White Paper gave a lead role to the local authority social services department, it was decided to use local authority boundaries as the reference point for the fieldwork. Two boroughs, one in Merseyside (Sea Borough) and one in Greater Manchester (Mill Borough), were selected, of comparable and sufficient population size (290,000 + 260,000) to allow for an adequate sample. The two boroughs otherwise offered differing characteristics in terms of the communities they serve, geographical spread, organization of services and size and activity of the local branches of the PDS. The fieldwork comprised of two parts: a questionnaire survey to all known people with PD and their carers, and 26 follow-up case studies.

The importance of contacting all potential service users when evaluating access to services and their effectiveness in meeting need, rather than restricting contacts to existing known service users, has been established by other researchers (e.g. Bewley and Glendinning, 1994). This, combined with the fact that mapping the incidence of PD and identifying people with the disease are complex and inexact (see Mutch, 1990), led to the adoption of a wide trawl for the survey, using various capture points to gather the sample for the study. Thus, people with PD were identified through hospital consultants' outpatient lists (in neurology and geriatrics); GPs; social services disability registers and disability services teams; and the PDS head office and branch membership lists (a newspaper article was also run in each borough but resulted in only one telephone contact and no actual returns). A different questionnaire for each group – PD people and carers – was used, with the facility for the questionnaires to be returned under separate cover. Although permission for the study had been obtained from the relevant medical ethics committees, the PDS was understandably reluctant to release names and addresses from its membership lists. A system of third-part anonymity, whereby the researchers kept identification codes only and the 'referrers' retained the matching of codes with names and addresses, was therefore used.

The drawback to this system was that some people received questionnaires from several sources – for example, via their GP, consultant and the PDS – and since referrers were ultimately unable to provide the administrative support to cross-check returns, it proved impossible to quote an exact return rate. However, after excluding those returns from people in residential or nursing home care, a total of 202 PD questionnaires and 140 carers' questionnaires were analysed. This represented 214 PD 'cases', since 12 carers' questionnaires were not matched with a PD questionnaire. A guesstimate which takes account of the numbers of respondents reporting that they had received several questionnaires suggests a response rate of around 50%. This figure is also consistent with the anticipated numbers in each borough, given an overall incidence of PD of 1 in 1,000 and allowing for those in residential care. Of the total sample, 55% of PD returns were from members of the PDS, as were 46% of carer returns.

The second stage of the fieldwork involved the compiling of 26 case studies to explore further the main findings of the survey and the subtleties of the way in which the caring network is operating. The case studies were selected from the questionnaire returns to illustrate a wide range of situations and individual profiles (e.g. people living alone, with a partner, having no services, in receipt of a care package, recently diagnosed or long-term sufferers). The case studies were built up through separate conversational interviews using an interview guide with the person with PD and the carer where there was one, and semistructured interviews with a range of health and social care workers from both formal and informal services making up the caring network. The interviews were taped and transcribed.

As well as the methodological problems alluded to above, a number of other difficulties in undertaking social research of this nature with people with PD should be noted. First, they are difficult to identify and contact in a community study. Hospital outpatient records do not contain the diagnosis and PD patients may be seen at a general neurology or geriatric medicine clinic; GPs do not always record this information except on the individual record card and GP databases are of varying reliability; social service departments normally do not record medical diagnosis on their disability registers, although they do record functional capacity; the fact that many people with PD are old, frail and poorly leads to referrers protecting contact details; the PDS membership list does not identify who is a person with PD and who, for example, is an interested professional.

Second, both the physical frailty of people with PD and communication problems caused by particular difficulties with writing and /or speech often led to carers completing questionnaires on their behalf, perhaps wanting to be present at their interview and sometimes 'taking over' both processes. Where the carer and person with PD choose to be interviewed together, for whatever reason, both may be inhibited in their responses.

Third, even where the person with PD participates directly, the effects of the illness and medication may lead to the provision of contradictory and incomplete data from both questionnaires and interviews (certainly, interviews should be carefully timed for each individual's 'best' time of day). A specific frustration in this study was that missing data resulted in small cell sizes in some cross-tabulations, although large numbers of people had answered one or other of the questions, thus limiting the degree of analysis which could be quoted as statistically reliable.

Fourth, there is a very wide range of professionals and services potentially involved whose worlds do not automatically connect and whose different identifications, roles and functions are confusing to the service user (e.g. some respondents referred to the PDS welfare visitor as the social worker); without careful cross-checking, this can lead to the collection of unreliable data. Thus, any study such as this wishing to explore the 'real lives' of people with PD in the community must accommodate contradiction and inexactitude as it trades the control of the clinical environment for the breadth, richness and variety of the outside world.

One final point which should be made is that it was not possible within the resources of this study to survey the views of service providers in the same way as the people with PD and their carers. Thus, the quantitative data gathered on assessments and service provision were accrued through the self-reporting of actual or potential service users. However, general trends were corroborated in the interviews with service providers and through cross-checking of different pieces of information – for example, numbers claiming to have had a community care assessment with those known to the social services department.

The picture of needs and problems

The profile of the survey respondents reflected the age, sex, onset and length of illness suggested by other epidemiological and descriptive community studies. PD respondents were predominantly male (64%) and carers were mainly female (72%). PD respondents were slightly older than the carers, but female PD respondents tended to be older than the male PD respondents. Male carers, however, tended to be older than female carers. The largest grouping in terms of length of the illness was those who had had PD for under five years (46%) and the average length of time respondents had had the illness was eight years. Half the carers in the sample had been caring for the person with PD for five years or less. Twenty-five per cent of the PD sample lived alone, but women were more likely to live alone than men. Seventy-seven per cent of carers lived with the person that they cared for, with male carers being slightly more likely to live with the PD person than female carers. Fifty-five per cent of the PD respondents and 46% of the carers were members of the PDS. Members with PD had similar characteristics to the PD sample as a whole, with a slight tendency to have had the illness for longer and to be receiving personal care from a partner. Carers who were members tended to be older, to live with the person that they cared for and to have been caring for longer.

In general, it is the physical symptoms of PD which are the most comprehensively studied and documented, but living with the disease may produce an enormous range of practical, social, psychological and emotional needs and problems for both the person with PD and the immediate family and friends, who are closely involved. This study needed to gather a holistic picture of individuals' needs, since community care

Table 2.1. *Degree to which symptoms were experienced (n = 202)*

	A little difficulty (valid %)	A lot of difficulty (valid %)	n
Tiredness	39	61	158
Walking	44	56	160
Tremor	58	42	156
Bowel/bladder	55	46	110
Speech	70	30	99
Dribbling	54	46	90
Swallowing	63	37	68

assessments should be needs led, comprehensive and multidisciplinary in approach. Respondents were asked about their problems and needs under the headings of health and medical care, daily living needs, and social and emotional needs, in an attempt to gain a holistic picture.

From a list of common physical symptoms, PD respondents were asked whether they experienced a little or a lot of difficulty in that area. Collapsing these categories revealed that the main difficulties for survey respondents revolved around tiredness, walking and tremor. Significant numbers experienced at least some difficulty with all the other commonly described clinical features. Sexual problems were reported by only 14% of respondents, although this represented 21% of male respondents and only 3% of female respondents. Reporting of sexual problems peaked in the 50–59-year age group and was highest (25%) among those who had had the illness for ten years or more. For those reporting them, however, sexual problems and sexuality issues often assumed major importance:

> Problem with Parkinson's is that it affects my sex life, it cuts it right in half sometimes.

The severity of the commonest symptoms also showed fatigue to be the overwhelming physical effect of the illness (Table 2.1).

A major difficulty often reported by people with PD in managing their illness is the fact that symptoms can vary so much, both over a longer period and, suddenly, over the course of the day. Forty-six per cent of the sample reported experiencing this level of symptoms all the time, 39% approximately half of the time and 13% said they experienced them occasionally.

Achieving and maintaining the correct drug regimen as the condition progresses is a problem for both patient and doctor. The interaction of medication with 'on' and 'off' periods, and the problems which may ensue, were graphically described by one respondent:

> The off periods are rather unpredictable, more so as the day progresses. There is a marked difference in my condition both mentally and physically when the medication is not controlling the symptoms. I often switch off very abruptly, experiencing some tremor in my right hand and forearm. At the same time I become both mentally and physically inhibited. Apomorphine injections have helped a lot to cope with this problem. I find it difficult to achieve the elusive balance with my drugs between [this and] not being completely switched on and experiencing the symptoms of an overdose – dyskinesia. Choosing between the two states is like asking whether you prefer to be burnt or scalded.

Severity of symptoms appeared to increase with length of illness. For example, 75% of those who had had PD for ten years or more reported a lot of difficulty with tiredness, compared with 62% in the six- to nine-year group and 44% of those who had had the illness for five years or less. Frequency of experiencing symptoms, however, showed the six- to nine-year group as those most likely to report that they experienced these symptoms most of the time (Figure 2.1).

These physical problems all have social consequences for those with PD and their families. The practical effects reported in terms of daily

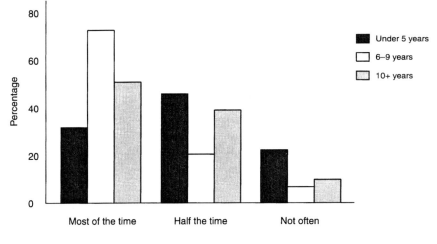

Figure 2.1. *Length of time with PD and frequency of worst symptoms (n = 183)*

living were significant. Ninety-three per cent had problems with walking and mobility, over a third needed a lot of help with personal care at least some of the time, 41% of carers said that they had to act as an advocate for the PD person (indicating a range of communication problems), and 67% needed help with domestic tasks at least some of the time. Data from the carers' questionnaires suggested even higher levels of help were being given – for example, 72% of carers said they gave a lot of help with household tasks. This discrepancy might be due to the fact that most of the carers were the spouse or partner of the person with PD, and housework, particularly among the older population, might be regarded as a normal part of household duties rather than 'receiving help' for many with PD. Carers were also giving intimate care which went beyond personal care assistance. Thirty-six per cent were giving what they considered to be nursing care and 78% were assisting with medication management, increasingly so the longer the person had had PD. Carers found it difficult to estimate the amount of care they gave, with over a third of those who answered this question saying they gave 24 hours' care a day, which tended to skew any average calculation. However, on average they reported giving 96 hours of care a week, of which 13 hours were devoted to personal care tasks. One carer described the daily routine thus:

> Our morning starts at six o'clock 'cos I start work at half past eight. He has medication for his tummy straight away, I see to his leg bag and everything and then go and give him his breakfast. Then he has his follow-up tablets 'cos he's on water tablets and Madopar as well and everything, and then I give him his clothes in the way he has to put them on, and then I leave him to wash and dress himself, keep an eye on him but give him about an hour, and then he comes downstairs with a chair-lift and has a shave. Before I go to work I empty his leg bag, and then if he's going to day care he's there till at the latest its five o'clock but some of them it's half past three, and then the evening starts with his medication, his meals and then just general supervision of him until we're going to bed about ten o'clock. I do his dressing every night because at least then I've not got that to mess with in the morning, and that's it, the full day.

The effects on social and leisure activities were also severe, 68% stating that they were not able to do the things that they wished to do and 62% saying that this was directly due to the physical limitations of their illness. Again, this effect was increased the longer the person had had PD, 87% in the ten years plus group saying that their social lives were restricted beyond that which they would wish. Holidays were particularly affected for some people (although 34% reported their holidays had not changed as a result of PD). Thirty-eight per cent reported that they did not go away on holiday at all and 28% stated that they did not go away because of their PD. Five per cent said that they went on holiday only where there were special facilities and 3% said that only special holidays for people with PD were appropriate. As with general leisure activities, the level of restriction was linked to the severity of symptoms and those with more severe symptoms tended to stay at home if possible. One respondent wrote:

> I refuse invitations to go on holiday or even on day excursions. I prefer to be uncomfortable and distressed in familiar surroundings.

The impact of the disease in emotional and psychological terms led to a number of problems which interacted with the social needs identified. Loneliness and isolation were highlighted by many respondents in their comments and were linked to both anxiety and depression. There was also a correlation with greater severity of physical symptoms. For example, in the case of mobility problems, 64% of those reporting loneliness also said they could only travel in a private car or taxi.

Anxiety was a common feature and was frequently related to fears about physical deterioration in the future (cited by 51%) as well as feelings of insecurity created by trying to manage the condition in the present. One 70-year-old man described it thus:

> I do get anxious because I go days and weeks without seeing anybody in this building.... The worst thing is getting into bed. Your body just goes dead once you lie down.

Forty-one per cent of PD respondents said that they had experienced depression. Again, a correlation was seen with severity of physical symptoms and their effects in social terms. For example, 60% of those who reported that they needed help with personal care all the time also said that they got depressed, compared with only 32% of those who either coped unaided or needed only a little help sometimes (Figure 2.2). Inversely, those who did not report depression were less likely to need high levels of personal care.

Similarly, of those respondents who had been unable to complete the questionnaire themselves, 59% reported depression, compared with 31% who did not need help, as well as being more likely to report loneliness and problems with accepting their illness.

The interaction between severity of physical symptoms, social consequences and emotional impact is illustrated by the following comments:

> The long periods of immobility are soul-destroying.... I can sense myself changing when I become immobile, also the way friends and relatives react to me.

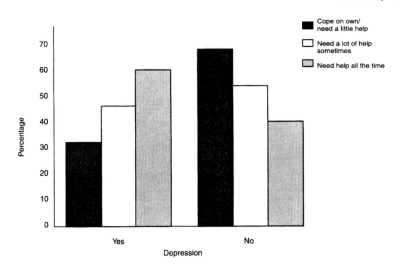

Figure 2.2. *Effect of levels of personal care needed on likelihood of PD respondents feeling depressed (n = 178)*

> I soon have trouble trying to talk, so I just sit there and listen. I don't always feel like listening. I just sit there and disappear into the background. Let them talk, talk and just listen. It's best like that.

A significant factor affecting social activities which both respondents and their carers reported was embarrassment. By and large, respondents did not point to the disabling effects of society in general failing to accommodate their physical limitations, except, and importantly, in relation to the high degree of public ignorance about PD and lack of awareness of the effect of the illness among the general public. (This would underline the validity of the PDS making public awareness a major plank in its campaign.) Thirty-three per cent of PD respondents said that they were embarrassed about their condition in public and therefore tended to shy away from social occasions:

> PD respondent: Parkinson's is not acceptable in company.

> Carer: Other people are unaware of PD problems such as shaking and spilling of food. The PD sufferer tends to lose confidence and is loathe to go out; therefore both the sufferer and the carer start to become house-bound.

Restriction of social and leisure activities increased with the length of time that the person had had PD, although, interestingly, reported embarrassment rose in the six- to nine- year group but fell slightly in the ten years plus group. This may suggest gradual acceptance by sufferers

Table 2.2. *Social and leisure activities by length of illness (n = 191)*

Length of illness	Not able to do all things wished	Limited by physical effects	Embarrassed in public	n
5 years or less	46%	45%	16%	89
6–9 years	84%	80%	50%	32
10 years +	87%	80%	43%	70

Table 2.3. *Relationship between severity of symptoms and limiting effects of embarrassment (n = 196)*

	Embarrassed in public (valid %)	n
Whole sample	33	196
Report a lot of tremor	54	65
Report a lot of difficulty with walking	46	88
Report a lot of difficulty with speech	50	30
Report a lot of difficulty with swallowing	32	25
Report a lot of difficulty with dribbling	42	41
Report a lot of difficulty with tiredness	43	96
Report a lot of difficulty with bowel or bladder	41	49

and those around them of the illness, or it may indicate self-limiting of social activities to those which are manageable without difficulty and embarrassment (Table 2.2).

Reporting of embarrassment increased, however, among those worst affected by physical symptoms, particularly symptoms such as tremor and difficulties with speech (Table 2.3).

Carers' needs

The help given by carers reflects the needs of the person with PD, but carers were also asked about their own needs. Only 42% of them reported that they were in good health. A further 38% stated that their health was 'okay' but that they often suffered with minor ailments and a substantial number (21%) reported that they actually suffered from a chronic condition themselves. What does give rise to concern is that this made absolutely no difference to the levels of care that they gave. However, the quality of care given could be less, as was illustrated by one woman with PD in the case studies, who talked about the effect her

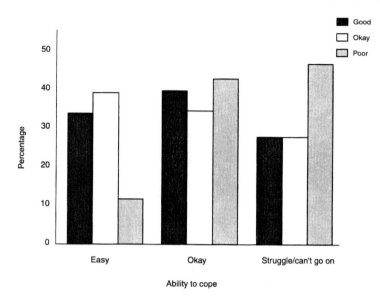

Figure 2.3. *Effect of carer's health on coping ability (n = 121)*

husband's health had on their social life because of his inability to push a wheelchair for long distances:

> With his heart being the way it is, he can't honestly push me very far because he starts getting angina pains and he has bronchial asthma and then he's gasping for breath.

Not surprisingly, carers who were in poor health were more likely to express problems with coping with the demands of caring. For those carers who reported that they were either in good or reasonable health, there was roughly an even divide between the three categories of those who stated that they found it easy to cope, those who thought they managed okay and those who either struggled to manage or did not know if they could carry on. However, for the carers in poor health, only 12% found caring easy and 46% found it a struggle or did not know if they could carry on (Figure 2.3).

The severity of the symptoms experienced by the person with PD was related to the health of the carer. For example, 70% of those who said that their physical health had been affected by caring reported that they were giving a lot of help with personal care (Figure 2.4).

Carers also reported social and emotional effects which mirrored the pattern seen among PD respondents. Forty-six per cent reported having

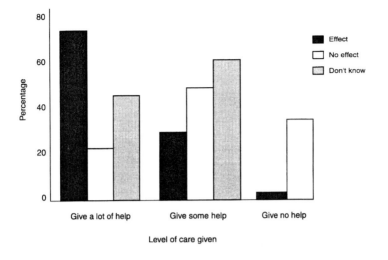

Figure 2.4. *Level of care given and effect on the carers' health (n = 97)*

had to make changes in their social lives, 36% stating that they had less opportunity to go out. Indeed, 64% of those providing substantial care reported that they never got a break from their responsibilities, or only very occasionally. A particular consequence of giving high levels of care for carers was the effect on their other relationships. While the pre-existing relationship between the person with PD and the carer is that most obviously affected by the experience of living with the illness, other relationships for both parties were also affected. For carers particularly, there was a correlation between severity of physical symptoms of the PD person (suggesting more intensive caring) and the reporting of adverse effects on their other relationships. For example, those carers who reported a negative effect on their other relationships were significantly more likely to be giving nursing and night-time care. Only 37% of those who said their other relationships were unaffected were giving night-time care, compared to 80% of those who said that their other relationships had been affected a lot (Figure 2.5). This often led to feelings of guilt:

As soon as he rings up I'll go ... and they always think I'm there for hours....
I'm torn between everybody.

Guilt was not the only emotional consequence. Forty-nine per cent of carers believed that their emotional health had suffered in some way. The main anxiety expressed was their ability to continue caring as they

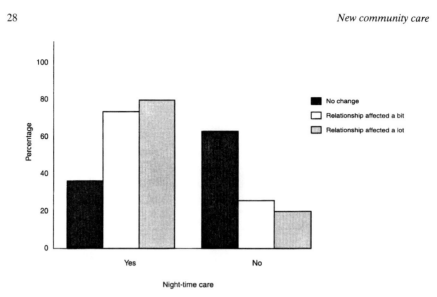

Figure 2.5. *Carer's involvement in night-time care and effect on other relationships (n = 124)*

grew older (38%) and in the face of declining health themselves. The next most commonly cited fear was concern about the health and well-being of the PD person (23%).

Feelings of depression and a sense of loss were also recorded:

> I feel depressed by my husband's inability to participate in conversation and other activities in the easy way that he used to.

Overall, carers' sense of wellbeing was directly related to both the number of breaks they had and to the severity of PD. When asked how well they thought they were coping, 29% stated that they found their caring responsibilities easy, 40% said they managed okay, 26% said that they found it a struggle and 5% said that they did not know whether they could carry on giving this level of care. Of those carers who said that their emotional health had been adversely affected, 72% never had a break or had only occasional breaks and, of those who never had a break, 46% reported either that they were struggling to cope or that they were not sure if they could carry on.

Summary

The survey confirmed the established picture that the physical symptoms of tiredness, problems with walking and problems with tremor are the main difficulties with which people with PD have to battle. However, what it also shows is the connection between severity of these symptoms and a whole range of social and emotional problems. The less controlled the physical symptoms, the greater is their effect on the practicalities of everyday life, with corresponding knock-on negative effects in social relations generally and emotional wellbeing. Carers become particularly caught up in this spiralling effect: those who reported the greatest degree of stress and damage to their own physical and mental health were those who were heavily involved in giving personal, nursing and night-time care. These carers expressed the greatest anxiety about the future and doubts as to how long they could carry on.

Case study

Mr and Mrs MacGregor demonstrate this spiralling effect of increasing practical, social and emotional needs arising from Mrs MacGregor's physical symptoms worsening and becoming less controlled by her medication. Mrs MacGregor, aged 67, had had PD for only two years, but its onset appeared to have been relatively rapid. Mr MacGregor continued to be in paid employment, but at the same time was having to do most of the household and domestic chores and increasing amounts of personal care for his wife. Their married daughter also helped out, and she was of the opinion that her mother could now do practically nothing for herself, citing the example of finding her mother eating a packet of crisps because she had been on her own all day and was unable to prepare any food for herself. Both Mrs MacGregor and her daughter felt that Mr MacGregor 'didn't want to know' how serious his wife's illness was because he could not face the future if he thought about it. The daughter, however, was becoming increasingly stressed and torn between the needs of her own husband and family and trying to help her parents. She felt that there should be far more input from formal services but, to date, Mrs MacGregor had had only a short course of physiotherapy treatment in addition to seeing her GP and consultant. They were, however, awaiting assessment from the social services department. Mrs MacGregor's greatest problem was mobility, and she had become very socially isolated, experiencing bouts of loneliness and depression.

Where has all the assessment and care management gone?

This picture of interrelated and spiralling needs would suggest that the management of PD in the community was crying out for the new arrangements. The White Paper highlighted the undertaking of individual needs assessments by the social services department, which would involve the procuring and managing of a multidisciplinary assessment where necessary. On the basis of such assessments, individual care packages are devised, implemented and managed.

The findings from this research about numbers and targeting of community care assessments are both alarming and perplexing. Only 9% of all PD respondents were certain that they had had a community care assessment (see Table 2.4). Moreover, there was considerable ignorance about these assessments – only 21% of all PD people and 37% of the carers thought they knew what a community care assessment was – and this degree of ignorance was reflected in the uncertainty expressed by some respondents as to whether or not a community care assessment had been carried out in their case. Nevertheless, the resounding majority were certain that it had not. These figures are corroborated by the low numbers supplied by the two social services departments of people with PD known to them, since a formal community care assessment cannot be undertaken without social services involvement.

The targeting of need is one of the imperatives for social services departments in implementing the new arrangements. Two approaches go hand in hand: the targeting of a *priority group* – which was at the time of the care management pilot studies, and continues to be, those frail elderly people whose needs are open-ended and potentially comprehensive and who are at risk of entering residential or nursing home care; and the targeting of the *highest-risk individuals* within any group, whose situations may reach crisis if their needs are not met (Association of Directors of Social Services and Social Services Inspectorate, 1991).

> Care manager: We've had to concentrate more on certain priority groups ... because ultimately they are the ones that if you did not give them a service they would be in residential care.

In practice, this targeting policy is translated into a number of 'priority indicators', if not hard-and-fast criteria:

- Is the (potential) service user both old and suffering from an age-related (or other) health condition which is likely to deteriorate?
- Does she or he live alone?
- Does she or he have continuous and intensive daily living and personal care needs?
- Is there a sole informal carer who may not be able to continue without support?

Taking the first of these indicators, we looked at community care assessments for the over-65s, who will automatically be dealt with by older people's services (now a priority category), irrespective of their PD. The over-75s group are also entitled to GP assessment, in their own home if they wish. Eleven per cent of those aged 65 and over, as compared with 5% of those under 65, said that they had had a community care assessment;

Table 2.4. *Receipt of community care assessments (n = 163)*

	Yes (valid %)	No (valid %)	Not sure (valid %)	n
Whole sample	9	75	17	163
Over 65 years	11	72	17	105
PD 6–9 years	16	61	23	31
PD 10 years or more	9	72	19	58
Lives alone	8	72	20	39
Lone carer	25	53	22	55
High personal care needs	17	64	19	58

72% of the over-65s asserted that they had never had a community care assessment. The absence of any real increase in assessments among the older group is particularly significant, given that the incidence of PD shows a marked increase in older age and 70% of this survey were aged 65 or over.

A more relevant factor may be the stage which has been reached in the illness. Of those people who had had PD less than five years, 5% had had a community care assessment; of those who had had PD from six to nine years, 16% had had a community care assessment; and of those who had had PD ten years or more, 9% had had a community care assessment. The slight surge in the middle category may reflect the fact that there is a tendency at this stage for the condition to be less controlled through medication, with consequent effects in wider areas of the life of the PD person and family. There is no obvious way of accounting for the slight drop in community care assessments in the ten years plus group, other than the possibility that people have made their own gradual accommodations and become used to managing their situation, having perhaps stepped up the level of help some years previously. Some may also be accounted for by people entering residential care at this stage, although it is to be hoped that this had been preceded by a community care assessment at some point.

The relationship between informal support being provided and community care assessments was at first sight puzzling, but actually reflected the preoccupations of social services departments. The numbers of PD people living alone who had had a community care assessment – 8% – was consistent with the general picture. In other words, living alone did not of itself appear to trigger priority. However, the presence of an otherwise unsupported informal carer was related to significantly higher levels of assessment. Where informal carers identified themselves as the *only* regular carer, 25% said the person they cared for had had a community care assessment. Of carers who said that they lived with the person (and these were predominantly spouses or partners), 24% said that there had been an assessment. The 1989 White Paper has as one of its six key objectives the support of informal carers. These responses would suggest – and this was confirmed in the interviews with social services care managers – that social services departments are concerned to give *enough* support to informal carers in situations which might otherwise break down, leaving formal services to meet the total needs:

> Social services team leader: We are only supporting carers and filling in the gaps.

However, there were instances where serious questions were raised about whether or not this support was enough:

> My mother is 76 and in ill health herself. She is not capable of caring for my father and I feel that she should be offered more assistance. Social services did put my father to bed at night but they said that it was too much for two women on their own, so they withdrew the service, leaving a 76-year-old woman with asthma and emphysema to cope on her own.

Given that community care assessments should be needs led, the priority indicator of the person having intensive daily living and personal care needs might reasonably be expected to be the one to trigger an assessment. Despite the evidence that where they knew there was a lone carer the social services were undertaking higher levels of community care assessment, there was equally strong evidence of carers just managing to cope with heavy demands without even an assessment of need being carried out.

Seventy-four per cent of those PD people who replied that they had *not* had a community care assessment were receiving personal care or assistance from a relative. This finding is more disturbing when the *level* of need is looked at more closely. Fifty-six per cent of those who said they needed help all the time with personal care tasks and 70% of those who said they needed a lot of help sometimes had never had a community care assessment. Similarly, 64% of those who said they needed help all the time with domestic and household tasks and 65% of those who said they needed a lot of help some of the time had had no assessment for community care services. The conclusion is unavoidable – that informal carers are meeting this high level of need without it even being noted by the agency responsible for both determining and planning for the needs of its locality, and for assessing and meeting the needs of individuals within its community:

> Independent care agency worker: Basically, as long as the main carer puts up with things, no one will pay any attention.

However, an important finding was that where a community care assessment *had* been carried out, carers were significantly less likely to say that they were not sure if they could carry on – 16% as opposed to 71% where there had not been a community care assessment.

The PDS sees information giving and advocacy as an important part of its role and, in one of the two boroughs studied, branch officials had been involved in consultation exercises set up by the local authority with regard to the implementation of care management. Respondents who were PDS members did have more knowledge about community care – 47% of carer members compared with 29% of non-members knew what a community care assessment was – but there were no significant differences between members and non-members in terms of actual numbers who had been assessed. Nevertheless, there was evidence of PDS welfare visitors in particular acting as advocates on behalf of individuals. The following account is both sobering for formal service providers and illustrative of positive intervention undertaken by the PDS:

> After a week in hospital in 1995 an Age Concern counsellor told me what an assessment was and I watched him for half an hour trying to arrange one for me on the telephone. Later that day, armed with another telephone number, I continued to try ... passing the buck from office to office ... effectively being given the brush-off. Some time later I got an assessment when the Parkinson's Disease Society sent a note to my GP and the GP got on to social services.

The formal community care assessment is the way into care management arrangements, but the incidence of community care assessments provides only a partial picture when exploring to what extent the health' and social care needs of people with PD are being assessed by professionals. Relatively high numbers thought their condition had been formally assessed by their GP (51%) and by a consultant (50%). People also recorded having been assessed by physiotherapists, occupational therapists, speech therapists, a PD nurse specialist and district nurses. The content of these assessments appeared, however, to be predominantly medical, with relatively little attention being paid to social and emotional issues and everyday living needs such as personal care (Figure 2.6).

Moreover, most of these assessments were not carried out in the person's own home. The inadequacy of such assessments to provide an accurate picture of the day-to-day realities for the person with PD and carer was pointed out by many respondents and highlighted by a PDS welfare visitor:

> The GP misunderstands them sometimes. They don't see them when they are struggling at home.... They come across like they can cope.

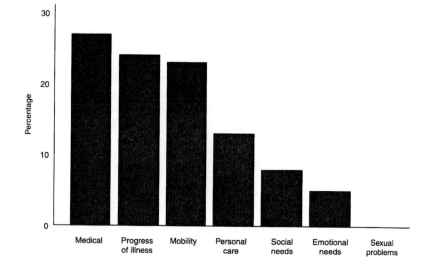

Figure 2.6. *Percentages of each type of assessment as a total of all assess-ments undertaken*

The wife of a man admitted in an emergency to hospital (who subse-quently died) commented:

> I think really that they didn't think he was as confused as what he was ... but now he's there in the hospital they say they don't know how I've coped.

This problem has been recognized more widely. Around half the old people assessed for community care packages in a study carried out by the Social Services Inspectorate and the National Health Service Ex-ecutive had been assessed in hospital (Department of Health, 1994b).

In most instances, it was not that medical and health care staff did not recognize that people with PD may have significant social care needs, but that they felt both their priorities and their expertise lay elsewhere:

> Consultant: I wish we had adequate time for everything but the medical prob-lem has to be prioritized ... they've come to me not as a social worker, they've come to me for my diagnostic and therapeutic ability.

> Consultant: The social aspect is much more problematic.... I wouldn't know where to begin.

> PD nurse: Because my service is evaluated by doctors, that's what I work to.... it's not much different from the way a doctor would assess.... *I'd like to*

know who they live with, the type of accommodation, how well they manage getting washed, dressed ... cope with meals.

Confining oneself to one's own specialist professional expertise is a legitimate position and a common model in multidisciplinary assessment. The problem that was identified in this study lay in the lack of referrals being made for social care services, and particularly for a comprehensive community care assessment. This, taken in conjunction with the fact that the vast majority (85%) had been seen by a hospital consultant at least once, appears to provide two important clues as to the low numbers of community care assessments being undertaken with people with PD. First, the starting point for their treatment is most commonly the specialist medical environment of the hospital consultant's outpatient clinic. Not only are very few of those being assessed by a consultant or a GP proceeding to a community care assessment (15% and 13%, respectively) but such clinics have no immediate social services link, such as being regularly staffed by a hospital social worker. The district nurse interviewed felt that coordination between the different community health services was good, but that communication with social services varied from 'okay' to 'poor'. This pattern was confirmed by the PD nurse, who covered a very wide area and therefore potentially liaised with the greatest number of agencies. The main problem she identified was that health workers are attached to GPs or consultants, whereas social services staff are organized in geographically based teams. Thus, common meeting places for the various health workers invariably did not provide the opportunity for liaison with social workers:

> PD nurse: I don't think I ever met anybody from Social Services in any of the clinics.

Second, there is no systematic screening of social care needs taking place at these clinics and very low numbers of referrals for social care services arising from the clinic visit. Nonetheless, respondents rated the potential importance of hospital visits as a way of accessing other services quite highly: 46% said this was very or quite important. However, 54% said the hospital was not much help or no help in referring them on. Further, when looking at a range of other services for which, potentially, a referral might be made from a hospital clinic, the percentages obtaining such help were low, markedly so in relation to those services for which a full assessment of need would be undertaken before provision. For example, only 4% had obtained respite care through a hospital referral, only 6% a home carer and only 15% had been referred to a social worker (Figure 2.7).

Contact with GPs seemed to lead in the main to referrals for other medical or paramedical services, with the most common referral being

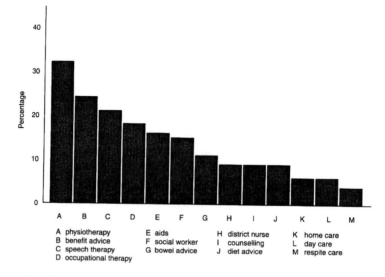

Figure 2.7. *Hospital referrals for other services (n = 160)*

to a consultant neurologist. Eighty-five per cent said that they had been referred to a consultant, and 46% said that they had been referred by their GP for other services (although there is some overlap between these two responses). Society members were more likely to be referred by their GP for other services – 51%, compared with 42% of non-members. Only 17% said that their GP had given them information about other services. The experience of this carer is probably not uncommon:

> We never had a social worker to give us advice or help. It was only in the last year of his life that I was put in touch with social workers, only to be told that there is a waiting list.

One social services team leader also expressed concern about this situation. Reflecting that his team (which dealt with all disabled and chronically ill people under 65 in the borough) had had contact with only three people with PD in the last year, he commented:

> It worries me a bit and I wonder why we are not reaching these people, or do they think the things we have to offer are no good?

However, some people *were* getting through to social workers. Twenty-six per cent claimed to have been assessed by a social worker since 1993, a significantly higher figure than those saying that they had had a community care assessment. When linked with other information about service provision, it is likely that this figure represents people assessed for a specific service provided through the social services department – such as a home carer or special aids or equipment – rather than those receiving a comprehensive assessment. Evidence that GPs were referring directly for such services, rather than for a community care assessment, further corroborates this picture. Nevertheless, single-agency assessments for a particular service are likely to leave worrying gaps in the management of a condition like PD, where not only does the close interrelationship of medical, social and emotional needs demand a holistic approach, but the changing pattern of the illness requires a monitoring system which can trigger assessment and reassessment, as necessary. If the care of people with PD remains largely outside the care management system, this is unlikely to occur.

Care manager: Someone who needs a one-off service, such as a telephone, would be priority four because that's not a complex assessment, it's just a quick go in thing. Sometimes you do go in and find a horrendous situation, but on the face of it it's a priority four.

Case study
Mr Thomas provides just such an example of the failure to follow through referrals and monitor the overall situation. Aged 70 and living alone in a first-floor flat accessed by stairs, he had had PD for 11 years. He was very aware of the risks in his situation but remained fiercely independent. He had attended a consultant neurologist's clinic since being diagnosed by a locum GP, and was generally satisfied with this treatment, particularly over the last few years. He tended to consult his pharmacist more than his GP, who, he felt, had handed him over to the specialists and was not very interested in PD. Mr Thomas had seen the PD nurse occasionally at the clinic, although she had not visited him at home. However, at least a year ago, she had written to the social services department on his behalf, after he himself had written requesting an assessment for bath aids and rails but received no response. At this point, the story becomes confused, as Mr Thomas was supplied with a rail for the toilet by someone, but the occupational therapy services (who were contacted by the researchers to be interviewed for the case study) had no record of him. Mr Thomas did not appear to have had a proper needs assessment by the social services department, commenting when asked whether anything other than the rail had been discussed, 'They didn't really give me the impression that they had much time to spare'. Until the week before being interviewed, Mr Thomas had had no other services. However, through a chance encounter with an old acquaintance, he had heard about a home care scheme run by a housing association, and he had just started with two hours a week of home help, for which he paid £6.32 out of his attendance allowance. This allowance he had only recently applied for, through a welfare rights adviser from a local voluntary organization. The organizer of the home care scheme, interviewed later in the study, confirmed that Mr Thomas had a basic domestic service for which he had applied

himself, rather than receiving the home care package through a social services referral. Mr Thomas was well aware of the health and safety risks he was running, admitting, 'I do get anxious because I go days and weeks without seeing anybody in this building.... I'm getting showered with one hand and holding on to the fitting with another.... I used to grill steaks but I find myself getting a bit frightened of burning myself, so I thought I'll go back to the microwave and even that now is a bit high'. However, whether through stubborn independence, or feeling rejected by the lack of an effective response from service providers, he feared intrusion into his life and talked of euthanasia rather than ending up dependent. He suffered from depression and had been prescribed an antidepressant for more than a year. Nevertheless, he had his own idea of the kind of low-key community support which would benefit someone like himself, particularly as he got older – 'I don't want someone to run my life. I don't want someone knocking on the door every five minutes saying are you all right? It would be nice for someone to call now and again.... I like this carer coming round.... It'd be nice if there was a young kid locally that could get something if you needed it.' Mr Thomas's situation would appear to be just that which a care management system, capable of providing individually tailored packages of care, taking account of the views of the service user, was designed to serve.

Service provision

The picture of need presented by respondents pointed to a complicated web of health and social care services which might be relevant. Thus, as well as looking at the services people were actually getting, the study explored the *processes* by which services were accessed or access was hindered, and the *relationship between* the health and social care sectors in delivering community care for people with PD.

The majority of PD respondents were in receipt of the basic medical services only. Eighty per cent reported services from GPs and 86% had seen a consultant. Figures for the receipt of all other services were below 40%. Thirty-six per cent of respondents had had special aids, 30% had had physiotherapy, 27% had seen a specialist PD nurse, 26% had been a hospital inpatient, a further 26% had seen a social worker, and 25% had had hospital outpatient services. Under 25% of respondents had had speech therapy, home care, occupational therapy, support group, adaptations to the house, district nurse, day care and transport services. Under 10% of respondents had had respite care, meals services, a night sitting service or specialist holiday services for people with PD.

In general, members of the PDS showed a slightly higher rate of receipt of services than did non-members, although in the case of support groups and special holidays members are most likely to be referring to the Society's own activities. The greatest differences were seen in members being more likely to have had special aids provided, physiotherapy and day care. Moreover, there was no service that non-members were significantly more likely to have received than members.

When carers were asked about services that the PD person received, responses were similar but not identical. Nineteen per cent stated that they had had a home carer, 17% stated that they had had district nurse services, 12% day care, 8% respite care, 3% special holidays, 6% meals service and 5% received a night sitting service. However, significantly fewer carers reported having had a social worker (19% as opposed to 26% of PD respondents) and occupational therapy (13% as opposed to 22% of PD respondents). The comparison of PDS members with non-members provided a few surprises, in that non-members were more likely to report receiving both a home carer and a meals service. One explanation could be that domestic and personal care assistance can be purchased independently of social service departments and therefore represent help which can be obtained even where the system of formal service provision is not understood. These findings may also reflect the very high numbers of member carers who are providing care full time and live with the PD person, and might be less likely to see a need for help with domestic and caring tasks within the home.

Those people who *did* report having a particular service were generally happy with it. Levels of satisfaction never fell below 66% for any one service, and were particularly high for consultant and hospital outpatient services. Satisfaction with GPs was similarly high, although 15% said their GP was helpful but too rushed, 12% said their GP was concerned with medication but little else and 12% said their doctor did not seem to be interested in PD. In terms of their GP's understanding of PD, 24% thought it was excellent and 35% good. In relation to this, it is worth noting that 74% thought that seeing a consultant improved the treatment they received from their GP. One of the consultant neurologists interviewed in the study expressed his fear that the development of a health service led by primary care might result in more GPs undertaking the care of PD patients themselves without recourse to specialist secondary health care services and a consequent diminishing in quality of treatment and overall care.

The tendency for users of services to express general satisfaction with them has been noted elsewhere (e.g. Nocon and Qureshi, 1996). However, two cautionary notes are sounded in this study. First, respondents repeatedly emphasized the importance of non-specialist workers having knowledge about PD and were equivocal about the extent to which general health and social care services understand and accommodate the particular needs of people with PD. Secondly, levels of satisfaction with their care in the community related directly to the level of domiciliary services which these people were receiving and bore no relationship to having good specialist medical care, which was reported as having improved or at least stayed the same through the 1990s changes in health care delivery.

Many respondents were happy with having GP and consultant services only and felt that they did not need to receive anything more. Some remarked that if they did need more help, it would be provided by social services:

> My wife had Alzheimer's disease and I nursed her for many years and the social services were very good. So I know what the social services can do, you know if I wanted any help, I'm sure that they would be the first to come and get it.

Slipping through the net

Although many people do not receive services because they are able to cope on their own, others have simply 'slipped through the net' and social services are unaware of the extent to which they are struggling by themselves. One respondent whose wife had recently entered a nursing home struggled to cope with his wife's illness by himself, until almost by chance social services became aware of the difficulties that they were experiencing. By this point, the only feasible option was thought to be for his wife to enter residential care. He explained:

> I'd seen notices about attendance allowance and so I went to the local place, because I was passing there one day, that's how chance it was, so I went in and they gave me two envelopes the size of big library books with all these questions ... there was two lots, one lot was apparently for the social security people and the other lot for the medical side. I took them to the doctor because he had to sign one part which he did and the next thing was I got phone calls from both the social services and the social security saying could they come and see me. So a representative of each came. They had a lot of things with them and I didn't really gather what it was all about really, I just answered all their questions because I was on for this 50 pounds a week. The social services person came back and said, 'I think your wife should be in a nursing home'.

Further exploration of the way in which people were receiving medical services provided a few clues as to why, possibly, they did not appear to be even considered for the social care services which their needs might demand. Contact with GPs was for the most part irregular and in connection with a particular problem rather than in the form of routine check-ups. Given the view from consultants that referrals to social services and other community services are most appropriately channelled through the GP, this may provide a clue as to why the feedback loop from health to social care is not working as well as it should be. Respondents were asked how frequently they saw their GP and whether this tended to be for a routine check-up or only when they had a particular problem. Only 10% saw their GP as often as once a month and 59% said they saw their GP at more than three-monthly intervals. Twenty-eight per cent said they went for routine check-ups but the vast majority (72%) saw their GP only when they had a specific problem. An overwhelming majority (92%) said that they usually collected a prescription without seeing their GP.

When these pieces of information are put together, the pattern emerges of most people seeing their GP infrequently for treatment, rather than routinely for monitoring of their situation; 79% of those who saw their GP at more than three-monthly intervals did so only when they had a problem. However, one 75-year-old woman who had had PD for 35 years, and who experienced numerous problems with medication, illustrated how this pattern of contact was not necessarily picking up problems:

> Well, I don't see ... [the GP] so much, when I go for my prescription being renewed, I don't see him. But then I've not been ill. I don't bother with him.

Of the 85% of people who had been referred to a consultant, 70% were attending hospital between two and four times a year, 9% only once a year and 21% for the initial diagnosis of their PD. As has already been seen, however, these consultations concentrate on medical treatment and rarely, in the time available, move on to screening for social care needs, unless the patient or carer raises these as of paramount concern. Even where social needs *are* noted, the link from the specialist secondary health care service to the social services department as the organizer of social care services, or even to some community health care services, appears to be fragile. This was reflected in comments from the various professionals interviewed. There were two problems: first, they did not know how to go about the referral procedure efficiently; secondly, everyone seemed to think it was someone else's job, or at least not their priority.

> Consultant: In the beginning I started to write to social services and it would be passed from one office to another.... I don't think this is a good use of my time, so unless I have a named contact, I would ask the GP to do that ... my main role is as a diagnostician and clinician.

> GP: The annoying thing is that we get asked to refer people for community care assessment, although it can come from anyone ... there are plenty of people out there who would benefit from being referred without us being involved.

Consultant: I rely on the Parkinson's Disease Society to identify a social work need.

PD nurse: I don't think I myself personally have referred more than perhaps three patients in two years for community care assessments. I will have referred to other agencies hoping that the appropriate choices were made ... it's much more difficult to work out who you refer to for community care assessments.

At the potential receiving end, the disability services team leader confirmed the result: only 3% of all their referrals come from GPs, they get the occasional contact from the local branch of the PDS, but, by and large, they are reliant on self-referral from the PD person or carer. Given the numbers in the survey who had no knowledge or understanding of community care assessment, this picture is disturbing.

Lack of coordination between and even within services was commented upon more by the workers interviewed than by either the PD respondents or their carers. The picture of a relatively tightly contained specialist medical service within secondary health care, which lacked the information and mechanisms to connect effectively with the sprawling world of social care which is delivering this 'new' community care, came across strongly:

Consultant: We don't know how it's working ... it seems fragmented in the districts, it's difficult finding the coordinator.... I'm not sure I really know how the system works.

Equally, from the social care end, there was a helplessness expressed about how to improve communication:

Social services team leader: There isn't a formal framework ... multi-disciplinary meetings or case conferences on just about every case would be overkill ... mainly it's ad hoc and informal.

From the service users' point of view, the effect of having one person who acted as a key worker and coordinator could be seen in relation to the difficulties and obstacles which people faced when trying to access services. Only 29% of the survey stated that they had one particular person who seemed to work on their behalf, but those respondents who did so were significantly less likely to cite difficulties in obtaining information about services (8% as opposed to 92% of those who did not have a key worker) and in finding out about their entitlements, and about which agency was responsible for providing which services. Fifty-eight per cent of these said having a key worker made it quicker and easier to get help. However, in many instances the worker referred to was someone from the PDS, probably a welfare visitor or branch official. In the worker interviews, it was the PDS welfare visitor alone who expressed optimism and energy concerning the coordinating role:

> We liaise with all the other services, for instance if they want home help we contact the home help service and if it's a nursing service, well then the district nurse.... In fact, every few months we have a meeting and the branch provides the cost. In a way, I'm all things to all people ... it does work very well.

The problem of adequate coverage remained, however. The data seemed to suggest that being a PDS member raised expectations about being able to find one's way around services and obtain what was needed, but that the combined effect of PDS membership and having an identified key worker was to raise frustration about obstacles and deficits encountered in the system.

Targeting of services

A major preoccupation for local authorities and health authorities in the delivery of care has been the development of (local) eligibility criteria for service provision. There are two ways of exploring who is getting services, both of which reflect targeting principles. One is to look at the general characteristics of the sample in relation to services received, and the other is to relate levels of reported need in specific areas to receipt of particular services.

Taking the first of these approaches, the characteristics of age, home situation, gender, personal care from a relative and length of time that the respondent had had PD were explored in relation to receipt of services. Those respondents who were aged 65 or over were more likely to receive all services except consultant, outpatient hospital services and PD nurse. Interestingly, they were actually *less* likely to receive these specialist services. This suggests that the older population are instead reliant on medical services from their GP. The higher proportion of all other services that those over 65 receive could be because they have had PD longer and therefore their symptoms are more severe, although severity of symptoms did not, on the whole, appear to increase with age alone. Furthermore, there is no correlation between being under or over 65 and the length of time that respondents had had PD. This suggests that the general trend in community services is to prioritize this group because of their age rather than their PD (Figure 2.8).

Many respondents were satisfied with their main care coming from the GP, but concern was sometimes voiced:

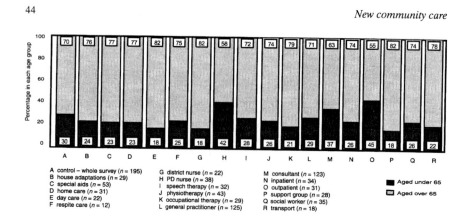

Figure 2.8. *Receipt of services by age of respondents*

I feel that my doctor, a very good man, tends to accept that little can be done for PD patients. No clinic support, a great lack.

At the present time my GP is treating my husband for PD and thinks this is the right thing to do. Whilst I value the help he is giving my husband, that is, we visit the surgery every four to six months, I do feel that perhaps he should be seen by a specialist

One of the consultants interviewed expressed his concern that in the new world of fund-holding general practices, increasing numbers of GPs would seek to manage PD patients within the practice, but because of the small numbers seen by any one GP, they would not have the necessary experience and expertise.

One aspect of the age divide (under and over 65) is the discontinuity in service provision that can occur when service users or potential service users reach the age of 65 and they find that different departments will now be dealing with their case. This discontinuity was summed up by one respondent who initially turned down offers of aids because she did not feel that she needed them then. Some time later, when she felt that they would be useful, she found that, as she was now over 65, different people would be dealing with her case.

An important variable influencing service provision might be whether or not the person with PD lives alone. Twenty-five per cent of respondents in this study lived by themselves, but as a proportion of all respondents who were in receipt of services, only 14% of those who received physiotherapy, occupational therapy and adaptations to the house lived alone, as did only 19% of those who received special aids and only 18% who had a support group. Furthermore, only 21% of all

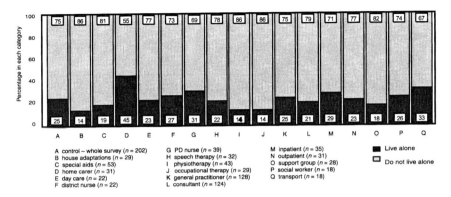

A control – whole survey (n = 202)
B house adaptations (n = 29)
C special aids (n = 53)
D home carer (n = 31)
E day care (n = 22)
F district nurse (n = 22)

G PD nurse (n = 39)
H speech therapy (n = 32)
I physiotherapy (n = 43)
J occupational therapy (n = 29)
K general practitioner (n = 128)
L consultant (n = 124)

M inpatient (n = 35)
N outpatient (n = 31)
O support group (n = 28)
P social worker (n = 18)
Q transport (n = 18)

■ Live alone
▫ Do not live alone

Figure 2.9. *Services received, by home situation*

those who saw a hospital consultant lived alone. This latter slightly lower figure relative to the actual proportion who lived alone is probably a reflection of the fact that those who live alone are quite likely to be widowed and also over the age of 65, and as such is another indicator of the existence of an elderly group who do not receive specialist medical services. An additional factor which also emerged in the study is the potential importance of a carer who can advocate on behalf of the PD person to obtain certain services.

On the other hand, those who lived alone were much more likely to have home care – 45% of all respondents who received this service. Similarly, they were more likely to receive transport services (33%) and to see a PD nurse (31%). They were also slightly more likely to have a district nurse and in-patient hospital treatment (Figure 2.9).

In keeping with the idea that women are more likely to live alone than men, when the receipt of services was correlated with gender it was found that, of all those who had home care, 48% of them were female, of all those who saw a PD nurse 41% of them were female and of all those who received transport services 39% of them were female. Since women constituted only 36% of the overall survey population, this suggests that being female and living alone increases the likelihood of being in receipt of these services. With regard to all other services, women were actually less likely to be in receipt of them than men.

The picture becomes even more complex when the length of time that respondents have had PD is correlated with services received (Figure 2.10). Of the whole survey population, 46% had had PD for five years or less, 17% had had PD for six to nine years and 37% had had PD for ten years or more. As would be expected, those who had had PD for five years or less were in receipt of fewest services, although of all

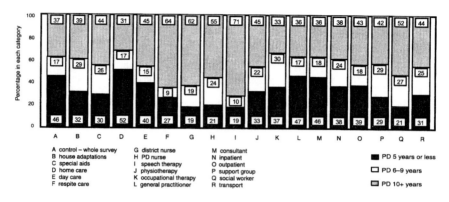

Figure 2.10. *Services received in relation to the length of time respondents had had PD*

those who had a home carer, 52% had had PD for five years or less. The six- to nine-year category also provided a few surprises: they were more likely than the other age categories (after adjusting for the overall age composition of the sample) to have had housing adaptations (29% of all those in receipt of this), special aids (26%), a PD nurse (24%), occupational therapy (30%), physiotherapy (22%), transport services (25%), a social worker (27%), a support group (29%) and hospital in-patient services (24%). However, with regard to respite care, the six- to nine-year category constituted only 9% of all those in receipt of respite services and with regard to speech therapy only 10% came from this group.

A substantial 64% of those who had respite care and 71% of those who had speech therapy had had PD for ten years or more. This group was also much more likely to have seen a district nurse (62%), PD nurse (55%) and a social worker (52%). Furthermore, on the whole, this group had an increased likelihood of being in receipt of all services although, interestingly, their share of home care (31%) and occupational therapy (33%) was lower than would be expected (Figure 2.10).

Members of the PDS a received slightly more services overall, and there was no service that they were significantly less likely to receive than non-members.

The relationship between service provision and levels of need was equally complex. Overall, services seemed to be appropriately targeted at those with high levels of need and not to be provided to those with less severe needs. However, worryingly, in every area of service provi-sion there were also people with high levels of need who were *not* getting a service – in other words, large numbers of people were falling through the net. This can be seen in each of the main categories of need. Thus, for example, in relation to medical needs, those with the severest symptoms are more likely to receive services, with the exception of those who experience a lot of difficulty with tremor. However, those who experience 'some difficulty' with their symptoms do not usually receive a proportional amount of service. Further, of those who are *not* receiving services, there is still a substantial number of respondents who experience a lot of difficulty with a particular symptom.

When it came to practical and daily living needs, although transport and housing adaptation services were being directed at those who are in most need, they are not reaching adequate numbers of PD respondents and as such their mobility and ability to perform tasks in and around their own home is limited. Those respondents who needed a lot of help with personal care at least some of the time are generally being reached by services, although there are still respondents who are in need and who are not in receipt of services. Home care is being directed towards those who have most need of help around the house but, again, they are not reaching adequate numbers. PD respondents who need help with communication are more likely to receive help from a support group; this may well be the local branch of the PDS.

Unmet need

The role of informal carers in bridging these gaps cannot be overestimated. What is therefore uncovered is a high degree of need which is either unmet, or being met, perhaps partially, through the 'service' provided by informal carers. An interesting but disturbing finding is that there is no relationship between the *carer's* health and the formal services provided. Those with PD and their carers in this study did not present as a demanding group. When asked about services which they required but did not receive, perceptions of unmet need among respondents indicated the highest shortfalls in adaptations to housing, physiotherapy and the provision of special aids: 30%, 29% and 29%, respectively, of those who did not receive these services stated that they would like to do so. In one instance, a respondent also pointed out that not only had he applied for a ramp to be fitted outside his house and been turned down, but that no adequate explanation had been given as to why this was so:

> Social services said that they can't give me a ramp, that I'll have to buy one myself and have one fitted myself. Going up those steps is murder.... I don't know why, they just wrote me a letter.

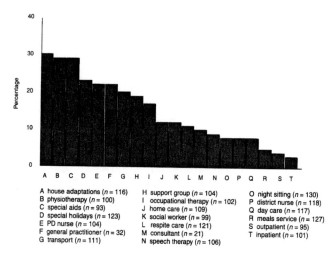

A house adaptations (n = 116)
B physiotherapy (n = 100)
C special aids (n = 93)
D special holidays (n = 123)
E PD nurse (n = 104)
F general practitioner (n = 32)
G transport (n = 111)

H support group (n = 104)
I occupational therapy (n = 102)
J home care (n = 109)
K social worker (n = 99)
L respite care (n = 121)
M consultant (n = 21)
N speech therapy (n = 106)

O night sitting (n = 130)
P district nurse (n = 118)
Q day care (n = 117)
R meals service (n = 127)
S outpatient (n = 95)
T inpatient (n = 101)

Figure 2.11. *Perceptions of unmet need by PD respondents*

The least shortfalls were in meals services and hospital out- and in-patient services; 5%, 4% and 3% of those who did not receive these services stated that they would like to do so (Figure 2.11).

Once more, perceptions among carers were similar but not identical: the highest unmet needs reported were for a PD nurse specialist (37%), occupational therapy (30%), a social worker (23%) and home care (20%). Lowest were for a district nurse (11%), a night sitting service (8%) and a meals service (7%).

Service users and carers actually showed relatively low expectations and demand compared with the frustration felt by workers. Both the social services team leaders expressed dissatisfaction with their inability to deliver the service they felt was required and hence their hesitation to uncover unmet need:

We don't feel we should have waiting lists for services which are growing daily. We don't feel that we should have waiting lists for assessments which are growing as well.

Whether someone is getting the right level of care or not is something they should be saying not me.... I know that certainly his wife is under a lot of pressure, so maybe we are not meeting all of her needs.

This was the perception held by the GP:

I don't think social services assess as favourably as they might do because they haven't got the resources.

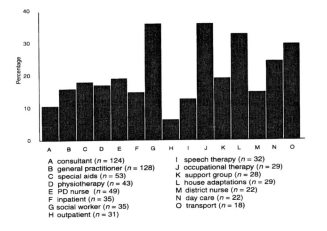

A consultant (*n* = 124)
B general practitioner (*n* = 128)
C special aids (*n* = 53)
D physiotherapy (*n* = 43)
E PD nurse (*n* = 49)
F inpatient (*n* = 35)
G social worker (*n* = 35)
H outpatient (*n* = 31)

I speech therapy (*n* = 32)
J occupational therapy (*n* = 29)
K support group (*n* = 28)
L house adaptations (*n* = 29)
M district nurse (*n* = 22)
N day care (*n* = 22)
O transport (*n* = 18)

Figure 2.12. *Percentage of respondents in receipt of services who express dissatisfaction*

This was a constant source of tension between professionals as they advocated and 'bartered' for their patients/service users, while these same people themselves often underplayed their difficulties:

> GPs are notorious for referring us to urgent cases and when you get there they say, 'What are you doing here?' But then you get someone who is self-referred who says, 'I just need a telephone,' and you get there and they are living in squalor and are really desperate.

One of the consultants, however, was firmly of the view that community services are a precious and scarce resource and it is part of his role to make rigorous judgements about who should most appropriately be referred:

> There's a fine dividing line ... you're happier sitting in a Jaguar but you can get from A to B in a Mini.

His judgement appeared to depend in the first instance on the degree of urgency and level of need conveyed by the patient.

Unmet need was also apparent among those who were in receipt of services. At least two-thirds of respondents who were in receipt of services were satisfied with what they received. However, this still leaves a relatively large number of people who found these services to be inadequate. In particular, 34% of people found their social worker or their occupational therapy to be inadequate. Services were perceived to be inadequate by 31% of those who had adaptations to the house, 28% of those receiving the transport services and 23% of those receiving day care (Figure 2.12). One carer explained:

> We did have one home carer once but she only used to come at dinner time for quarter of an hour just to make his dinner. I mean to me it was neither use nor ornament really. A quarter of an hour is nothing is it ... in and out to do a sandwich, well there's no time for him is there?

In some instances, respondents had by-passed formal service providers, or made good the shortfall by purchasing or obtaining services or aids/equipment for themselves, rather than receiving them through the formal channels. Thirty-eight per cent said that they had made their own arrangements. In terms of extra spending which they had incurred arising from PD, 34% said they had spent extra on heating, 29% on equipment or aids, 14% on adaptations to the house, 11% on medicines or dressings and 16% on other miscellaneous expenditure. This was an issue of which the PDS welfare visitor was particularly aware:

> There are things available but at what cost? With aids, a lot of people are actually purchasing them themselves. It's the same with incontinence pads – it all adds up and it costs a lot all the time.

If people are unable to make good the shortfall, the knock-on effects of a specific unmet need may be pervasive, as illustrated in several of the case studies. For example, the couple hoping for an electric wheelchair were experiencing: a serious threat to the carer's health through struggling to push an unsuitable chair (he had angina and bronchial asthma); feelings of isolation; difficulties in doing the shopping; and increased financial expenditure through greater use of taxis and needing to keep the heating on because they were staying in the house most of the time. A man who had been refused a ramp in place of some very steep steps, although he had arthritis and high blood pressure as well as PD and the family were on income support, explained how if he could not get out of the house, everything seemed to fall apart. As a young man he had run for a club, and he now managed his PD through a regular exercise programme:

> I've got to get out 'cos when I'm in the house I feel terrible. I'm all right in the fresh air walking around.

Overall, 45% of respondents believed that they would need other services in the future. Nevertheless, the picture which emerges is of a group of people who have made incremental adjustments in their daily lives to cope with the illness as it progresses. Too many had therefore reached a point where they were struggling with their difficulties without substantial, sometimes any, outside help, but who did not anticipate being able to carry on indefinitely. The primary reason for increasing levels and range of help not being provided in response to increasing needs lay in the weaknesses in communication and interagency working at the interface between health and social care.

Case study
Mr and Mrs Hollins illustrate many of the themes and issues raised. They lived in Mill Borough and owned their own house. Mrs Hollins was aged 75 years, and had had PD for 35 years. Mr Hollins was also aged 75 years and had himself had two strokes and was diabetic. Mrs Hollins saw her GP rarely, but over the last three years had had hospital appointments with the consultant neurologist every three to six months. Mr Hollins felt that this had resulted in much better treatment and management of his wife's illness but, unfortunately, this had been counteracted by the effects of some bad falls, so that over the last two years Mr Hollins said he had had to assume total responsibility for running the house and caring for his wife. She had deteriorated mentally to a considerable degree as well as physically, and it was this combination, rather than the severity of her physical symptoms (although she had difficulty with tremor, walking and bowel/bladder problems), which led to the need for total care. Intervention from formal services seemed to have been triggered by hospital admissions, which had themselves been because of Mrs Hollins falling and sustaining fractures, or because of the need to change her treatment, or Mr Hollins' own emergency admissions. These hospital admissions had triggered the provision of bath aids (which proved unsuitable but had not been replaced), a ramp, an alarm service and a one-off visit from the district nurse. Mr Hollins refused the full financial assessment for a stair-lift, preferring to purchase that for themselves. Although they had had contact with the hospital social work service and occupational therapist, after one hospital admission, they did not appear to have ongoing social services contact or to be care managed. Mr Hollins was very unclear about whether they had ever had a community care assessment, although it was probable that an assessment of need was completed (by the hospital social worker), despite his refusing the means assessment. The couple had little contact with their sons and their families and were socially quite isolated. Mr Hollins would have liked his wife to have day care, in order, he said, to provide her with some other company, but he was suspicious of respite care as he was adamant that she was not going to end up in long-term residential care. Mrs Hollins reflected on what a long time she had had to cope with the illness, and Mr Hollins was on antidepressants and complained of stress. They were members of the PDS, but said it was too difficult to attend branch meetings. They had had an occasional visit from the PDS welfare visitor. Mr Hollins said the single thing which would most help them would be to have one worker whom they could easily contact and who would periodically call on them at home to check on them. To this end, he had been interested in what he had read about the PD nurse scheme in the PDS newsletter.

Negotiating the health and social care network

To summarize, it would appear that people with PD are for the most part receiving at least some specialist medical input and are reasonably satisfied with their medical care; there is even a tendency to believe that medical care is better now than it was before the 1990s changes. However, the study uncovered a number of problems in the extension of this medical treatment to other health and social care services, which have the potential between them to provide holistic care to assist in the everyday management of PD. These problems can be listed as follows.

- A high percentage (85%) are referred to a consultant neurologist (or geriatrician with a specialist interest in PD), but very few proceed from there to receive either other health care or social care assessments or services.
- Consultants see their priority in the limited consultation time available as being the diagnostic and medical treatment needs of the patient and will address social problems only if presented by the patient/carer; similar prioritization precludes the completion of complicated referral forms for other services and the pursuit of community referrals.
- Most people with PD lack the knowledge of procedures or information about potential services either to raise wider issues or to self-refer.
- Contact with GPs is predominately limited to routine collection of repeat prescriptions, with infrequent direct consultation only when there is a specific problem.
- Secondary health care services expect the primary health care team to make referrals for community services (although this is less so for geriatricians than for neurologists), but GPs do not necessarily see this as their role; one of the reasons lies in the fact that some GPs regard the care of the PD patient as appropriately belonging to the expert.
- While consultants may write to GPs after the patient's visit to the hospital clinic, other referrals, even where suggested, are at the discretion of GPs and may not be picked up and followed through, because of the lack of routine contact between PD patients and GPs.
- Social services are in contact with a very small proportion of the total population of PD patients (slightly higher in those over 65 years) and both communication from health care professionals to social services and feedback from the latter on action taken are acknowledged to be poor, being both ad hoc and infrequent.

The world of health and social care which emerges can perhaps be understood by conceptualizing it as a number of relatively self-contained systems (e.g. secondary health care, social services), each working in its own way. While the White Paper envisaged the development of a 'seamless service', the reality appears to be that these separate systems are sustaining interconnections only at the macro level of operations – such as joint planning committees. A reiterated complaint from both the professionals and the people with PD or their carers concerned the lack of communication between the different health and social care professionals, and the fact that frequently it was the patient/service user who provided the only feedback from one worker to another. This was seen by the workers who participated as a major failing of the system and its capacity to deliver integrated holistic care. In an ideal world, a comprehensive network of specialist liaison workers would deal with the referral and communication problems identified in this study, which are preventing people with PD from receiving the information, support and overall management of their care which their condition potentially requires. PD is a chronic degenerative disease in which medical diagnosis and treatment are paramount but whose increasingly pervasive effects create sometimes extensive social care needs. At the minimum, this requires the pivotal link – envisaged in the Department of Health's (1994a) implementation guidance, of the GP between secondary health care and both community health and social care services – to work considerably more effectively than was demonstrated in this study. Only a handful of respondents identified being referred to, or given information about, agencies or services which might lead directly or indirectly to a comprehensive needs assessment.

A comprehensive network of liaison and attached workers could include the attachment of care managers to general practices and hospital outpatient clinics. However, there are two major obstacles to the implementation of such a system. First, such measures demand large amounts of professional time. Secondly, they draw on a model of service delivery which fans out from the specialist medical core. While there is logic and coherence in this model, it no longer fits with the world of social care delivery, which has its own core and cannot comprehensively resource worker attachments to other systems *at the level of specialist operational units*. The now much-reduced hospital social work service never could provide the comprehensive coverage required, even at the zenith of its operation: indeed, the proactive worker in outpatient clinics quickly became overwhelmed by the volume of referrals, in much the same way as the PD nurse in this study described the clinical nurse specialist scheme as having been overtaken by its own success. The hopes vested in the 1980s in the multidisciplinary teams, for achieving coordinated service delivery and interprofessional working, suffer from a similar problem of scale. Multidisciplinary teams work best in a tightly coordinated, narrowly focused environment and all too often are spread too thinly in the community to be effective. The interprofessional endeavour requires resourcing in itself, and as one of the hospital consultants in this study argued forcibly, diverting the energies of a specialist in this way (into multidisciplinary meetings, for example) may actually reduce the quality of care provided to the patient. Such teams are unlikely to be set up in all provider units at the point of delivery to the service user, as recommended in the neurological charities' consultative report on service standards (Neurological Alliance, 1992). A more likely scenario is the one described in this study, of ad hoc 'interested party' meetings, prompted by a specific need or problem.

The recommendations from this study therefore focus around seeing the person with PD and the carer as a communication and liaison resource, to procure services which may well be available but whose effective delivery is not being achieved. This is a significant shift from the established view of seeing the person with PD as a (relatively passive) service user and the carer as a resource primarily as an alternative service provider. Thus, one set of recommendations is aimed at resourcing the PD patient and carer in the self-management of their care pathway. The most illuminating finding of the research is that the people who demonstrated a successful negotiation of their pathway (or 'career') were the people who had been able to control that process *themselves*, usually through a combination of personal resources, available external resources and the ability to access those resources in the way which best suited their individual circumstance. It is possible that this is the underlying explanation for the findings in the study's 'ten years plus' group, who did not display the picture presented in the Society's own discussion document (Parkinson's Disease Society, 1994, p. 16):

> During the final phase, typically some ten years after diagnosis, drugs cease to be very effective. The patient suffers from multiple disabilities.... The needs in this phase are for intervention from a fully skilled, domiciliary, multi-disciplinary team.

Some of the people in the study had learnt to manage over 20 or 30 years, and were no more likely to be receiving some key community care services than the six- to ten-year group. This is not to say that they did not struggle sometimes, or that there had not been unnecessary obstacles encountered when trying to obtain help. Further, unmet need was found.

These, however, were the survivors in the community. At the same time as resourcing such people, checks must be in place to identify those people – most likely the very frail, severely affected and those who do not have an informal carer capable of acting as an advocate on their behalf – who are unable to be actively involved in their own care management in this way. This should assist in the early targeting of people whose need for intensive support through the care management system is such that they are otherwise greatly at risk of requiring entry to residential or nursing home care. Thus, while the adoption of such measures might in some instances result in greater take-up of services, it should, overall, lead to more effective use of services at an earlier stage, both maintaining situations which might otherwise break down (thereby creating a sudden, intense and costly demand for formal services) and delaying the need for total care in residential settings in other situations. It also uses the presently largely untapped resource of the service user to resource the multidisciplinary endeavour, which current practice suggests the services themselves are unable to resource adequately.

In brief, four interrelated, overarching problems are posed by the findings of this study:

1 how to increase numbers of assessments and improve the comprehensiveness of assessments for PD people;

2 how to improve coordination between the different health and social care sectors, in particular, how to create sustainable links between a specialist medical service and general social care service;

3 how to open up the social care sector for people with PD as a preventive measure – before deterioration and breakdown;

4 how to achieve the above objectives in the context of limited public resources.

The following recommendations seek to address these problems:

1 The person with PD or the carer should become the 'communications centre', assisted by:
   • information packs;
   • advice on assessment procedures;
   • a 'self-help' needs-registration and needs-monitoring form;
   • extension of the PDS counselling, advice and advocacy services.

2 There should be a simplification of referral systems for social care services, using the above needs-registration/monitoring form.

3 The role of GPs as the link between hospital and community should be strengthened through the standardization of *routine* contact with the PD patient and the use of the needs-registration/monitoring form.

4 The PD nurse scheme should be extended to fulfil a community liaison function; this service could be purchased by GPs (e.g. for

medication management) and social services departments (e.g. for care management).

5 There should be key workers in complex cases. This function could be fulfilled via an extension of the PDS welfare visiting scheme where no one professional is intensively involved.

6 The PDS should work with social care agencies at the level of organizational management to make existing health and social care systems more effective for people with PD. In particular, it would be useful to monitor the use of respite care, home care and housing adaptations.

Some of these recommendations are also aimed at the PDS establishing its place in this 'new world' of health and social care so as to achieve a better service for people with PD, thus extending the success which it has arguably had in influencing medical care. The very high number of respondents who have been seen by a hospital consultant, for the most part a neurologist or geriatrician with a special interest in PD, must be an encouraging finding for the Society, which has fought for specialist diagnosis and treatment over the past decade. Organizations such as the PDS represent an important arm of the 'third sector' in community care, that is, support and services provided through independent voluntary organizations or private businesses. The PDS has not, to date, extended its provider activities to any great degree, although it continues to provide holidays, volunteer visitors and some paid welfare visitors. It remains a promoter of research and a campaigning organization, with the particular aim of raising public awareness. At the level of the individual member, it sees itself as primarily providing information and offering support and advocacy. The emotional and 'moral' support derived by members who are strongly engaged with their local branch was clear from both the comments sections of the questionnaire responses and the case study interviews. It is also possible to see that PDS members are more knowledgeable about health and social care in general terms and have greater expectations about their needs being met. However, the positive impact of PDS membership on community care outcomes, as measured by assessments undertaken, services received and successful negotiation of the system of health and social care, was not significant, except in relation to one or two services which have been specifically targeted by a particular branch.

It cannot be assumed that any of these recommendations would achieve a comprehensive improvement in meeting the *emotional* needs which were highlighted by the study. It is always the case that the right worker in the right situation at the right time will continue to understand the need for counselling at particular times (e.g. at diagnosis, when deciding whether to enter residential care) and will continue to respond sensitively at all times to the underlying emotional dimension. However, to bolster such examples of good practice, the PDS should consider the feasibility of extending its confidential telephone help/counselling line services to local areas. Some of the people who identified most strongly their need to talk to 'someone who understood' were also those who would not attend branch meetings, even though they recognized the emotional support which might be available. A help line could also serve as a research and monitoring device to log clusters of difficulties and problems experienced with services; this could be done without breaching individual confidentiality. There is no agency which could provide this service as appropriately as the PDS, and although its effects could not easily be measured, it is arguably one of the most valuable contributions which the Society could make in sustaining people with PD and their carers.

Conclusions

The 'new world' of community care is not really operating as such for people with PD. However, the 'old world' of self-contained health and medical care appears to be providing at least as good, if not better, a service as before 1993. The disappointment lies in the fact that community care in its true definition, involving a comprehensive and integrated network of health and social care, is not being delivered, despite the sometimes extensive social care needs which living with PD may raise. Even allowing for the fact that help from informal carers may be the preferred option for the person with PD and their relatives or friends, there is considerable room for improvement in the buttressing of that informal care by formal services. In some instances, high levels of need are remaining unmet by either formal services or informal arrangements. Perhaps the saddest comment on the 'seamless service' came from a district nurse, who had not been in post before the new community care arrangements and who made the point that she was generally happy with the way things worked. However, she relayed the fact that patients quoted a different experience:

> Most of the things patients want doing they used to get from home care and now they have this variety of services and it's bits from here and bits from there, and they get confused and end up struggling to do things themselves because they don't know who all these different people are.

In their own way, the people with PD and their carers in this study underlined her words:

Married woman helping her elderly father care for her mother: I don't know what's happening to the care in the community, whether they're going to keep it.

Elderly widow, diagnosed with PD eight years ago: I don't know of any community care ... nobody has ever suggested anything ... there must be some kind of help.

Acknowledgement

Some sections of this chapter have been reproduced from the research report (Lloyd and Smith, 1998). I am grateful to the contribution made by the project research associate, Maria Smith, in undertaking and reporting this study.

References

ASSOCIATION OF DIRECTORS OF SOCIAL SERVICES and SOCIAL SERVICES INSPECTORATE (1991) *Care in the Community Project: Care Management and Assessment.* London: DOH/SSI.

BEWLEY, C. and GLENDINNING, C. (1994) *Involving Disabled People in Community Care Planning.* York: Joseph Rowntree Foundation.

CHALLIS, D. and CHESSUM, R. (1990) *Case Management in Social and Health Care.* London: Whiting and Birch.

CHALLIS, D., DARTON, R., JOHNSON, L., STONE, M. and TRASKE, K. (1995) *Care Management and Health Care of Older People: The Darlington Community Care Project.* Aldershot: Arena.

DEPARTMENT OF HEALTH (1989) *Caring for People,* Cm 849. London: HMSO.

DEPARTMENT OF HEALTH (1994a) *Implementing Caring for People: The Role of the GP and Primary Health Care Team.* London: DOH/HMSO.

DEPARTMENT OF HEALTH (1994b) *Implementing Caring for People: Community Care Packages for Older People.* London, DOH/HMSO.

DEPARTMENT OF HEALTH and SOCIAL SERVICES INSPECTORATE (1991) *Training for Community Care: A Joint Approach.* London: HMSO.

GRIFFITHS, R. (1988) *Community Care: Agenda for Action.* London: HMSO.

LEWIS, J. and GLENNERSTER, H. (1996) *Implementing the New Community Care.* Buckingham: Open University Press.

LLOYD, M. and SMITH, M. (1998) *Assessment and Service Provision under the new Community Care Arrangements for People with Parkinson's Disease and their Carers,* arc Research Reports No. 13, University of Manchester.

MEANS, R. and SMITH, R. (1994) *Community Care: Policy and Practice.* Buckingham: Open University Press.

MUTCH, W. (1990) Aspects of the epidemiology of Parkinson's disease. In *The Parkinson's Papers.* London: Franklin Scientific Projects.

NEUROLOGICAL ALLIANCE (1992) *Living With a Neurological Condition: Standards of Services for Quality of Life.* London: Neurological Alliance.

NOCON, A. and QURESHI, H. (1996) *Outcomes of Community Care for Users and Carers.* Buckingham: Open University Press.

OLIVER, M., ZARB, G., SILVER, J., MOORE, M. and SALISBURY, V. (1988)

Walking into Darkness: The Experience of Spinal Cord Injury. Basingstoke: Macmillan.

PARKINSON'S DISEASE SOCIETY (1994) *Meeting a Need?* London: Parkinson's Disease Society.

WARBURTON, R.W. (1994) *Implementing Caring for People: Home and Away.* London: DOH/HMSO.

WISTOW, G., KNAPP, M., HARDY, B. and ALLEN, C. (1994) *Social Care in a Mixed Economy.* Buckingham: Open University Press.

WISTOW, G., KNAPP, M., HARDY, B., FORDER, J., MANNING, R. and KENDALL, J. (1996) *Social Care Markets: Progress and Prospects.* Buckingham: Open University Press.

Chapter 3

The needs of people with Parkinson's disease and their families: The Parkinson's Disease Study, Devon and Cornwall, 1989–92

Robert Jones, Carol D'eath, Jane Harnsford, Heather Hutchinson, Linda Hyde, Linda Thurlow and Lorraine Spanton

The purpose of this project was to identify and assess the needs – physical, emotional/psychological, social and spiritual – of people with Parkinson's disease (PD) and their families within general medical practices in Devon and Cornwall, and to measure how well, and by whom, these needs were being met. The intention was that the results of the study would indicate priority areas of educational input for general practitioners and other primary care professionals.

The study sample

Five hundred and twenty-one people with PD and 318 of their carers were interviewed in their homes. Originally, 1,000 people with the disease had been notified to the project by 284 general practitioners. However, for a variety of reasons, it was not possible to interview 479 (48%) of these. In fact, these figures are in line with the experience of Mutch *et al.* (1986), who, in their Aberdeen study, were notified of 1,325 patients but whose interviewed sample eventually numbered 267 (i.e. 20%).

The names of people with PD were provided to the project secretary by general practitioners. The accuracy of diagnosis was not confirmed by specialist examination. Other studies suggest that about 15% of people with Parkinsonism (i.e. Parkinsonian symptoms) do not actually suffer from PD (see Chapter 1). However, it is impossible to identify people with PD clinically with certainty before post-mortem (and 25% at post-mortem prove not to have had the disease). In this study, all patients notified by general practitioners as having PD were included, the justification being that we are concerned with the needs of people and the carers of people with Parkinsonism rather than with cellular or biochemical exactitude.

Of the 521 patients interviewed, 146 (28%) were members of the Parkinson' s Disease Society (PDS) and 375 (72%) were not. One out of three of the men interviewed were members, whereas for women the figure was only one in four.

Age and sex structure of the sample

In Table 3.1, the age structure of the present sample is compared with that of Oxtoby (1982) and Mutch *et al.* (1986). Mutch's sample was similar to that in the present study. The Oxtoby sample (by questionnaire from PDS members) contained more middle-aged and fewer elderly patients than the other two studies.

Degree of disability

It may be misleading to compare the percentage disability discovered in the three studies because three different measures of disability were used: Oxtoby derived an overall measure of handicap by 'combining the answers to ... three questions on tremor, walking and speech'. Mutch

Table 3.1. *Age distribution (%) of men in the study samples*

Patient' s age	Study		
	Oxtoby	*Mutch*	*Jones*
Men			
< 55 years	11	12	5
55–69 years	52	27	37
70+ years	37	61	58
Totals	129	109	278
Women			
< 55 years	12	2	2
55–69 years	62	14	21
70+ years	45	83	77
Totals	123	140	243

Table 3.2. *Percentage of PD patients by degree of disability in three surveys*

Survey 1 – Oxtoby Oxtoby	%	Survey 2 Mutch Hoehn and Yahr scale	%	Survey 3 – Jones Barthel index	%
Little or no handicap	10	Mild, Grade1 Mild, Grade 2	14 13	Independent (20) Mild functional loss (15–19)	40 35
Partial handicap	55	Moderate, Grade 3	23	Moderate functional loss (10–14)	15
Severely handicapped	19	Severe, Grade 4 Severe, Grade 5	35 10	Severe functional loss (5–9) Very severe functional loss (0–4)	6 46

Table 3.3. *Marital status of those with PD in two surveys*

Marital status	Percentage in study	
	Oxtoby	Jones
Men		
Single	4	4
Married	85	77
Widowed/divorced	11	16/3
Women		
Single	17	13
Married	51	38
Widowed/divorced	32	46/3

used the Hoehn and Yahr scale (see Chapter 1). In this study, the Barthel ADL index was used. It has been validated as a standard measure of physical disability independent of cause. In Table 3.2 the percentage of people with PD found to be disabled in the three surveys is compared. It will be seen that the percentage of severely disabled, as opposed to independent or mildly disabled, people is considerably lower in this study compared with the other two. This finding has major educational and service implications.

Marital status and household composition

Tables 3.3 and 3.4 show the marital status of the men and women with PD who were interviewed and their household composition, again compared with those recorded by Oxtoby (Mutch has no comparable figures). There are several notable differences between the present study and the earlier survey. First, many more women with PD seen in this survey are now widowed or divorced. Secondly, while a large number of women still live alone, fewer are living with their sons and daughters.

Table 3.4. *Household composition (%) of samples in two surveys*

	Men		Women	
	Oxtoby	Jones	Oxtoby	Jones
Alone	7	11	27	22
With spouse	62	74	37	34
With son/daughter	20	2	18	8
Residential home	4	11	7	33
Other	7	2	11	3

Table 3.5. *Age and sex distribution of carers in the present study*

Age	Total	Men	Women
0–49	33	6	27
50–54	19	1	18
55–59	30	3	27
60–64	40	5	35
65–69	63	21	42
70–74	51	11	40
75–79	47	22	25
80–84	27	11	16
85 and over	9	4	5
Totals	319	84	235

Thirdly, residential homes have become one of the main providers of accommodation for people with PD, particularly women. Although part of this last apparent change may be due to underreporting in the Oxtoby survey, the standards of care provided within residential homes for people with PD must be seen as a major matter of concern.

The carers

The total number of carers interviewed was 318. Of the 203 patients whose domestic carers were not interviewed, 108 lived in residential homes. The remainder either lived alone or had no available carer (e.g. were independent and their 'carer' was out). The age and sex distributions of carers are shown in Table 3.5. Whereas 83% of male carers are aged over 65, for female carers the comparable figure is 54%. It is notable that whereas 88% of female patients are over 65 years old, 46% of female carers are less than 65 years old. These figures have implications for service provision, for employment and potential financial need.

The disease and its symptoms

Disability/dependency

The overall disability figures by age and sex of the 521 patients interviewed are shown in Table 3.6. With regard to grades of functional disability, the following categories by Barthel index score are used

Table 3.6. *Level of disability among the survey sample, by sex and age (number of subjects)*

	Men, by age group				Women, by age group				Total
	<60	60–79	80+	Total	<60	60–79	80+	Total	
Independent	20	103	15	138	11	48	13	72	210
Mild	6	51	23	80	2	61	40	103	183
Moderate	2	25	14	41	0	24	12	36	77
Severe	1	8	4	13	0	11	6	17	30
Very Severe	1	2	3	6	0	5	10	15	21
Total in age groups	30	189	59	278	13	149	81	243	521

throughout this text: independent = 20, mild = 15–19, moderate = 10–14, severe = 5–9, very severe = 0–4. As well as confirming the greater percentage of women (33%) than men (21%) with PD who are aged over 80 years, this table shows that many more men with PD are independent (50%) than women (30%), and that many fewer men are severely disabled (7%) than women (13%).

Swings in disability

It is a well recognized feature of PD that the severity of disability varies from day to day or even during the day. Patients and carers talk about 'good days' and 'bad days'. Table 3.7 shows that people who have mild or moderate disability are much more likely to suffer disabling swings than people who are independent or who are severely affected.

Table 3.7. *Variability of level of disability among survey sample*

Functional category	No. of patients in category on a good day	No. who lose 5+ points on a bad day	Percentage who drop a category on a bad day
Independent	210	13	6
Mild	183	52	24
Moderate	77	30	39
Severe	30	4	13
Very severe	21	0	0

Table 3.8. *Functional disability by time since diagnosis in years*

Years since diagnosis	Functional disability					
	None	Mild	Moderate	Severe	Very severe	Totals
0–4	99	67	22	8	11	207
5–9	61	55	22	9	1	148
10–14	33	27	15	5	3	83
15–24	14	29	15	4	4	66
25+	3	5	3	4	2	17
Totals	210	183	77	30	21	521

Speed of development of disability

It is recognized that some people with PD deteriorate rapidly whereas others progress very slowly. In Table 3.8 it can be seen that of the 166 patients who had been diagnosed more than ten years earlier, two-thirds are still independent ($n = 50$) or mildly functionally affected ($n = 61$), whereas of the 207 diagnosed less than five years earlier, 9% are already severely ($n = 11$) affected.

It would be very valuable if the likelihood of fast or slow deterioration could be clinically assessed early in the disease process: this is a priority for future research. The identification of the existence of 'fast' and 'slow' tracks would have educational implications.

Development and frequency of symptoms

In Table 3.9, the symptoms suffered at different stages of the disease (as measured by the severity of functional impairment) are enumerated. A number of aspects are particularly interesting:

1 A large number of symptoms are suffered by a large number of patients at all stages in the disease.
2 The only symptoms whose frequency changes consistently with severity of disability appear to be bedsores and swallowing, which get worse with increasing disability, and cramp, which improves with increasing disability, being at its maximum during the independent stage.
3 Worry and depression (as expressed by the patient) are at their highest in the mildly disabled stage.
4 There is a high level of symptoms in the independent stage – there is a lot going on in this stage.
5 The frequency of different symptoms varies widely.

Table 3.9. *Symptoms suffered by men and women patients, enumerated by severity of functional impairment*

	% with symptom	Independent (n = 210) n %	Mild (n = 183) n %	Moderate (n = 77) n %	Severe (n = 30) n %	Very severe (n = 21) n %
Balance	74	67 (141)	80 (147)	83 (64)	60 (18)	76 (16)
Dribbles	62	47 (99)	74 (135)	66 (51)	83 (25)	57 (12)
Weak	54	48 (100)	61 (111)	49 (38)	63 (19)	52 (11)
Reduced talking	52	37 (77))	52 (103)	62 (48)	87 (26)	71 (15)
Constipation	51	39 (81)	57 (104)	66 (51)	57 (17)	61 (13)
Cramp	50	59 (124)	51 (94)	40 (31)	30 (9)	19 (4)
Dizzy	45	38 (79)	53 (97)	45 (35)	57 (17)	33 (7)
Worry	44	41 (86)	51 (94)	40 (31)	39 (12)	19 (4)
Pain	43	37 (72)	48 (87)	44 (34)	43 (13)	62 (13)
Confusion	40	29 (61)	49 (89)	42 (32)	60 (18)	52 (11)
Sleep	40	39 (82)	43 (78)	42 (32)	37 (11)	38 (8)
Urine	36	27 (57)	39 (72)	44 (34)	37 (11)	76 (16)
Breathless	36	30 (64)	49 (89)	23 (18)	33 (10)	38 (8)
Reduced weight	26	24 (51)	22 (41)	34 (26)	37 (11)	33 (7)
Difficulty swallowing	26	12 (26)	30 (55)	39 (30)	43 (13)	43 (9)
Cough	17	13 (28)	20 (36)	21 (16)	17 (5)	24 (5)
Reduced appetite	17	16 (33)	16 (29)	19 (15)	20 (6)	19 (4)
Nausea	12	13 (27)	12 (22)	19 (15)	27 (8)	14 (3)
Vomiting	7	3 (7)	7 (12)	10 (8)	17 (5)	10 (2)
Bedsores	6	1 (0)	4 (7)	12 (9)	23 (7)	38 (8)
Diarrhoea	5	3 (7)	6 (11)	8 (6)	7 (2)	5 (1)

These figures are of great relevance to both the education of general practitioners and service provision. When the number of symptoms recorded is compared with the number of symptoms reported (i.e. known to the doctor or nurse) (Table 3.10), the so far largely unsuspected need for general practitioners and consultants to carry out careful assessment of symptoms during the earlier stages of the disease is clearly demonstrated. During the independent stage, almost 50% of symptoms are unreported.

Confusion/dementia

These cognitive symptoms were measured at interview with all patients using the Hodkinson Abbreviated Mental Test (scores of 0–3 indicate

Table 3.10. *Under-reporting of symptoms by patients in present survey (from list of 22 symptoms)*

No. of patients by function category	No. of symptoms recorded	Average per patient	% of symptoms not reported to doctor or nurse
Independent (n = 201)	1362	6.5	47%
Mild (n = 183)	1577	8.6	38%
Moderate (n = 77)	669	8.7	40%
Severe (n = 30)	272	9.1	32%
Very severe (n = 21)	182	8.7	26%

demented, 4–6 some confusion, 7–10 not confused) (Table 3.11). The figures do not suggest that confusion is higher in old people with PD than in people of the same age who have not got the disease, although (as our interviewers have confirmed) patients may often appear to be confused.

Anxiety/depression

Anxiety and depression were evaluated using the Hamilton Anxiety and Depression (HAD) scale. It is clear (Table 3.12) that over one-third of people with PD are clinically anxious and almost a third are depressed. Although maximum anxiety is found during the stage of moderate disability and maximum depression at the stage of severe disability, a considerable number of people are affected during the independent and mildly disabled stages.

Additional clinical problems

In Table 3.13, additional diseases suffered are listed by patients' age, for men and women. In Tables 3.14 and 3.15, information is provided about

Table 3.11. *Confusion/dementia (% of survey sample) by age and sex*

Degree of confusion	Men(age, years)			Women (age, years)		
	< 60 (n = 30)	60–79 (n = 189)	80+ (n = 58)	<60 (n = 13)	60–79 (n = 149)	80+ (n = 78)
None or slight	97	92	69	100	85	77
Some confusion	3	6	17	0	9	12
Demented	0	2	12	0	7	12

Table 3.12. *Percentage of patients with clinical anxiety and depression (as indicated by scores over 8 on the HAD), by functional disability*

Functional disability	Anxiety	Depression
Independent (*n* = 210)	29	19
Mild (*n* = 183)	34	31
Moderate (*n* = 77)	42	42
Severe (*n* = 30)	40	47
Very severe (*n* = 21)	29	33
Total average (*n* = 521)	36	29

the clinical problems suffered by carers. Many patients and carers had more than one complicating disease – the figures provided related solely to their prime complaint.

Although the numbers are small, it is notable that of patients aged less than 60 years only 15% of women had no other disease whereas the figure for men was 60%.

The majority of both male and female carers had clinical problems. Overall, 67% were affected in ways which could adversely influence their ability to provide domestic care.

Patients' feelings and carer strain

The feelings of PD patients and carers, the amount of carer strain and marital stress were enquired about during the interviews.

Table 3.16 relates to patients' emotions as described at interview. Although at first glance they appear to be predominantly happy, with low figures for irritability and depression, this contrasts with 44% who confessed to anxiety and 44% who said they were depressed when asked about these symptoms directly. It also contrasts with the 36% found to be clinically anxious and 29% found to be clinically depressed according to the HAD scale. For carers, a similar picture emerges (Table 3.16).

When those patients and carers who have said they are usually happy, rarely low or depressed and who rarely worry are matched against their HAD scores (Table 3.17), the disparity between what they say and what they are becomes plain. The implications for assessment and for education concerning assessment in these figures are clear.

The Robinson Caregiver Strain Index was used to judge the degree of strain under which domestic carers are living. Using the criterion that seven or more items on the Index indicates a greater level of stress (e.g. lost sleep, physical strain, emotional problems, feeling overwhelmed), carers at all stages showed evidence of strain, with levels rising steadily

Table 3.13. *Additional prime medical problems among patients surveyed (number of subjects)*

Age	Arthritis	Cardiac	Stroke	Lung	Psychological	Eyes	Ears	Other	None
Men									
< 60 years (*n* = 30)	6	1	–	–	–	–	1	4	18
60–74 years (*n* = 128)	22	21	2	2	1	7	1	29	43
75 years and over (*n* = 120)	22	12	3	3	2	14	3	24	37
Total (*n* = 278)	50	34	5	5	3	21	5	57	98
Women									
< 60 years (*n* = 13)	3	1	–	0	1	1	–	5	2
60–74 years (*n* = 88)	17	11	2	–	2	4	5	26	21
75 years and over (*n* = 142)	40	9	8	8	12	9	3	26	27
Total (*n* = 243)	60	21	10	8	15	14	8	57	50

Table 3.14. *Number of carers with clinical problems*

	Men (n = 77)	Women (n = 211)
Arthritis	6	27
Cardiac	11	28
Stroke	3	1
Respiratory	9	5
Psychological	2	11
Eyes	3	5
Ears	2	5
Others	25	52
Total	61	134

Table 3.15. *Percentage of carers with clinical problems, by age group and sex*

Age group (years)	Male carers (n = 77)	Female carers (n = 211)
< 60	50	37
60–74	70	70
75+	94	89

Table 3.16. *Frequency of emotions felt*

Emotion	Frequency (no. of subjects)				% with emotion usually or often
	Usually	Often	Sometimes	Rarely	
Patients					
Happy	332	64	81	29	78
Tired	60	197	167	85	50
Irritable	6	46	191	266	10
Frustrated	15	130	202	160	28
Depressed	12	68	188	234	16
Worried	31	111	175	193	28
Forgetful	14	100	200	193	22
Carers					
Happy	215	40	37	13	84
Tired	19	102	132	54	39
Irritable	3	42	144	116	15
Frustrated	4	55	132	116	19
Depressed	6	22	123	154	9
Worried	12	66	113	114	26
Forgetful	3	31	122	149	11

Table 3.17. *Clinical anxiety and depression (as indicated by HAD score) among patients and carers who deny these symptoms*

Emotions volunteered	No. volunteering these emotions	% (n) clinically anxious	% (n) clinically depressed
Patients			
Usually happy	332	25 (84)	22 (72)
Rarely low/depressed	234	16 (37)	15 (35)
Rarely worry	193	19 (37)	22 (22)
Carers			
Usually happy	215	27 (59)	7 (15)
Rarely low/depressed	154	21 (32)	4 (6)
Rarely worry	114	17 (19)	22 (7)

Table 3.18. *Strain among carers in survey*

Functional disability of patient	% of carers with a positive strain level
Independent (n = 132)	11
Mildly disabled (n = 102)	32
Moderately disabled (n = 44)	61
Severely disabled (n = 20)	70
Very severely disabled (n = 7)	71

from those 'looking after' independent patients to those caring for the very severely disabled (Table 3.18). Altogether, 94 out of 318 carers were under a high level of strain.

Social needs

Mobility

Of the 247 patients (47%) who possessed a car, 123 (50%) were still driving and the domestic carers of 119 (79%) of them were also driving. Of the PD drivers, 119 (97%) were independent or only mildly affected, two were moderately affected and (fortunately) only one severely affected.

Carer relief

Overall, 42% of carers would not leave their charges by day and 73% would not leave them at night. More detail is provided in Table 3.19.

Table 3.19. *Carers' perceived opportunities for respite (%)*

% of carers	By day	By night
Not safe to leave	5	5
Never would	37	68
Would leave for up to 4 hours (8 hours at night)	22	9
Would leave for over 4 hours (8 hours at night)	36	18

Availability of respite

Of the 521 patients, 176 had heard about the possibility of respite care (club/group, day centre, day hospital), whereas 345 (66%) had not. The numbers who attend respite care are shown in Table 3.20. As can be seen, the vast majority do not.

Domestic and financial support

In general, the amount of domestic and financial support is thought to be adequate by domestic carers (Tables 3.21 and 3.22), although there must be some doubt as to their level of knowledge of what could be available. Certainly, the level of support increases with the severity of disability (Table 3.23).

Spiritual needs

Among people living at home, of the 190 (45%) who used to go to church regularly half do so now, and although 78 (19%) receive a church visitor at home, a further 67 (10%) would like to do so.

Professional services

Continuing care

In order to improve the services received by people with PD and their carers, it is necessary to know first by whom these services are currently being provided. Table 3.24 shows that most surveillance is carried out by general practitioners, with little contribution from other professionals. When asked whom they considered to be their chief professional supporter, people with PD volunteered their general practitioner ($n = 293$), specialist ($n = 63$), district nurse ($n = 11$), physiotherapist ($n = 3$),

Table 3.20. *Respite care used by patients in survey*

Type of respite care	No. of patients who attend		
	Regularly	*Sometimes*	*Never*
Club/group	66	14	431
Day centre	21	2	475
Day hospital	11	6	480

Table 3.21. *Domestic and financial support (patients at home: n = 413)*

Service received	No. in receipt		No. (%) of patients who think they need more help (n = 413)		No. (%) of carers who think they need more help (n = 318)	
Home help	132	(32%)	25	(6%)	17	(5%)
Shopping	90	(22%)	10	(2%)	6	(2%)
Laundry	82	(20%)	10	(2%)	4	(1%)
Equipment	197	(48%)	25	(6%)	19	(6%)
Meals	32	(8%)	4	(1%)	1	(–)
Finance	174	(42%)	25	(6%)	26	(8%)

Table 3.22. *No. (%) of patients receiving financial help*

	No.	(%)
Attendance allowance	141	(34%)
Mobility	52	(13%)
Invalid care	1	(3%)
Other	79	(19%)

Table 3.23. *Total numbers at home receiving domestic and financial help by disability*

	Independent (n = 201)		Mild (n = 140)		Moderate (n = 46)		Severe (n = 19)		Very severe (n = 8)	
	n	*%*	*n*	*%*	*n*	*%*	*n*	*%*	*n*	*%*
Home help	38	19	62	44	18	39	8	42	6	75
Shopping	26	13	3	29	18	39	4	21	3	38
Laundry	26	13	34	24	17	37	3	18	2	25
Equipment	38	19	95	68	39	85	17	9	8	100
Meals	13	6	14	10	5	11	0	0	0	0
Finance	32	16	74	53	41	89	19	100	8	100

Table 3.24. *Number (%) of patients being monitored by health and social services personnel*

Professional seen	How often seen			Chief support	
	Regularly	Never	Sometimes/ have to ask		
General practitioner	223 (43%)	6 (1%)	290 (56%)	293	(56%)
Consultant	135 (26%)	253 (49%)	128 (29%)	63	(12%)
District nurse	77 (15%)	395 (77%)	41 (8%)	11	(2%)
Physiotherapist	35 (7%)	406 (79%)	70 (14%)	3	(<1%)
Occupational therapist	15 (3%)	394 (76%)	106 (21%)	2	(<1%
Speech therapist	5 (1%)	488 (95%)	18 (4%)	0	(0%)
Social worker	7 (1%)	443 (86%)	62 (12%)	?	(?%)
Health visitor	8 (2%)	461 (91%)	39 (8%)	10	(2%)
Other	55 (11%)	403 (81%)	30 (6%)	73	(14%)
		415 (83%)			

occupational therapist (*n* = 2), health visitor (*n* = 10), or other professional (*n* = 73).

Altogether, 82 (16%) had been an inpatient in a hospital during the previous year, 192 (37%) had been seen by their general practitioner in the surgery and 238 (46%) had been seen at home.

Clinical history

The same pattern is revealed when the situation at the time of diagnosis and early management is reviewed. The majority of people (57%) received the diagnosis from a general practitioner, 30% from a specialist, 6% from others, 5% from no one and 12 patients did not know the diagnosis. Furthermore, 91% received their first treatment from a general practitioner – few other professionals were involved.

Communication

General dissatisfaction was expressed by patients and carers over the way the diagnosis had been given (Table 3.25), with 49% of those told by general practitioners and 43% of those told by specialists thinking that it had been poorly done. Unfortunately, the situation is not improving (Table 3.26).

Table 3.25. *How well did patients/carers think diagnosis had been given*

	By GPs (n = 288)		By specialists (n = 43)	
Very well	47	(16%)	25	(17%)
Well	37	(13%)	27	(19%)
Fairly well	63	(22%)	29	(20%)
Not well	66	(23%)	32	(22%)
Not at all well	75	(26%)	30	(21%)

Table 3.26. *No. (%) of patients/carers reporting that communications are better now than at time of diagnosis*

	Diagnosis 0–4 years previously		Diagnosis 5–9 years previously		Diagnosis 10 or more years previously	
GP	(n = 113)		(n = 79)		(n = 87)	
Good	29	(26%)	24	(30%)	21	(24%)
Neutral	26	(23%)	21	(27%)	17	(20%)
Poor	58	(51%)	34	(43%)	49	(56%)
Specialist	(n = 55)		(n = 40)		(n = 51)	
Good	17	(29%)	20	(50%)	15	(29%)
Neutral	11	(19%)	2	(5%)	16	(31%)
Poor	27	(48%)	18	(45%)	20	(39%)

A desire to know more about the illness was expressed by 148 patients (31%) and 103 carers (36%), although equal numbers said firmly they would not.

Summary of findings and implications

Confirmation was provided that PD is largely a disease of 'old age', with a small but significant cohort of younger sufferers. Perhaps as a corollary, the number of people with PD cared for in the 'family situation' is falling, and there are large numbers of old people with PD (particularly women) who now live in residential homes. Among female carers, almost half are below the age of 65 (i.e. are of working age). The large majority of people with PD are independent or only mildly disabled because, in most people, the disease develops slowly; of people diagnosed more than ten years earlier, more than 60% are independent or mildly disabled. In a small percentage, the disease appears to develop fast. Nonetheless, at all stages of functional impairment (from none to very severe), people with PD have many symptoms. At all stages of the disease, a high percentage have not informed doctors or nurses about their symptoms. People with mild or moderate functional impairment suffer the most self-reported symptoms. Although a large majority of patients and carers say that they are happy, that they do not worry or 'feel low', a significant proportion are in fact clinically depressed or anxious. The level of 'confusion' in old people with PD is no higher than in old people without it. Respite and day centres are not generally used, as many domestic carers are unwilling to leave patients either in the day or at night.

Communication at diagnosis, in both general practice and hospital, is considered poor by about half the patients, and the process of communication has not improved over the past decade. General practitioners are seen as the main professional support by most patients and the number of non-medical professionals involved with people with PD is small.

A lack of information was a pervasive finding, which is surely linked to the fact that fewer than one out of three people interviewed were members of the PDS.

Summary of research findings

The following research findings have implications for service provision and for education:

- Confirmation that PD is largely a disease of 'old age', with a small but significant cohort of younger sufferers.
- The number of people with PD cared for in the 'family situation' is falling.
- There are large numbers of old people with PD (particularly women) who now live in residential homes.
- Among female carers, almost half are below the age of 65 (i.e. are of working age).
- The large majority of people with PD are independent or only mildly disabled.
- In most people, PD develops slowly: of people diagnosed more than 10 years earlier, more than 60% are independent or mildly disabled.
- In a small percentage the disease appears to develop fast.
- At all stages of functional impairment (from none to very severe) people with PD have many symptoms.

- At all stages a high percentage have not informed doctors or nurses about their symptoms.
- Even people with PD who are independent and have no functional disability have many unknown symptoms, with unrecognized anxiety and depression.
- People with mild or moderate functional impairment suffer the most self-reported symptoms.
- Although a large majority of patients and carers say they are happy, that they do not worry and do not 'feel low', a significant proportion are in fact clinically depressed or anxious.
- There is a high level of multiple pathology among both patients and carers. In particular young patients have (unexpected) multiple pathology.
- The level of 'confusion' in old people with PD is no higher than in old people without PD.
- Communication at diagnosis, in both general practice and hospital, is considered poor by about half the patients.
- The process of communication has not improved over the past decade.
- General practitioners are seen as the main support by most patients.
- The number of non-medical professionals involved with people with PD is small.
- Lack of knowledge and lack of use of respite and day centres are the rule.
- Many domestic carers are unwilling to leave patients day or night.
- In general, the uptake of benefits is high.
- Regarding spiritual needs, the lack of church visitors is regretted by a minority.
- Less than one out of three people interviewed were members of the PDS.

Endnote and acknowledgement

This study took place during a time of great organizational change within general practice, the magnitude of which could not be anticipated when the study was designed and started. Although a large number of practices were willing to participate, the increase in their workload meant that instead of a one-stage recruitment of the sample by post, multiple approaches to general practices followed by personal visits were necessary. Visits to patients and carers consequently had to be extended up to the completion date of the project. The research nurses and secretary deserve many congratulations and much gratitude for their flexibility, enthusiasm and persistence, without which this study could not have been completed.

Chapter 4

Members' 1998 survey of the Parkinson's Disease Society of the United Kingdom

Stella Yarrow

The Parkinson's Disease Society (PDS) commissioned the Policy Studies Institute to carry out a survey of members. The aim was to gather data on the composition of the membership, to examine members' needs and investigate their views of the PDS. A postal self-completion questionnaire was sent to 2,500 members, one in ten of the membership. A total of 1,693 usable questionnaires were received, a response rate of 68%. The fieldwork was carried out between November 1997 and January 1998. The survey largely replicated research carried out by the PDS in 1979 (the Oxtoby report – Oxtoby, 1982). The 1979 study was a survey of members and other contacts who had Parkinson's disease (PD). Where possible, data from the two surveys were compared.

The Society's membership

For the first time, the survey provides evidence about the breakdown between various categories of member. It also investigated how representative members are of the general population, and members with PD are of people with PD generally. It is estimated that there are a minimum of about 92,800 people with PD in the UK. Estimates of the population with PD vary and this figure, based on an epidemiological study in Aberdeen in 1984 (Mutch *et al.*, 1986), is at the lower end of the range. At the top end, one estimate proposes a prevalence of about 120,000.

From the results of this survey, it appears that slightly less than a fifth of these belong to the PDS. The PDS offers all its services (with the exception of the newsletter) to all people with PD and their relatives, regardless of whether they are members or not. However, if certain groups of people are less likely to be members, they may also be less likely to be in contact with the PDS and use its services. Members are also vital by providing support to others, participating in running the organization and helping to raise funds. For this reason, the question of whether the PDS is reaching all its potential constituency is very important. The findings suggest that it is recruiting or retaining some types of people as members more successfully than others.

About two-thirds of respondents had PD, while 12% were carers and 10% were former carers of a person with the condition. This finding may underplay the role of carers in the PDS, however. The survey sampled the person in the household registered as the member and people with PD may be more likely to be the member than the carer. Among respondents, men were far more likely than women to have PD. Women were twice as likely to be current carers than men, and five times as likely to be past carers.

Three per cent of respondents belonged to the PDS because of their role as professionals, while another 9% belonged for other reasons, most frequently because they were relatives or friends of someone with the condition. Among the professionals, only three people worked in social care rather than in the health services. This suggests that the PDS could do more to publicize its role and encourage membership in both social services departments and the private social care sector, such as residential homes.

The average age of respondents was 68, and two-thirds were aged 65 or more. Carers had a slightly younger age profile than people with PD, while former carers had the highest proportion of those aged 75 or more. Among respondents with PD, older people (those aged 70 or more) appeared to be underrepresented. However, older people may have been less likely to respond to the survey. Older people were, however, better represented in the PDS than when the previous survey was carried out in 1979.

The proportion of men and women in the PDS was roughly equal. However, one would expect to find a higher percentage of women, bearing in mind that the proportion of women in the population grows with age and that the age profile of members is relatively high. Women appeared to be particularly underrepresented among members with PD; they comprise only 40% of this category of members. Women seemed to be even less well represented among people with PD than they were in 1979.

A third group who appeared to be underrepresented were people who were, or who had been, in manual occupations. Only 15% could be classified as manual workers, compared with 70% who were non-manual workers. (The rest did not answer or could not be classified.) Among men with PD, the proportion of members classified as non-manual workers has declined since 1979. It is not possible to make a comparison for women as data are not available from the earlier survey. Only 14% of members were now working, either full or part time; seven out of ten were retired.

About two-thirds of members were married or living with a partner. Among people with PD, the proportion of people who were married had increased slightly since 1979. This is perhaps surprising, as the higher proportion of older people might have been expected to lead to a greater likelihood of respondents being widowed.

The proportion of people with PD who lived with their partner or spouse alone had risen since 1979, while the percentage living with other members of their family such as a son or daughter had dropped. This reflects the decline in the general population of older people living with relatives other than their spouse alone. However, in other ways, the living arrangements of members with PD had not followed demographic trends. Although the proportion of older people in the general population living alone has increased, this is not the case among members with PD. This finding is perhaps unexpected, considering the higher age profile of the sample in the new survey and that the likelihood of living alone increases with age. In addition, the proportion of respondents in institutional care had dropped slightly. This is, again, somewhat unexpected, both because the proportion in the general population doing so has risen and because of the greater percentage of older people in the 1998 survey. It appears that people with PD living alone and in institutional care may be underrepresented in the PDS.

Less than 1% of members classified themselves as belonging to an ethnic group other than white. However, it appears that people from ethnic minorities were only slightly underrepresented because there is a lower proportion of non-white people among older age groups. As the ethnic minority population ages, PD will become more common in these groups. The PDS should therefore consider how to encourage the participation of ethnic minorities. It already has an outreach service for people from ethnic minorities, but insufficient people from these groups responded to the survey to allow any evaluation of its effectiveness.

There is evidence to suggest, therefore, that women, older people, people living alone or in institutional care and in manual occupations were underrepresented among both members with PD and members generally. There may be an association between these factors, as there is a greater proportion of women living alone and in institutional care and of women among older people. In order to ensure that there is equitable access to the PDS and its services, it is recommended that it should consider further the possible reasons for the underrepresentation of particular groups in the membership and what action it could take to address this issue. For example, it could investigate whether the problem is one of recruiting members in the first place or of retaining them.

Some form of monitoring of the membership might be one step forward. Although this survey provides useful baseline data, it is only a snapshot taken at a moment in time. In order to assist future monitoring of trends in the membership, it would be advisable for the PDS to start holding data on characteristics of members such as age and sex. As noted above, it is not necessary to be a member to use its services. The question of whether services are provided equitably therefore also entails investigation of how non-members use services and whether particular groups are underrepresented among them. The monitoring of service use is discussed further below.

There was also a disproportionate number of members in the south as opposed to the central and northern regions of the UK, compared with the percentage of people in the general population living in these locations. The PDS could also consider why this is the case. PD may be more prevalent in some regions than others (perhaps because the population is older). The disproportionate number of southern members might reflect differences in the level of statutory services (although our other findings did not find such differences). Alternatively, it could be due to factors connected to either the historical or the current organization of the PDS. It was beyond the scope of this study to investigate these organizational issues.

Members with PD and their health

The majority of members with PD were men aged 65–84 and either married or living with a partner. However, one member in five lives alone. Most commonly, they were diagnosed when aged 55–64; the average age at diagnosis was 60.

The survey asked respondents with PD to assess their own health, in order to provide a greater understanding of their needs. They were asked whether they had difficulty with a number of symptoms and activities (e.g. turning over in bed). As in 1979, most respondents (96%) were affected by the problems associated with PD. About three-quarters were affected by at least six. These problems were more likely to be experienced with increasing years since diagnosis.

Respondents were also asked whether they were affected by other (more general) health problems. Ninety-five per cent reported such problems, which may be associated with PD and its drug treatment, but some of which can also be unrelated. Forty per cent suffered five or more of these conditions. Sensory impairments were relatively common, particularly among those aged 75 or more.

The symptoms of PD can vary dramatically. About 80% reported some variation in symptoms, and about half said that there was a big difference. People diagnosed within the last five years were less likely to say that there was a big difference. The rate at which symptoms changed varied widely. The survey attempted to measure the difference between people's 'best' and 'worst' times for three functions: tremor, walking and speech. There appeared to be most variation in the case of tremor. The scores for these questions were also combined to give an overall score for disability. However, high proportions of respondents with PD did not respond fully to these questions, particularly the older members, making these measures of limited value.

Ninety-five per cent of respondents were taking drugs for PD and 87% felt that the drugs were helping them, 45% considerably and 42% moderately. Two-thirds of those taking drugs were having, or thought that they might have, side-effects. People diagnosed more than five years earlier were more likely to find drugs helpful but also more frequently reported side-effects.

Use of health services by respondents with PD

About half of the respondents with PD saw their general practioner regularly. This proportion was similar in 1979 but the level of home visits had dropped sharply in the new survey. This may be related to the fact that respondents with PD were much more likely to have a car in the household now. Nonetheless, it is important that people should still be able to have a home visit if they genuinely need it. The drop in home visits indicates that this could be a problem, but the survey findings do not confirm this one way or the other.

The proportion of respondents who had ever seen a specialist hospital doctor about PD was no higher now, at 80%, than in 1979 (86%). However, respondents were more likely to have had frequent outpatient appointments in connection with the condition now than at that time. Some groups seem to have worse access to hospital services for PD than others. People living alone and older people were less likely to have seen a hospital doctor. It is not possible to tell from this survey why this is the case, but it should be of concern to those commissioning or providing health services. In 1979, older people were even less likely to have seen a hospital doctor. The higher proportion of older people in the sample for this survey may explain why the percentage of those ever seeing a hospital doctor has not risen since 1979.

Other health professionals, such as occupational therapists, speech and language therapists, physiotherapists and dieticians, can make a contribution to the management of PD. However, only a fairly small minority of respondents had ever had an assessment or been treated by a member of any of these four professions (17%, 20%, 27% and 6%, respectively). People were more likely to have seen a speech or language therapist than in 1979 but the same did not apply to physiotherapists and occupational therapists. Only small percentages had ever had a visit from a district nurse, social worker or health visitor. It is not clear whether the relatively low use of these services was because respondents did not need them or because they had not, for one reason or another, had access to them. Again, those concerned with commissioning or providing local health or social services should give this matter further consideration. About a quarter of respondents had seen a PD nurse specialist.

There did not appear to be differences in the use of health services according to age, sex, living arrangements, occupation or region, apart from those mentioned above in relation to hospital doctors. The only other exception was physiotherapy: respondents in the central region were less likely to have had an assessment or treatment than those in the other two regions. The geographical units used in the analysis (the three PDS regions) are very large. Inequalities in the provision of services between different locations may, therefore, have been masked. There were insufficient numbers of respondents from ethnic minorities to determine whether they have equal access to services. Further research would therefore be necessary to examine this question.

In recent years, much emphasis has been placed on more effective communication between health care professionals and patients. The findings suggest, however, that there is still some way to go. Less than half of the respondents thought they had had a clear explanation of PD and its treatment when they were first diagnosed. Diagnosis was, for some people, many years ago. However, there is no evidence of an improvement in recent years because people diagnosed recently were not more likely to say that they had had a clear explanation, or any explanation at all. Nor were they more likely to say that they had had an opportunity to ask questions. People in manual occupations were less likely to say that they had had a clear explanation or an opportunity to ask questions. Almost four out of ten thought that their drugs had been only partially explained to them, or explained inadequately. People living alone and people over 65 were more likely to say this. People's expectations of the information they want or need may have risen, which might explain the apparent lack of improvement. Health care professionals should review how they communicate information to people with PD, so that it is appropriate to the needs of individuals.

Further work also needs to be done to improve the understanding by hospital staff of PD and how it affects people. This applies particularly to the need for people with PD to be able to follow their drug regimen when staying in hospital. Only about a quarter of those who had had an inpatient stay over the last five years felt that staff understood how PD affected them. When respondents were asked if they had any further comments about the topics raised in the survey, a major concern was the lack of experience, awareness and understanding of PD among health and social care professionals.

Members with PD and everyday living

The majority of respondents could manage most aspects of their personal care independently. Smaller proportions managed making meals and housework by themselves, but this was partly because 28% (mostly men) did not do these activities at all. Where people did get help, the source was more frequently family or friends than a paid or professional helper. Paid or professional help was mostly with housework, but only 11% of members received this.

The proportion of people who carried out personal care tasks by themselves had changed little since 1979, even though there were more older people in the sample for this survey. Then, as now, family members were the most important source of support. Respondents were, however, less likely to get help from family with preparing meals and housework than in 1979, perhaps reflecting the fact that a smaller proportion now live with family members other than a spouse or partner alone. Between about a fifth and a half of members needed help with each of a number of practical tasks such as fixing things round the house, decorating or home improvements, and writing letters.

Some subgroups of members were more likely to need help with particular tasks. People living alone were more likely than others to manage personal care, meals and housework independently, but more frequently needed help with jobs such as fixing things round the house and shopping. Manual workers were more likely to need help with finances, writing letters and taking medication. People aged 75 or over were more likely to need help with aspects of personal care and housework. Men were more likely to need help with writing letters than women, but women more frequently needed help with everyday shopping than men.

Only a very small percentage of respondents received community services such as visits to day centres, meals on wheels and day and night sitting. The only exceptions were home help services (received by 24%) and personal care (received by 21%). It was not possible to distinguish whether these services were provided by statutory authorities or bought privately by the individual. The take-up of most of a range of local authority services to help people with disabilities with such things as housing, transport and leisure was also very low. The services most likely to be received were orange badges for parking (by 46%), welfare benefits advice (by 16%) and housing adaptations (by 12%). Small percentages of people said that they needed these local authority services but were not getting them.

Most respondents did not find public transport easy to use (apart from taxis). Although access to a car in the household had increased dramatically since 1979, about a quarter still did not have this. Women, older people and those in manual occupations were more likely to find certain forms of public transport difficult or impossible, and were also less likely to have access to a car. About half the respondents would have liked to do more activities outside the home, or do them more often. Lack of transport or somebody to accompany them featured among the reasons why they did not do so. However, as noted above, respondents were unlikely to be using local authority leisure or transport services that could help overcome these problems. It is not clear why people said that they did not need these services.

Respondents also mentioned environmental problems that made outside activities more difficult for them. Local authorities and other owners of public buildings and leisure facilities should take these findings into account, particularly in view of the provisions of the Disability Discrimination Act. Nonetheless, the vast majority of respondents carried out a wide range of activities both at home and outside. Eight per cent, however, said that they did not go out. Visitors were much more likely to be relatives or friends than someone from formal services, churches or other religious institutions or a community or voluntary organization.

Research shows that income tends to be lower for people with a chronic illness or disability but that their living costs are higher. The majority of respondents thought that they were managing their finances quite well. Manual workers were less likely to say this. The benefits that respondents were most likely to be receiving were not means tested: the retirement pension, attendance allowance and disability allowance. Although only 1% said that they were getting into financial difficulties, 6% were receiving income support, an indicator of a low income. As discussed above, people in manual occupations are underrepresented among PDS members. Among people with PD in the general population, the proportion on a low income is likely to be higher. Two-thirds of respondents said that they had to spend more money on living expenses because of PD.

The question of why only relatively small proportions of respondents used formal services (and often said that they do not need them) deserves further consideration. Some who do not use services may genuinely not need them. On the other hand, they may need them but not have access to them. This could be because people are unaware that such services exist, or because there is inadequate local provision, or because services are not appropriate to individual needs, or because people cannot afford to pay a charge for services or buy them privately. The last possibility seems less likely to apply to members, most of whom appear to be reasonably comfortable financially. They may not be seen as a priority by local authorities for this reason, or may prefer to buy services privately.

It is possible that non-members are even less likely to use services, as they may be less aware of what is available than members. Alternatively, the higher proportion of people on low incomes in the general population might make them more likely to be in touch with, and receiving services from, local authority social services departments. Research among non-members would be needed to examine this subject.

The needs of carers of people with PD

The majority of respondents who were carers were looking after a spouse or partner, and most lived with the person with PD for whom they were caring. They had been caring for the person with PD for an average of nine years. Carers were more likely to carry out activities such as keeping the person company or doing household chores than to carry out aspects of personal care such as turning the person over in bed or helping with dressing and undressing. This is consistent with the perception of people with PD that they are more likely to get help with household activities than with personal care. The extent to which carers did provide personal care varied widely.

Four out of ten carers managed without help from anyone else with caring. They may not need such help or may prefer to do it themselves. However, they may want or need help but not be able to find it. Other findings of the survey suggest that carers did have unmet needs for help. Where they did get help, it was most likely to be from a relative of the person with PD rather than from formal services. This ties in with the view of people with PD that most care is provided by friends and family.

Fewer than half the carers had access to all but two of a list of items that could help them (namely being able to talk to a health professional and getting a break from caring for a few hours). The items that they felt were most important were getting expert advice about PD and its treatment, getting a good night's sleep and being able to talk to a health professional such as a nurse or doctor. Short-term breaks for a few hours or in the case of illness were also high priority. For several types of help, less than a quarter of those carers who thought an item important actually got it. Less than one in three carers was aware of the legal right to have an assessment by social services of their own needs. Only a minority wanted one, but demand might be stimulated if carers were more widely aware of this right.

About four in ten carers felt that caring had affected their own physical or mental health, most commonly causing stress, anxiety and fatigue.

About three-quarters had at least one health problem, which is unsurprising considering that about six out of ten were 65 or more, and about a quarter were aged at least 75. Arthritis was the most common health problem, affecting half. Most who had discussed how caring affected their health with their general practitioner felt that he or she understood the issue, but almost four in ten had not had such a discussion.

The problems identified most frequently with caring were difficulty in understanding the needs of the person with PD and other psychological and communication difficulties. More information and expert advice, such as from speech and language therapists or clinical psychologists, might assist with these problems. Some found providing round-the-clock care difficult. However, they did not often express the view that lack of support on the part of either formal services or friends or family was a problem. They may not perceive receiving support from outside sources as being part of their role as carers, or they may have low expectations of any such support being forthcoming. Support from other people or organizations seemed to play a relatively minor role in their lives, and only small percentages said that they had found such support helpful.

From the responses of both members with PD and those who are carers, it is clear that people with PD require a wide range of support and that the majority of this task falls to informal helpers. Carers are getting relatively little help from formal services. The reasons for this are not entirely clear from this research. The importance of their role justifies further research in order to explore their needs for help and whether services are accessible to them in more depth. The data from this survey are being made available to the PDS to carry out further analysis on this question.

Members' experiences of the Society

The survey gathered data on the views and perceptions of members about the PDS, in order to inform its policy making, in particular with regard to how it should prioritize its resources and activities. The findings in this section are, in many ways, complex. This reflects the complicated nature of many of the issues people were asked to consider and the fact that people often hold views which may, on the face of it, appear contradictory. As a result, the evidence does not necessarily point to a single clear-cut direction for the PDS. It would be unwise, therefore, to pick out individual findings to determine future policy. Instead, the full range of evidence needs to be carefully weighed up and balanced. The results are best seen as a starting point for an informed debate.

The most common way of finding out about the PDS was through a doctor or health professional. This was a much more frequent source of information than in 1979, but still only an overall minority of people find out about it in this way. Some means of informing people about the PDS seem to be under-used, in particular television and radio, and social workers. The latter findings, together with the fact that so few social care professionals are members, suggests that it needs a higher profile in this sector. On average, there was a gap of four and a half years between respondents with PD being diagnosed and first making contact with the PDS. One reason may be that it takes some time to find out about it after diagnosis. As noted earlier, many respondents felt that they had not had adequate explanations or opportunities to ask questions at diagnosis. Health care professionals may not be making the most of this opportunity to tell people about the PDS, for example by giving them a leaflet to look at when they get home.

Almost two-thirds of members had used one of the PDS's services in the last five years. However, most individual services were used by only a small minority of members. By far the most widely used service (by 49%) was the provision of books, information packs and leaflets. Other services that were relatively well used (by at least 10%) were the information service, branch welfare visitors, videos and the telephone helpline. Some subgroups were more likely not to use services than others, in particular non-branch members, those aged over 75 and people living alone.

People may not be using services because they do not need help, get it from other sources, or may not be aware of them. Some services are aimed at particular niches of the membership, or have not been running for long, and so lower usage would be expected. However, the PDS could consider whether the current levels of take-up of services by members are optimal or whether it might wish to target some for improvement by, for example, increasing publicity or investigating why they are not used. In order to ensure equitable access to services for members, it should also examine why some types of members are less likely to use services. This would require monitoring who uses services. Services are also open to non-members. In order to evaluate how well the PDS's services are meeting the needs of all people with PD and their relatives, data would need to be collected on non-members' use too. The most widely appreciated aspect of the PDS's activities was the provision of information, which is probably related to the fact that it is the most commonly used. Meetings and social activities were also appreciated.

The percentage of respondents who were members of local branches has grown from 23% in 1979 to 60%, reflecting the increase in the number of branches. There were no significant differences in the likelihood of different subgroups of members belonging to a branch, apart from respondents in the south being less likely to do so than those in the north. Branch members with PD were more likely to have been diagnosed for more than five years than non-branch members, and to have several problems associated with the condition. There seems to be scope for increasing branch membership, as about a quarter of non-branch members said that they would like to join one. The reasons why they had not done so are unknown but lack of awareness about branches might be one.

The most common reason non-branch members gave for not joining a branch was that they did not need help now. Practical problems such as lack of transport or lack of a nearby branch did not seem common. Further investigation could explore whether this group of non-joiners do, in fact, have needs that could be met by branches. They may be unaware of what branches offer, or alternatively branches could provide other activities to meet their needs.

Almost a third of branch members had attended seven or more meetings in the last year. However, half had attended only one or two branch meetings in the last year, or none. This may be related to the profile of the membership. Almost four members in ten said that it was difficult or impossible to get to branch meetings. People with PD were less likely to have attended several meetings than carers and were also more likely to say that getting there was difficult or impossible. People aged 75 or more were also more likely to say this. The most common reason was transport problems. This seemed a more important factor in deterring people from attending branch meetings than from joining a branch at all. Poor health and disability were other major factors. In order to encourage greater attendance, particularly by people with PD and older people, the PDS needs to consider how to address the obstacles. Alternatively, meetings may not be the best method for the branch to reach these groups.

Branch members had a strong demand for information from expert sources. Talks from professionals such as doctors, therapists and social workers were the aspect of branch activity most appreciated. Meeting people and companionship were, however, almost as important. A minority of members had taken part in PDS activities at other levels, most commonly by belonging to the special interest group for Young Alert Parkinsonians, Partners and Relatives (YAPP&Rs) or attending a regional or area meeting. Membership of YAPP&Rs is, however, restricted to only a small proportion (14%) of its target group of members aged under 60.

Attendance at branch meetings may be lower than indicated in this survey, as active people may be more likely to respond to the questionnaire. Use of the PDS's services may also be lower, for the same reason.

The survey investigated which of the PDS's objectives was thought to have the highest priority. Ranking a number of objectives, all of which may be considered desirable, is not an easy task for people. The results indicated that members most commonly considered the provision of advice and information to have the greatest priority. Encouraging and providing funds for research into PD was much less likely to be thought to have top priority. When the scores were adjusted to take into account rankings other than that of first, there was less distance between them. Nonetheless, providing information and advice was still the top priority. However, when members were asked to say what the PDS should spend additional resources on over the next ten years, they most frequently nominated medical research. There was only minimal support for spending more money on advice and information services. This may appear contradictory, but different formats for the two questions may have elicited different responses. People also may perceive research as needing a greater investment of resources than information services.

When respondents were asked to prioritize five different types of research, the vast majority gave top priority to medical research investigating the causes of PD and developing new treatments. Research into ways of helping people with PD was much less likely to be considered of first importance, although when the scores were adjusted to take into account other rankings, the distanced narrowed dramatically. People may view other types of research, for instance into personal and family relationships, or the contribution of a therapist, as secondary to the mission of finding a prevention or cure.

When members were asked for further comments about the PDS, the majority of those who responded expressed appreciation of it or of some aspect of its activities. However, members also had some criticism and suggestions for change.

Members' needs for information about PD

The majority of members wanted more information on PD and how to cope with it. Members with PD were even more likely to want information than they did in 1979. This might be because people now have higher expectations that they will be involved in looking after their health or because of the current drug regimens are more complicated.

Members wanted more information on a wide range of issues, but most frequently on medical subjects such as new treatments, drugs and their side-effects, and specific health problems related to PD. In view of this demand for medical information, it is unsurprising that two of the sources of information most likely to be thought useful were hospital doctors or consultants and general practitioners. Nonetheless, hospital doctors or consultants were rated more highly as useful sources of information than general practitioners. Almost the same proportion found their general practitioner not very useful as those who found him or her useful. While respondents were more likely to find hospital doctors or consultants a useful source of information now than in the 1979 survey, the same did not apply to general practitioners. Members are likely to have much more regular contact with their general practitioner than with a hospital doctor. It is worth considering, therefore, how general practitioners' abilities to provide information about PD could be improved, although it is not clear if lack of expertise, time or communication skills is the problem.

The methods of getting information most likely to be found helpful were the traditional ones of *The Parkinson* newsletter and leaflets and booklets. People aged 75 or more were less likely to favour a number of methods, including *The Parkinson* and leaflets and books, although a majority still found them helpful. The PDS should consider the best ways of communicating with this age group.

A proportion of members have sight or hearing problems. There was some demand for audio cassettes and large-print material, which would be of use to people with impaired vision. The Internet could be a useful way for the PDS to reach some groups of members with communication difficulties. It could also be used by members to communicate back to the PDS, and would be particularly helpful for some of the large proportion of people with PD who have difficulty in writing. Only 6% at present said that they would find the Internet useful (9% of members with PD said that they had a computer). The percentage with access to the Internet is likely to grow, however.

References and further reading

BERTHOUD, R. (1998) *Disability Benefits. A Review of the Issues and Options for Reform.* York: Joseph Rowntree Foundation.

BERTHOUD, R., LAKEY, J. and McKAY, S. (1993) *The Economic Problems of Disabled People.* London: Policy Studies Institute.

HEALY, J. and YARROW, S. (1997) *Family Matters. Parents Living with Children in Old Age.* Bristol: Policy Press and the Joseph Rowntree Foundation.

MUTCH, W.J., DINGWALL-FORDYCE, I., DOWNIE, A.W., PATERSON, J.G. and ROY, S.K. (1986) Parkinson's disease in a Scottish city. *British Medical Journal*, 292, 534–536.

OXTOBY, M. (1982) *Parkinson's Disease Patients and Their Social Needs.* London: Parkinson's Disease Society.

ROWLANDS, O., SINGLETON, N., MAHER, J. and HIGGINS, V. (1997) *Living in Britain. Results from the 1995 General Household Survey.* London: HMSO.

Chapter 5

Quality of life with Parkinson's disease: views of Scottish consumers and providers

*Rosemary Chesson, Diana Cockhead
and Debbie Romney-Alexander*

This chapter reports two studies funded by the Parkinson's Disease Society (PDS) which together help to provide a better understanding of the expectations of and satisfaction with health care of people with Parkinson's disease (PD), especially with regard to the provision of therapy and quality of life. Both investigations were undertaken within the context of major changes occurring in health and social care following the implementation of the NHS and Community Care Act (1990). Not only were changes in organizational structure required, but also health care providers had to develop new ways of thinking and new models of care. In particular, patients, as consumers, needed to be given a greater say in decision making, and partnerships had to be forged. Indeed, current government policy, as reflected in the White Papers *Designed to Care* and *The New NHS: Modern, Dependable* (Department of Health, 1997a,b), emphasizes patient involvement. Hence the studies described here, in which patients' as well as professionals' voices can be heard, have a significance for service planning for the twenty-first century.

The two studies

In 1993/4, a study on the availability of therapy services – occupational therapy, speech and language therapy, and physiotherapy – to people with PD living in Scotland began. This included Scotland-wide surveys of Scottish PDS members, their therapists, general practitioners and consultants. It emerged from this work that psychosocial factors and, specifically, quality-of-life issues associated with the disease were identified more frequently by patients than professionals, who tended to focus on physical dysfunction. This finding led to the second study, on health-related quality of life in 1996, which explored aspects important to people with PD and examined the relationship between patients' and their therapists' perceptions of quality of life. Whereas in our first survey a large number of people were contacted so that we might obtain as broad and as representative a picture as possible, in the second we restricted the numbers so that we could attempt to achieve an in-depth understanding. Thus the two projects should be regarded as complementary.

This chapter begins by describing briefly the wider context of the research, before outlining the aims and objectives of each study and describing the research methods employed. Subsequently the findings of each study are presented in turn. In the final section, the work overall is evaluated and its implications discussed.

The social and research context

The successful management of PD patients has been seen to depend on 'a network of medical and paramedical services working together to ensure the best possible quality of life for both the patient and family' (Whitehouse, 1994, p. 448). Speech therapy, physiotherapy and occupational therapy may help with the clinical features of the disease. Research over the years has investigated the timing and nature of such interventions, as well as their effectiveness. However, the evaluation of therapy is beset with difficulty and much of the evidence is inconclusive, although there are a few studies where patients' own assessment of benefit is included. Nevertheless, of all three therapies, speech and language therapy is most widely acknowledged to have demonstrable benefits, not only for those with communication difficulties, but also for those with swallowing disorders (Scott and Caird, 1983). Physiotherapy has for many years been advocated for people with PD, as it is primarily concerned with disorders of movement, whether musculoskeletal or neurological in origin, although a substantial body of supportive research is lacking. Nevertheless, the nature of physiotherapy provision is changing, with fewer people being treated in hospitals and more in community settings (health centres and general practice surgeries, for example). Home visits are being increasingly recommended, since they provide therapists with the opportunity to assess the patient in a real life environment and may enable closer cooperation with partners and relatives. Occupational therapists, on the other hand, have a long established tradition of home visiting, where clients and carers are advised on the best methods of coping with PD, and appliances and equipment may be provided to help achieve maximum independence (Beattie, 1991).

There appear to have been low levels of service usage among those with PD living in the community. In 1982, Oxtoby reported that of the 261 respondents in a survey of people with PD, 13% had received occupational therapy, 17% physiotherapy and only 3% speech and language therapy. As a result of these findings, therapy working groups were set up by the PDS to provide an information resource for the therapy professions and to publicize the value of their expertise in helping people with PD (Baker and McCall, 1991). Yet in their community study of the prevalence of PD in Aberdeen, Mutch *et al.* (1986) found that 25% of the 227 patients assessed had seen an occupational therapist, 7% a physiotherapist and 4% a speech and language therapist. Since referrals to the paramedical professions are made largely by medical practitioners (hospital consultants and general practitioners), their views regarding accessibility, efficacy and priorities are of crucial importance.

Before the 1990s, clinical investigation and quality-of-life research tended to remain apart. But with an increased emphasis on cost-effectiveness and the development of the QALY (quality-adjusted life year), health care professionals have had a growing interest in the concept. However, quality of life is an elusive concept; it has been likened to happiness, in that it is a term we all understand but it defies definition (Slevin, 1992). Indeed, a good quality of life may be expressed in terms of happiness as well as satisfaction, contentment, fulfilment and the ability to cope (Calman, 1984). Specifically in the clinical context, it has been proposed that the more focused term 'health-related quality of life' (HRQL) be used, defined as 'the individual's ability to function in a variety of social roles and to derive satisfaction from them' (Jette, 1993).

Healthy psychological functioning and the ability to adjust and adapt to different illness states may be crucial to a good quality of life (Fallowfield, 1990). As might be expected, researchers have reported that quality of life is of primary concern to people with PD and their families. Yet there has been very little research on therapy and quality of life. In fact, most therapy research has focused on functional outcome, and has been concerned with therapist-defined rather than patient-defined aspects of treatment.

It is hoped, therefore, that the two studies presented here start to fill some of the gaps in our knowledge and understanding, as well as stimulating debate on key issues relating to therapy and quality of life.

Research objectives of the study 'Availability of therapy services'

The main objectives were to:

1 establish how those with PD gain access to therapy services;

2 delineate patterns of service use (e.g. level of input, timing, frequency) with particular reference to disease course;
3 investigate the role of general practitioners and voluntary agencies, such as the PDS, in the provision of services;
4 identify users' perceptions of the benefits of therapeutic intervention in relation to improved quality of life;
5 determine perceived future needs for this client group and the potential demand for services.

Research objectives of the study 'Health-related quality of life'

The main objectives were to:

1 describe the perceptions of people with PD of their current quality of life and priorities for improved quality of life;
2 assess the congruence between health professionals' and patients' perceptions and expectations regarding quality of life;
3 establish the congruence between therapists' and patients' priorities with regard to quality of life.

Research design and methods of the study 'Availability of therapy services'

The study had five main elements:

1 questionnaire survey of Scottish PDS members;
2 survey of therapists;
3 questionnaire survey of general practitioners and consultants;
4 telephone survey of local voluntary agencies;
5 face-to-face interviews with 'experts'.

This chapter is concerned with the results of the first three elements. The results of the voluntary agency survey and expert interviews are given in the full report (Chesson *et al.*, 1996).

1. Questionnaire survey of members

During spring 1993, a questionnaire was developed for members and was piloted in Sussex. Following minor modifications in June, the PDS mailed 2,496 questionnaires directly to all Scottish members included on its membership list. This was undertaken by the Society in order to ensure confidentiality. A major concern related to the quality of the list, in particular regarding its inclusion criteria and the extent to which it was up to date.

The main topics covered in the questionnaire were:

i respondents' age and gender; date of membership and diagnosis; extent of disability; home circumstances and informal care networks;

ii past and current contact with services; frequency and duration of therapy input (if any); contact with general practitioner and voluntary agencies;

iii perceived need for services; perceptions of value and limitations of services; and prediction of future needs.

2. Survey of therapists

First, a questionnaire was sent to therapy managers and then telephone interviews were conducted with therapists employed by the National Health Service (NHS) or local authority social work departments (hereafter referred to as practitioners).

The questionnaire survey was intended primarily to investigate 'managerial' issues – for example, patient numbers, policy, procedures and priorities relevant to patients with PD – as well as to facilitate the identification of the therapists most involved in the treatment of people with PD. All managers (89 were contacted) were employed in the same geographical areas as the questionnaire member respondents. Managers were requested to provide the names of therapists who could be telephoned to discuss issues relating to 'hands on' work. A high response rate (79 managers, 89%) facilitated the compilation of a list of therapists to be interviewed by telephone.

All 79 therapists 'volunteered' by their managers agreed to participate. There were 29 occupational therapists, 33 physiotherapists and 17 speech and language therapists. The interviews took place between November 1993 and February 1994 and were mainly concerned with the referral of and current treatment methods for patients with PD. All interviews were carried out by the same interviewer (DC).

3. Questionnaire survey of general practitioners and consultants

Questionnaires were sent to 44 general practitioners and 25 consultants (neurologists, geriatricians and physicians) during February 1994. The former were randomly selected, while the latter were a purposive sample; both were selected from lists of practitioners from the geographical areas from which PDS members had responded. The questionnaires were short and limited in scope in order to encourage their return. They were concerned specifically with reasons for referral of patients with PD to therapy services and perceptions of the role of the therapies. Before reminders were sent, over half of all those contacted had responded.

Research design and method of the study
'Health-related quality of life'

Qualitative design

A qualitative approach was regarded as appropriate given the major objectives of this study and it was believed that in-depth interviewing offered the greatest opportunity for people with PD to voice their views, expectations and priorities. Through interviews, it was hoped that the concept of quality of life might be explored, enabling the patient to focus on self-determined, rather than researcher-determined, issues.

Also, it was envisaged that interviews with therapists would be more useful than questionnaires, since the interviewer could ensure that the therapist had accurately recalled a patient. In addition, they would enable issues to be examined in more depth.

The study group

Volunteers with PD were recruited via the local PDS branch in Aberdeen and through specialist outpatient clinics in Glasgow and Dundee (where there are no PDS branches) as well as therapy departments within Tayside, Aberdeenshire and Strathclyde. These three areas were chosen for their differing socio-economic characteristics, varying PDS activity and diversity of therapy available. By studying these three district locations, it was hoped that a picture of the quality of life of people with PD across central and north-east Scotland might emerge. The three regions each has a large city (Dundee, Aberdeen and Glasgow) and includes a large teaching hospital. However, despite their urban centres, each region also has many rural parts, with small local hospitals providing local care and therapy to the elderly and people with chronic illness.

Volunteers were recruited via local branches of the PDS and non-members from clinical settings. Volunteers were selected for participation if they had been in receipt of therapy (occupational therapy, physiotherapy or speech and language therapy) in the preceding nine months.

This was both so that a long time period had not elapsed between therapy and study participation, thus facilitating patient and therapist recall, and so that the volunteer's illness or social situation was unlikely to have altered significantly since therapy. Permission to recruit volunteers was sought and obtained from relevant regional ethical committees.

People with PD who took part in the study came from a diversity of locations, ranging from council-owned high-rise flats in the inner city, to quiet residential areas on the outskirts of town, as well as from isolated rural cottages. The therapists were based at large teaching hospitals, day hospitals, local community hospitals and in the community.

The pilot study

Before any of the research instruments were used in the study, they were tested for effectiveness and acceptability on a small number of patients and therapists in South Wales (six in total). Participants for the pilot study were recruited from a Welsh branch of the PDS, and each had to meet the same selection criterion used in the main study.

The interviews

The volunteers were visited once in their own home by the same researcher (DRA). After participants had completed the Nottingham Health Profile (the results of which are not reported here), the researcher proceeded to interview them to discover what was important to them regarding their quality of life, how this has changed since developing PD and what their views were on the therapy received. Interview questions were open ended. The questions used by Farquhar (1991) in her study on the measurement of quality of life were used as a guide, but were adapted and implemented to meet the specific needs of this study. Unlike in Farquhar's study, they were not coded on a Likert scale. Direct quotations from patient interviews are presented below to let the participants speak for themselves, and to avoid some of the distortion which occurs when responses are 'forced' into a limited number of categories.

Therapists were interviewed, again by the same researcher, after the client interviews. Before interview, therapists were asked about their experience of quality-of-life measures and were requested to grade each patient's level of disability using the Hoehn and Yahr scale of physical disability (Hoehn and Yahr, 1967) (see Chapter 1), as used by Clarke *et al.* (1995) and Lee *et al.* (1994) in their study of the medical, social and functional profile of patients with PD. The therapists were asked similar questions to their patients, to enable comparisons to be made between the two sets of responses. Patient and therapist interviews began in January 1996 and were completed in August 1996.

All interviews were tape recorded, to allow for a detailed content analysis. Permission was sought from each participant to use a tape recorder. The researcher also took notes to act as a 'back-up' in case the tape playback proved to be of poor quality. This was the case in a small number of interviews where the person's speech had been adversely affected by PD, or where there was a high level of background noise.

Some observations on our research methods

A major problem regarding our first questionnaire to members was that we could not have access to the membership list. This had major implications for the study, since we were not able to scrutinize the list and exclude carers and benefactors, for example, even though our questionnaire was designed solely for people with PD. As is evident from Table 5.1, only approximately half the respondents fulfilled this criterion. Fundamentally, it meant that as researchers we lost control of the research process, as we had to depend on the Society with respect to all contact with members.

Regarding our second study, we had difficulties in recruiting participants as so few people had had therapy in recent months. It is significant that our contact with the many people who expressed a wish to help revealed that a large proportion had had therapy in the past (including many years previously) and the fact that there was considerable discrepancy between the numbers who had been seen by a therapist and who had actually received a course of therapy. This, in fact, reinforced the findings from our first study.

In both studies, a considerable volume of data was generated. Moreover, the analysis of end-opened questions was very time consuming. However, we are convinced that our findings should facilitate a greater understanding of people with PD and their problems and expectations, and doubt that a similar level of understanding would have been possible from a pre-coded questionnaire. Moreover, the interviews enabled people to set the agenda and express their opinions in their own words, which we do not believe often occurs in health settings. However, this does not lend itself to the 'executive summary' type of reporting which is often required by the health care manager bombarded by information. This is indeed a challenge for the future, since without doubt there is a need to develop methods of reporting qualitative data which make it accessible to health care managers making major decisions regarding service delivery.

Main findings of the study 'Availability of therapy services'

PDS members

Following reminders to non-respondents, 1,388 questionnaires were returned, representing a 62% response rate. Although people with PD were the single largest group to reply, representing 47.9% of respondents, significant numbers of questionnaires had been completed by a wide range of individuals, including carers and health care professionals (Table 5.1). There were also some questionnaires which were partially completed. Here we consider solely the 665 completed questionnaires returned by people with PD.

Health care professionals: therapists and general practitioners

Levels of response varied between professions, from 81% (13/16) for occupational therapists in social work departments to 94% (18/19) for speech and language therapists. Of the 79 named therapists, all of whom participated, 29 were occupational therapists, 33 physiotherapists and 17 speech and language therapists. Questionnaires were returned by 29 general practitioners, representing a 65.9% response rate, and by 15 of the 25 consultants.

Characteristics of respondents

Questionnaires were returned from people with PD living throughout Scotland. Approximately half (53.6%) were men and the overwhelming majority (86.8%) were over 60 years of age. The age distribution of men and women was broadly similar. Nearly two-thirds of respondents owned their own homes. Approximately one-quarter lived alone but most people (471) lived in two-person (or more) households (most commonly

Table 5.1. *Respondents to the 'Availability of therapy services' questionnaire*

Respondents	No.	%
People with PD	665	47.9
Carers	298	21.5
'Professional' members	52	3.7
Questionnaires incomplete (or unusable)	308	22.2
Other	65	4.7
Total	1,388	100

with spouses). However, 62.2% of those living with a partner or relative considered that they would not be 'able to manage' living alone. Less than a tenth of respondents reported living in sheltered housing, even though approximately 80% indicated that they were either moderately or severely affected by PD. Indeed, when asked if they were 'able to turn over in bed', only 34% indicated that this could be achieved.

The therapy manager respondents comprised 40.5% physiotherapists, 36.7% occupational therapists, and 22.8% speech and language therapists; 76% described themselves as managers, while 24% were senior therapists.

The therapists were distributed throughout Scotland and over a quarter (26.6%) reported working in the community – these were largely occupational therapists within social work departments or health service speech and language therapists. Most commonly, NHS therapy managers were located within departments of neurology or care of the elderly. A small number of respondents reported working within rehabilitation. As expected, given the method of recruitment, the practitioner therapists reflected the profile of the managers regarding, for example, geographical location, speciality and work setting.

General practitioners who responded were working throughout Scotland, from Thurso to Dumfries and Oban to Aberdeen. Both fundholding (7) and non-fundholding (22) practices were represented. Of the 15 consultant respondents, 13 were geriatricians and two neurologists.

Access to therapy services

Nearly half the members with PD who completed the questionnaire (47.5%) had received therapy. Approximately one in ten of all respondents, and one in five of all who had had therapy, had received all three therapies (Table 5.2). Of the 104 respondents who had had two therapies, the most common combination was occupational therapy and physiotherapy, and more people received physiotherapy (80.1%) than any other therapy (Table 5.3). Across all three therapies, 8.5% of respondents (27) in receipt of therapy had seen a therapist, usually a physiotherapist, in private practice. A quarter of respondents indicated that their local branch was able to arrange therapy, but nearly 75% of these people lived either in Edinburgh or Glasgow, where multidisciplinary clinics were run by the PDS.

Patterns of referral were broadly similar in all therapies, although more of the physiotherapy referrals were from general practitioners and greater numbers of self-referrals were reported in occupational therapy and speech and language therapy (Table 5.4). Eighty-two per cent of

Table 5.2. *Number of therapies received by respondents*

No. of therapies	No.	% of all who received therapy	% of all respondents
Three	58	18.4	8.7
Two	104	32.9	15.6
One	316	100.0	47.5

Table 5.3. *Type of therapy received*

Therapy	No.	% of all who received therapy	% of all respondents
Physiotherapy	253	80.1	38.0
Occupational therapy	161	50.9	24.2
Speech and language therapy	122	38.6	18.3

Table 5.4. *Source of referral, by therapy*

Source	Occupational therapy (n = 111)		Physiotherapy (n = 201)		Speech and language therapy (n = 97)	
	No.	%	No.	%	No.	%
Consultant	41	36.9	74	36.8	41	42.3
General practitioner	30	27.0	71	35.3	28	28.9
Self	20	18.0	22	10.9	17	17.5
Health visitors/ district nurses	20	13.5	34	16.9	11	11.3

respondents said that if they felt they needed therapy services, these would be requested, and nearly two-thirds indicated they would ask their general practitioner.

Approximately two-thirds of respondents were able to state the number of visits during their most recent course of therapy – nearly one in five of those who reported receiving therapy had had one session, but 7.5% had over 15 sessions. Those who had occupational therapy were more likely to have received it in their own homes but had had fewer sessions compared with the other two therapies. Sixty-two per cent of those who replied thought that they might need therapy services in the future and nearly one-third considered that they might require all three therapies. Nearly half stated a preference for any future therapy to be at home.

Therapists' accounts of service provision

Both therapy managers and practitioners indicated more than one main source of referral. However, 67 NHS therapy practitioners cited geriatricians (44.8%), GPs (29.2%) and neurologists (11.9%).

'Assessment' was given as the single most common reason for referral. Surprisingly, only eight of the 158 respondents (six were social work department occupational therapists) reported referral for activities of daily living or aids and adaptations.

When managers were asked at what stage in the disease course they were most like to see a person with PD referred, approximately half (49.9%) thought that this should occur either at diagnosis or within a year of it. The majority of managers (70.9%) thought that once people with PD were referred, they should be assessed on a regular basis, such as every six months.

Although treatment was provided in a range of different settings (Table 5.5), which reflected the distinctive working patterns of the different therapists, it occurred most frequently in hospitals rather than people's homes.

Managers were asked specifically if they felt voluntary agencies should provide services such as information, the provision of transport, equipment and therapy for people with PD. Above all else 'information

Table 5.5. *Location of treatment, by therapy*

Location	Occupational therapy		Physiotherapy		Speech therapy	
	No.	%	No.	%	No.	%
Outpatient/hospital departments	40	28.6	111	46.8	61	54.5
Home	44	31.4	29	12.2	18	16.1
Hospital	20	14.3	42	17.7	15	13.4
Outpatients, hospital and home	16	11.4	15	6.3	6	4.1
Hospital and outpatients	6	4.3	18	7.6	7	6.3
Hospital and home	12	8.6	14	5.9	2	1.8
Other	2	1.4	8	3.4	4	3.6
Total	140	100	237	100	113	100

about access to services' received the highest support (91.1% of managers), and nearly a quarter (24.1%) thought that voluntary agencies should provide therapy services.

General practitioners' referral and access to therapy

All respondents were able to refer patients directly to physiotherapy. Referral to either occupational therapy or speech and language therapy, however, was not possible for three general practitioners.

Main findings of the study 'Health-related quality of life'

Patient interviews

Twenty men and ten women participated in the study, the number reflecting the availability of patients who met our criteria. Twelve, eleven and seven respondents were recruited from Aberdeen, Tayside and Glasgow, respectively. All interviews were held in participants' homes and interview duration ranged from 30 minutes and two hours. Variation often reflected the severity of PD, as well as differing personalities. Eleven patients (36%) had their speech affected in some way. Speech problems ranged from mild, where the voice was quiet, to severe, where the speech was extremely difficult to understand. Generally, those with less severe symptoms had less to say, as they perceived that their lives were not greatly affected by the disorder. Some patients with more severe symptoms, whose social life was restricted, said that they were glad to have somebody to talk to about the disease, and to have a chat with a visitor. Carers were present at 14 interviews and occasionally contributed. Carers' responses have been included in the findings where relevant.

Patient characteristics

Ten patients had less severe PD as indicated by a Hoehn and Yahr score below 2, although there were eight people with scores of 4 and one of 5 (for full details of the study participants, see Table 5.6). Seven of the eight people who lived alone had a Hoehn and Yahr score of 3 or more, six of whom were women. Eighteen of the participants lived with their wives, two with husbands and three with either a son, daughter or brother. None of the interviewees were currently employed. When the women who were described as housewives were excluded, the participants were

Table 5.6. *Characteristics of interviewees with PD*

Patient	Gender	Age	Length of PD (years)	Hoehn and Yahr score	Former occupation	Lives with	Home status
A	M	63	42	3	Cook	Wife	Tenant
B	M	65	14	1	Steward	Wife	Tenant
C	F	59	10	3	Machinist	Alone	Tenant
D	F	81	2	2	Teacher	Alone	Owner
E	M	60	17	3	Lecturer	Wife	Owner
F	M	70	13	4	Joiner	Wife	Tenant
G	M	63	5	1	Gardener	Wife	Owner
H	M	77	9	3	Rail guard	Wife	Tenant
I	F	74	14	4	Mill worker	Alone	Tenant
J	M	78	5	1	Clerk	Wife	Tenant
K	M	74	3	3	Teacher	Wife	Owner
L	M	88	5	4	Veterinary surgeon	Wife	Owner
M	F	61	1	2	Shop assistant	Son	Owner
N	M	57	7	3	Lecturer	Wife	Owner
O	M	71	1	3	Shop owner	Alone	Tenant
P	M	80	8	5	Farm manager	Wife	Tenant
Q	M	61	16	2	Teacher	Wife	Owner
R	M	82	12	4	Clock maker	Wife	Tenant
S	F	73	1	3	Housewife	Alone	Owner
T	F	66	1	3	Canteen worker	Alone	Tenant
U	M	69	1	2	Bricklayer	Wife	Tenant
V	M	85	2	3	Office foreman	Wife/ daughter	Owner
W	F	69	2	2	Clerk	Brother	Owner
X	M	77	2	4	Self-employed	Wife	Owner
Y	M	71	2	1	Housewife	Husband	Owner
Z	F	71	7	4	Policeman	Wife	Owner
AA	M	67	2	2	Labourer	Wife	Tenant
BB	F	79	10	4	Clerk	Husband	Owner
CC	M	76	6	3	Farm manager	Alone	Tenant
DD	F	71	34	4	Shop assistant	Alone	Tenant

equally divided between manual and non-manual occupations on the basis of their previous employment. Manual occupations included a cook, gardener, rail guard and a bricklayer. Nearly half of the former white-collar workers had been teachers or lecturers but there were also two farm managers, three clerks and a veterinary surgeon. The majority of interviewees who had professional and managerial backgrounds were home owners, and these comprised half of the study group. Membership of the PDS, however, appeared to be associated with geographical location rather than socio-economic status.

What is quality of life?

When asked what quality of life meant to people with PD, patients equated the concept with a number of aspects of living: 'It's how you get about, how you enjoy life, being able to do what I did before, being independent' (Patient B). These aspects were mentioned frequently by other interviewees, although all four were not necessarily mentioned in combination. However, these factors were the most widely regarded as the key aspects of quality of life.

Patients often referred to enjoyment: 'Having interests which allow you to enjoy your days without being bored or miserable' (Patient D). Patient L, who was very elderly and fairly disabled (Hoehn and Yahr score of 4) said that quality of life was 'The joy of living. If there is joy in it', while Patient Y, one of the least disabled participants, thought that it was 'Being able to enjoy life the way you did before'. Apart from enjoying life, Patient Y also said that being able to do what she did before was part of quality of life, a view expressed by many of those interviewed. In order to maintain former activities, reference was often made to mobility. 'To be able to move around and do the things that you like to do' (Patient H). Others highlighted the relationship between mobility and social contact. Quality of life is 'How you are able to get out and about and meet other people and enjoy yourself' (Patient W) and for Patient I essentially it meant 'Getting out and about and social-ising', as it was also the case for Patient G: 'to be able to get out and about. It's pointless dwelling on Parkinson's. You have to accept it and get on with it. You can't make everyone else's life hell.'

Many people felt that attitude of mind was related to quality of life. For instance, Patient G believed that having a good attitude was impor-tant and said 'Nothing gets me down', a view reinforced by Patient V: 'You've got to accept what you get'.

Only one patient (Patient O) equated material possessions with qual-ity of life and said 'Standard of living, I suppose'.

Evaluating quality of life

Patients usually were able to evaluate their quality of life and a third of people (11/30) taking part in the study described it as good. A further 11 patients did not evaluate their quality of life as either being particu-larly good or bad, or did not evaluate it at all. 'I would say I suppose it's all right. I don't do an awful lot. I take care of the house and do the shopping.... I don't have a great lifestyle or anything. I never did go mad of course.'

Patients with greater disability were more likely to describe their qual-ity of life as poor: 'Well, when you ask that, I'm comparing with what it was like before. Now I can't walk.... Now I'm confined to a chair, it's poor, my quality of life is poor' (Patient P). Patient Z likened it to being a 'Prisoner Cell Block H'. As he came to have tears in his eyes, his wife added 'This is something we don't talk about usually. We try to pretend our life is normal. Probably the fact that you are talking about it brings it to the surface.... We try to keep in touch with people, but we're in a different world to everyone else.'

Medication

The majority of people interviewed believed that without their drug regimen, their quality of life would be reduced, even though difficulties regarding dose and side-effects were reported.

Patient M explained that the drugs initially made a big difference to her life, but when the dose was increased by half a tablet four times a day to help improve her walking, she experienced side-effects, particularly of confusion: 'I was away with the fairies.... I didn't know how to cook or what to buy or what to eat.' Now on a lower dose, she said: 'I'm perfect'.

Many interviewees highly valued their drugs and saw them as central to their quality of life, which would be threatened should they become ineffective. 'You can say you get no quality of life until you get that tablet. I don't know where I'd be without my tablet. I swear by it. The only way to describe it is like a car without petrol until, I get my tablet,' said Patient C. Her greatest fear was: 'My tablet just stopping. Just not working on me. What would I do? I often worry about that. I live in horror about that. It's a real dread I have.'

A number of patients mentioned that their tremor was significantly helped by medication, and some thought that it improved general mobility. 'I had trouble turning in bed at night, but I'm much better since my new medication' (Patient Y). Patient Z, despite having ten injections for his freezing said, 'I've been taking these frozen periods where I feel as if I've been nailed to the ground.... I can be frozen for anything up to five hours.... Once I take the injection, the frozen period disappears.'

Factors related to quality of life

During the course of an interview, a participant was likely to refer to a wide range of factors in the context of quality of life. Combinations, however, were unique to particular individuals. Nevertheless, particular activities or considerations were mentioned repeatedly and these have been subsumed within broad categories, under the headings below.

Mobility, movement and tremor

Nearly two-thirds of people interviewed referred to difficulties with mobility, although different aspects were highlighted.

Ability or inability to walk was mentioned by 13 interviewees: 'Sometimes I can walk all right and other times I can't walk at all. Sometimes it just stops, like your battery running out and you just stop' (Patient F).

Transfers also were problematic for some people. Patient X described major difficulties in 'Getting in and out of bed', whereas Patient Y regarded her problems as: 'Getting up off a low chair. I'm a bit embarrassed if I'm visiting anywhere. I wonder if I'm going to be able to get up okay without help.' Several people raised problems regarding comfort and turning in bed. One patient said: 'At night it affects my sleeping and is in itself quite alarming.... When you're lying in bed at night, the weight of the covers and the inability to get comfortable means one spends a lot of the time being awake. It's a constant battle to try and be at ease to fall asleep. The simple operation of trying to turn over with covers on is a bit frightening. You feel as if you're going to die. As a consequence I frequently get up at night and come downstairs to try and experience freedom of movement.' Patient AA also had problems getting comfortable in bed and had problems turning over, as did Patients A, F, I, J and Y. Patient R had a different source of distress: 'I have to sleep in the bed like a little child in a cot, railings on both sides in case I fall out.'

'Off' periods were described as difficult to live with: 'I was in hospital for three weeks to try to sort out my medication. One afternoon, I was I bed and I couldn't move the whole afternoon.... When I explained I was frozen, they asked me if I wanted another blanket' (Patient Z); 'The mind doesn't tell the body or the legs to move and if you force it you fall. I find it hard to answer the door, to get started. If the postman knocks, he is gone before I can reach the door' (Patient H).

Tremor was mentioned by half the interviewees as being a significant problem: 'My hand shakes like anything.... I'm not able to do things properly, like model making' (Patient G). For Patient I, her tremor was regarded as a real nuisance, as were her involuntary movements. Patient T's main concern regarding her tremor related to going shopping: 'It's just the shaking. Once I get to the shop, the nerves take over. The shopkeeper had to take the purse off me because my hands were shaking so much.' Other patients with tremor also said that it was worse in situations of stress, or if they were in a hurry. Patient J also believed his tremor was worse when he was aware of people watching him: 'If I'm somewhere where there's people it's [the tremor] worse. Going to the bank for instance or booking a holiday I find that when it comes to writing [in public] it's a problem.'

Communication and speech

Patient M concluded that 'Being able to speak to people' was one of the most important things to her quality of life: 'Until I was on that drug I had no interest in anybody. I wasn't able to speak, I couldn't speak and I felt I was in the room with people but I felt far away.' Patient A discussed how he was frustrated by his speech problems, especially when people did not take the time to listen to him, or spoke for him. Patient J found it embarrassing because he spoke so quietly: 'People lean forward to hear you.' Patient N, who previously was a lecturer and did much public speaking, now feels inadequate when addressing a group: 'Unless I concentrate now, my sentences run out of power.... I can't think on my feet and change track any more. If I get a phrase in my head I have to come out with it regardless, whereas before, I used to be able to improvise and be spontaneous and enthusiastic.... I very rarely feel in charge in a group. I perceive to myself that I have lost that capability.'

Activities of daily living

Problems with things such as dressing and undressing, bathing and eating were mentioned by nearly all those interviewed (28/30), with 17 stating that they experienced major problems of living.

Psychological impact

Loss of confidence, worry and anxiety, loneliness, embarrassment and depression were all raised by interviewees.

Attitude towards the disease was mentioned specifically by over a third of patients (12/30) as important in maintaining quality of life. Patient N, who regarded himself as preoccupied with his condition said: 'As time goes by and the disease gets a stronger hold, actually gaining some relief from the disease seems to be one of the main points of living. It's not a very inspiring spectre.... As you approach each stage of decline with the Parkinson's you're concerned about what the next stage will bring.... I'm concerned about what the future holds. Sometimes, from a personal point of view, I think it would be rather nice just to slip away. Though, of course, one doesn't say that sort of thing to one's family.... Before my horizons were always dotted with ambition, whereas now there's the realization of receding opportunities, which is a gross restriction on my hopes. I'm more conscious of my physical state, my health, than ever I was before. It's also frustrating to see one's powers of communication and mobility so sadly declining. It seems a one-way journey, which is depressing.'

Patient Z's wife also thought that PD could take over: 'I try to keep our life normal ... we just don 't talk about it.... The only way you can survive is by playing a game, and you hope you don't draw on all the pretence you have, because what would happen then?... Sometimes I feel I'm going to explode with it. Instead of crying, it just takes you over. I can't explain: it's just so sad and all consuming.'

Six participants, however, appeared to accept their situation and were 'making the best of it'.

In terms of the psychological aspects of living with PD, six people spoke of the emptiness, loneliness or sense of isolation they felt as a result of the disease: 'I used to be a right gad-about.... I don't mix with people so much. I've a different nature entirely. It was as if I went away and somebody else came in my place' (Patient AA).

Some patients mentioned anxieties at the time of the diagnosis: 'The name frightens me. I didn't know what Parkinson's disease was' (Patient U). Patient D, too, was alarmed when she was told she had the disease: 'I think the thought of having Parkinson's bothered me for a while. I thought "what's this going to come to?" But I've lived with it for two years. I think the thought of being told I had it did upset me at first.' Patient D did not tell her family she had PD for about one and a half years after her diagnosis, and revealed: 'Very few people know. Not that I'm ashamed to admit it, but I don't want their pity because people will feel the way I felt about Parkinson's.'

A few participants appeared poorly informed. For example, one interviewee enquired, 'It doesn't actually kill you does it?' (Patient O). Similarly, Patient F said, 'I'm not aware what's going to happen, you don't know what's coming next. Does it kill you in time? I don't know much about Parkinson's except that it causes people to shake' (Patient AA).

Family, friends and neighbours

Patient A stated that: 'I live for my family.' He resides with his wife, and his children and his 12 grandchildren live nearby and visit almost daily. Patient AA, married for 42 years, said in response to being asked what would make his life worse, 'If I lost my wife'. Patient D, who lives alone, but has children close by, said her family were the most important aspect of her quality of life: 'The feeling that there is somebody looking after you, which is important at my age.... It gives you a feeling of safety, knowing you can just pick up the 'phone and they will do what they can.'

Family relationships frequently were mentioned in relation to quality of life and those with less disability generally referred to their family less often than those with greater disability. Those who were more disabled often saw fewer friends and found their social interaction reduced, leaving the family often as the main source of social contact: 'The only thing now is my family, being there for them. I haven't anything else that's important. I don't want to be a burden too' (Patient S).

Many people mentioned the importance of friends, neighbours and the company of others: 'The neighbours round here are really marvellous. Upstairs they are really good to me, even cook me a meal sometimes' (Patient O). Patient U said that being able to get out and chat to people was one of the factors most important to his quality of life: 'I meet plenty of people in the street. I talk to everybody who comes up and down the road. I'm not lonely or isolated.' Diminished social contact was seen by others as a consequence of their disability.

Patient V, who was unable to meet people when he would like to, missed being up to date with the news in his local community: 'I used to go down the road every morning to the shopping centre for half an hour which I can't do now.... I miss all the banter and the scandal.' Patient X was very aware of his own and his wife's diminished social life and, being a very jolly person who was always telling jokes, he regretted the loss of this part of his life: 'We used to go out more, we used to go to shows every week, used to go to restaurants every week. All that's gone now. We don't entertain friends any more.... The biggest help to Parkinson's is the television.'

Apart from the effects on their own lives, some people worried about how their symptoms might spoil occasions for others: 'It's the shaky hand at bingo and the like, it's getting in the way and I feel it's annoying others, not so much myself' (Patient B). Lack of understanding by others was sometimes seen as adding to people's problems: 'I think one of the problems is that certain people treat me as if I was an imbecile' (Patient P); 'I would like to be able to walk into a room without people staring and folks looking at you queer' (Patient A).

The PDS was praised as a valuable support system for people with PD and their carers: 'I expected to find it [the PDS meeting] depressing, but I didn't. Your carer is there too, so you're not sitting with a load of invalids.... I've found them quite jolly honestly, I enjoy the meetings.... I think it helps. You see people who are bad, but you see that they are coping. Most people are really jolly. I would recommend anyone who has it to go' (Patient D).

Leisure and interests

Every participant mentioned some aspect of how their interests and social life had been affected by the disease. When asked about ways in which their quality of life had changed since developing PD, three-quarters (22) referred to changes in these areas. However, a few people (largely those with lower Hoehn and Yahr scores) thought that their quality of life had not been significantly affected in this respect: 'No, I don't think so.... The only thing I've given up really is the golf. Everything else is as it was' (Patient J).

Many men missed being able to participate in sports: 'Now I can't walk.... In 1989 I climbed three mountains in a week. I wouldn't be able to do that now. These are some of the things about my quality of life which I miss' (Patient P). Dancing was particularly missed by women: 'I haven't got the energy to dance any more, which I miss, but at least I can go out and watch others enjoying themselves' (Patient C). Dancing was mentioned by one man too: 'I wish I could go dancing. Even at 87 I would like to go dancing' (Patient X).

Several patients said they missed playing a useful role in society and felt a loss of status as a result of having PD. Patient P was formerly an elder in his church, and was no longer a member of his club because there is no wheelchair access to the meeting room. Patient N, too, was a fairly prominent member of his local community but now felt restricted as he was no longer not able to play a full part.

Independence

Being able to do things for oneself and not having to rely on others was often mentioned as being a significant element of quality of life. Patient BB regarded it as 'the most important thing' to her quality of life, and she wanted 'To be able to get up and clean the house and clean the windows and not have to watch somebody else doing it for you.' Loss of independence was mourned by the people interviewed and many dreaded having to be dependent on others. Loss of freedom was mentioned even by those with positive attitudes.

Therapy, therapists and day hospitals

The majority of patients (18) thought their therapists did have an understanding of their PD problems: 'Definitely. The people here are very good and patient' (Patient X). Some patients (five), on the other hand, felt their therapists lacked understanding of their specific problems. The remaining seven people were either not sure if their therapist understood them or did not express a definite opinion.

Several patients highlighted a lack of continuity in the therapist treating them and how this affected understanding of their problems: 'I wouldn't think so, maybe perhaps. It was a different one each time I'd gone. I only got about quarter of an hour and it wasn't always the same exercises' (Patient J).

Patients hoped for some improvement in their condition, or maintenance of their abilities, although some felt there was little that therapy could realistically do for them.

A further five people hoped for equipment to help them: 'I got a seat for in the shower and a few other things' (Patient I). Patient CC valued the equipment her occupational therapist provided, but she appreciated 'Company most of all'.

Seventeen participants thought that therapy was beneficial: 'Yes. It hasn't helped my balance, but it keeps me going and it keeps me moving. I do enjoy going to therapy' (Patient BB). One patient (X) appreciated therapy because he felt 'something was being done. I enjoy her company [the physiotherapist]. She's a most interesting person.... I quite enjoyed going and it definitely helped me to relax' (Patient D). Patient X, while believing that therapy was beneficial, found it tiring: 'When I finish I have the self-satisfaction that I've done something to help myself. It's tiring. It's not enjoyable but it's bearable.'

Overview of patient interviews

1 Patients had few difficulties in attempting to define quality of life.
2 Descriptions of quality of life related closely to physical disability and severity of PD (as indicated by Hoehn and Yahr scores).
3 One patient's global description of quality of life well summarized many interviewees' viewpoint: 'It's how you get about; how you enjoy life, being able to do what I did before, being independent.'
4 The four most consistently mentioned aspects of quality of life by all patients were: family; social life; getting out and about; not being a burden. Important to note is that the less disabled did not want to become a burden and valued their independence, while the more severally disabled regretted being dependent and more than anything wished for independence.
5 Effective medication was seen as contributing to people's quality of life. Many participants were anxious therefore that it might cease to be effective or that they would have to take increasingly stronger doses.

6 In terms of evaluating quality of life, 27 patients were able to judge the worth of their quality of life: 13 said that they had a good quality of life; five regarded it was moderate; and nine rated it as poor.

7 The main problem of PD mentioned in the context of quality of life was tremor, which often caused much embarrassment, as well as frustration.

8 Difficulties with activities of daily living most commonly centred around dressing, but slowness was repeatedly mentioned in interviews. Problems with personal care and tasks requiring precision were often described.

9 The impact of the disease on the carer's quality of life emerged during interviews.

10 Patients without family or relatives living nearby appeared to be the most distressed and lonely and often reported that they received little by way of care from social agencies.

11 The social aspect of therapy and the supportive role of the therapist was important to patients, who often said they enjoyed therapy.

12 Seventeen patients considered that they benefited from therapy and seven thought that they did not. Very few interviewed made reference to quality-of-life issues when discussing the benefits of therapy.

Therapist characteristics

All 22 therapists approached were willing to be interviewed and expressed interest in the project. Ten were occupational therapists, nine physiotherapists and three speech and language therapists. They worked in a range of settings, including private practice (one physiotherapist), hospital (day and general) and the community (see Table 5.7). Therapists' experience covered a broad spectrum, and they had qualified between 1960 and 1993 (mean 13.7 years). When asked to self-rate the extent of their experience with patients with PD, six felt they had extensive experience, with the remainder equally divided between moderate or limited experience. Twenty-one were women.

All of the 22 therapists interviewed had treated at least one of the patients included in our study. However, two therapists had seen two patients each, three others had seen three patients and one had seen four patients. A physiotherapist had treated one patient who was also receiving occupational therapy (see Table 5.7). Only a few therapists had difficulty recalling a patient. Interviews were held in the work setting and lasted approximately 45 minutes, but where a therapist had treated more than one patient they lasted longer.

Table 5.7. Therapist characteristics

Ther-apist	Patients treated	Therapy	Designation	Year of quali-fication	Experi-ence
1	Patient D	Physiotherapy	Private practice	1984	Limited
2	Patient C	Physiotherapy	General hospital	1977	Extensive
3	Patients A, N	Speech	General hospital	1981	Extensive
4	Patient B	Speech	Community	1963	Limited
5	Patient G	Occupational	Community	1978	Limited
6	Patient I	Occupational	Community	1973	Moderate
7	Patients K, R, S	Physiotherapy	Day hospital	1990	Extensive
8	Patient F	Physiotherapy	Community	1982	Moderate
9	Patient L	Physiotherapy	Day hospital	1987	Limited
10	Patient E	Occupational	Community	1971	Moderate
11	Patient P	Physiotherapy	Day hospital	1983	Limited
12	Patient M	Physiotherapy	General hospital	1990	Limited
13	Patient Q	Speech	Community	1970	Limited
14	Patients O, CC	Occupational	Community	1989	Limited
15	Patient T	Occupational	Day hospital	1989	Moderate
16	Patient R	Occupational (and physiotherapy)	Day hospital	1990	Moderate
17	Patients X, Y, Z, AA	Physiotherapy	Day hospital	1960	Extensive
18	Patients U, V, W	Occupational	Day hospital	1979	Extensive
19	Patient DD	Occupational	Community	1986	Moderate
20	Patient H	Occupational	Day hospital	1993	Moderate
21	Patient J	Occupational	Day hospital	1991	Moderate
22	Patient BB	Physiotherapy	Day hospital	1989	Extensive

Use of quality-of-life measures

Despite the fact that only two therapists had used quality-of-life measures, all were familiar with, had used, or were using functional measures of some kind, ranging from simple in-house checklists of activities of daily living to standardized measures such as the Functional Independence Measure and the Barthel index.

Therapists' views of patients' quality of life

When asked if they consider quality-of-life issues when assessing or treating patients, ten therapists indicated that they were: 'I think we try and look at the effect on a person's life not just what the problem is. We look at their lifestyle and try to see how things (therapy wise) will fit in. I do anyway and I'm sure others do too' (No. 2); 'For some, improved quality of life is the ultimate goal; for others, improvement in physical outcome is more important' (No. 9).

Other therapists drew attention to the approach of their profession: 'The OT assessment is a holistic approach. We look at all aspects of a person's life.'

The remaining 12 therapists were less definite regarding consideration of quality-of-life issues. All said it probably was taken into account, but not formally: 'I don't know if we consider it under that title, if you see what I mean, and yet any sort of assessment of people's communication with their fellow man is bound to touch on quality of life isn't it? ... I think when you're dealing with communication, you do have to be knowing about what makes a person tick, and how he ticks. I often say to people, it's not like I can just sit here and peel the corn off your toe and say goodbye without knowing what's inside you. When I'm working on how you're communicating, there's got to be a bit of you in it' (No. 4).

Four therapists felt unable to describe their patients' quality of life because they felt it was a concept which was difficult to define. Therapists who offered an opinion did so by evaluating their patients' quality of life, while others listed activities patients could achieve and referred to dependency levels. In terms of evaluating patients' quality of life, therapists identified nine patients who had a good quality of life and six who had a poor quality of life. Therapist 7 thought Patient R's quality of life was 'Quite poor. He's having problems at home with his marriage. He feels very trapped in his own body and feels he's a huge burden on his wife.... He's had it [PD] for so long. Thirteen years progressively getting worse, so I would say in the last two or three years, he would say his quality of life has gone down.'

Many therapists identified aspects of activities of daily living as being patients' main problems in the context of quality of life: 'The main areas are functional problems he's having in the house. In the kitchen, opening tins, preparing vegetables, that sort of thing. He was having problems with transfers, on and off the toilet. He was given a toilet seat ... and something to help him get in and out of the bath, a high chair and dressing aids' (No. 14).

Therapists' awareness of psychological aspects

Many therapists were well aware that PD has psychological as well as physical dimensions, and that these affect quality of life. Therapist 1 felt it important to know about a person's emotional reaction to the disease in order for therapy to be more effective. Some therapists thought that embarrassment could be a major feature of the disease.

Therapist 5, an occupational therapist, believed that a significant part of her role was responding to psychological aspects of the disease and helping people to feel confident in themselves: 'I always feel with people, even if you can't help them physically, if you can help them come to terms with it, that often in a way is an improvement in itself and you can't only work on the physical side. One has to work on the mental aspect.... Counselling is a very important aspect and I think OTs can handle that more than physios actually.'

Therapist 18 thought that sometimes having a family who were willing to do too much could have a detrimental effect on a person. Therapist 7 said how important it was to Patient R's quality of life to be as independent as possible.

A few therapists thought that help from health professionals could sometimes make a patient *more* dependent. Therapists 5 and 18, both occupational therapists, thought this could sometimes happen: 'OT isn't about organising everything for a person, it is about encouraging them to organise things for themselves. And I think this is so important. Particularly with the home helps. There's plenty of people who I think could manage with such a small amount of home help but once, you've put in that home help, the person really quickly becomes reliant on them.'

Therapist 3 felt that speech difficulties hindered Patient A's social interactions: 'If his communication was more consistent, I have no doubt that would make him feel more happy and confident about himself in social situations.' Similarly, another speech and language therapist (No. 4) was concerned that if Patient B experienced a 'deterioration of his condition and probably, particularly, his speech, [then this would detract from his quality of life] if it were to become worse; because as I say, he's very sociable. He needs that.... He also worries about other people's reaction to his speech.' Indeed, several therapists said that a patient's social life had been affected by PD.

Therapist 19 pointed out the Patient DD's social life was of prime concern: 'He doesn't have much in the way of family so his social life is very important to him.... He is determined to get out and about despite his arthritis.... Getting out and about and seeing people, his networking and keeping up with the local gossip.'

Therapists' understanding of problems associated with PD

When asked if they understood their patients' problems, therapists gave a number of responses. Some said that all patients were different and that they should be treated as individuals. Others said that while they could never fully understand another person's problems, they could perhaps empathize or sympathize. Therapist 18 did not think PD was any more difficult to understand than other conditions.

Therapists 22 and 12 thought it may be easier to understand patients' problems through seeing them in their own environment: 'I think it's difficult to understand totally. I think we see patients through a medical model rather than a social model and therefore don't see the whole picture.... I'd like to think I have an idea of the problems, but I doubt if I understand the true complexity of them. It's difficult when you see someone in a ward setting or day hospital. It would be different if we saw people in their own environment. I think that's where an OT has a slight advantage, in that they see people in their own homes' (No. 22).

Some therapists thought that experience of working with people with PD helped in understanding their problems: 'I think over the years you learn to understand. You can't put yourself in their place, but I think you have to understand their problems if you're going to help them. I think that one of the biggest problems with PD is the lack of understanding of the disease, although I do think this is improving, especially when clinics like our own are set up. I do think it's a problem for GPs who may only see one or two cases a year. They don't have the experience and they're maybe not referred to the neurologist as soon as they should be, as many of the earlier symptoms are similar to these of old age. So they are not diagnosed as quick as they might be' (No. 17).

Therapist 4 thought that being ill herself perhaps gave her a better insight than somebody who had not experienced ill health: 'I have a chronic illness myself. I feel that I'm a little better at understanding chronic illness having it myself. But I think it's terrible if a therapist has to be old and ill before they can understand.'

Therapists' understanding of patients' expectations of therapy

Several therapists thought that the social element of seeing a therapist or attending therapy was some patients' objective. Therapist 17 also said one of the most important aspects of therapy for many is 'The fact that someone is taking an interest in them and you have a link'. The chance of maintaining independence was also regarded as a common objective of patients.

Most therapists thought that patients were expecting some improvement. A few occupational therapists thought that some patients did not know what to expect of therapy: Therapist 19 remarked, 'I find most people don't know what we do, what's available, and how we can help them.' Therapist 7, a physiotherapist, said: 'I always ask what the patient wants to achieve and I try and make my goals what they want to achieve if they are realistic. If they're not realistic, we try and modify what they would like. One of my questions is always, what do you want me to do for you, what would you like physiotherapy to offer?'

Medication

Medication for PD, and medical care generally, was mentioned by therapists during the interviews. Some expressed frustration at the limitations of medication, and the fact that much of what they did was dependent on the patient's drug regimen. Therapist 2 referred to this: 'As a lot of PD symptoms are controlled by drugs, I find it frustrating, in that most changes in the patient are the result of the drug regimen and very little is the result of physio input. As therapists see the problems, they may outline these to the prescriber, but it can be as much as three months before any changes to medication are made. It can take many months sometimes before the drug regimen is adequate.'

Outcomes of therapy

When asked if they saw any benefit in their patients after therapy, therapists thought this to be the case with 14 patients, thought it not to be so with eight, and were non-committal with regard to the remaining eight patients. Many therapists believed that therapy helped patients to gain more independence. However, therapy was not always seen as beneficial: 'I think in a way she probably thought she knew better than I did and she was just going to do what she wanted to do. I don't think she feels she gained much from coming to see me' (No. 2).

Some therapists saw benefits as more related to the provision of information on the service and future use, rather than 'hands on' work. Therapist 19, referring to Patient DD, remarked: 'I think in his case, because he was managing quite well and did not need much OT intervention, my visits served more as a foot in the door and an introduction for him as to ways in which we could help him in the future if the need arises. It was also a way of discussing any other problems. He knows now what we can offer him and that he only needs to telephone if he wants further help.'

Many therapists emphasized the importance of patients having access to information on PD, and some saw it an important aspect of their role. The PDS was mentioned specifically as a useful source of information for patients.

Many therapists spoke of the fact that patients enjoyed therapy and that the opportunity for social interaction and enjoyment was of major benefit.

Day hospitals

Several therapists regarded attendance at a day hospital as a vital social link for many patients. On the other hand, day hospitals were not seen as appropriate for all patients. Therapist 17 thought that although Patient AA was not benefiting from attending day hospital in a physical sense, he was gaining psychologically.

Overview of therapist interviews

1 While some therapists were concerned about quality-of-life issues, most appeared to consider the physical aspects of a patient's disease as their priority.
2 Many therapists thought there should be someone to take responsibility for quality-of-life concerns (emotional, psychological and social) but the majority did not consider that it was their responsibility.
3 Most therapists (15/22) were unfamiliar with specific quality-of-life measures. Very few had used them previously (2/22) and none were currently in use.
4 Despite lack of familiarity with quality-of-life measures, most therapists (14/22) thought that it would be useful to have access to this type of information on patients.
5 Therapists with longer experience of treating PD (or exceptionally a special interest in the condition) appeared better informed and more interested in all aspects of a patient's life than those with little experience or interest.
6 Tremor as the main problem for patients was mentioned during only eight therapist interviews (four with occupational therapists, two with physiotherapists, and two with speech and language therapists).
7 Therapists thought that improved function and independence or practical considerations such as rehousing or equipment would improve quality of life for patients.
8 It appeared that the quality of the relationship with a patient and duration of the therapeutic relationship affected therapists' awareness of quality-of-life issues for a patient (greater awareness was associated with more positive feelings and a prolonged period of contact).
9 While therapists said that they considered quality of life on an informal basis, nine seemed unaware of some aspects of patients' lives which crucially affected their quality of life. Twenty-one, however, were aware of a patient's home circumstances. In general, occupational therapists seemed more aware of quality-of-life issues than physiotherapists.

Overview: congruence between patients and therapists

1 Overall, there was agreement between patients and therapists regarding how patients evaluated their quality of life.

2 In half of all cases, therapists identified accurately key aspects of the patient's quality of life. Of the 14 therapist interviews where there was incongruence regarding essentials of quality of life, nine were with occupational therapists, and five with physiotherapists.

3 More therapists disagreed with patients with regard to what would improve their quality of life than agreed. Therapists generally referred to functional factors and improving independence on a practical level. Patients, while citing these aspects, either more often emphasized social aspects of their lives, or else were content with their situation and did not identify anything which would improve their quality of life.

4 In general, therapists suggested improvements to their patients' quality of life which were achievable, whereas some patients had unrealistic expectations, such as wanting a cure for PD.

5 Patients and therapists agreed that any deterioration in physical condition would be the main factor adversely affecting quality of life.

6 Most patients felt their therapists understood their problems, whereas most therapists felt they could never fully understand, although they could empathize. The majority of therapists agreed on the main problems associated with PD for the patient. Lack of concordance was evident in six cases, in five of which patients referred to tremor as a major problem, whereas this was not mentioned by therapists. Indeed, tremor was referred to by half of all the study participants, but by only a quarter of the therapists. Pain was frequently referred to by therapists as detracting from patients' quality of life but was mentioned by only three patients during interviews (in two instances seen as unrelated to PD).

7 Most patients believed therapy was beneficial in treating PD, compared with approximately half the therapists. Therapists, however, thought their patients gained in some way from therapy, although much of this was of a psychological or social nature, and was not related to physical outcome. Psychological benefits did not appear to be rated as highly as functional outcome.

8 Regarding all aspects covered during the interviews, there was evidence of more congruence between patients and therapists than incongruence.

Discussion

The findings presented well demonstrate a close relationship between the two studies; our second investigation often amplifies issues raised the first. Six main themes emerged from our work:

1 participation and involvement in PD research;
2 professional and patient perspectives on PD;
3 the local and national picture regarding therapy provision;
4 the role of therapy and potential benefits;
5 educational needs (patients, general public and health care professionals);
6 the role of the PDS.

1. Participation and involvement in PD research

Throughout both studies we experienced widespread support, despite the apparently low proportion of replies to our membership questionnaire (62%). As noted earlier, however, the response rate we regard as an underestimation because of difficulties regarding the membership list. Nevertheless, people with PD who did respond often provided much additional comment and some spontaneously volunteered to help us further. Moreover, all the people with PD approached in our second study agreed to participate in the interviews and they were unstinting in the time they made available to us. It should also be noted that, especially in our quality-of-life project (as reflected in the quotations given), people with PD were willing to discuss with us not only their physical problems but also details of emotional difficulties and intimate relationships.

Similarly, we were impressed by the considerable commitment shown by health professionals in completing questionnaires and participating in interviews. In particular, the high rate of participation of therapists is perhaps indicative of their interest in the treatment of patients with PD.

2. Perspectives on PD

There were no major differences in perceptions either between health professionals or between therapists and people with PD regarding a number of disease-related factors. Patients and those treating them identified similar physical difficulties as well as functional problems. However, generally, those with PD approached the concept of quality of life in a different manner to their therapists. Clearly, the concept was meaningful to people with PD, and very few interviewees had difficulty with definition. In fact, those who found quality of life easiest to describe were the most disabled, perhaps reflecting that awareness is heightened with loss.

Patients were able to bring together disparate elements of their lives – the physical, psychological and social – for the purpose of the definition. Their answers reflected their lives in their own homes, in which diverse elements are present and interact. This may be seen to contrast with the hospital, or therapeutic setting, where aspects of individuals' lives often are isolated before treatment begins. For example, therapists in this study tended to focus on the physical problems of patients and, indeed, often seemed to be uneasy regarding the concept of quality of life. Frequently they had greater difficulty than their patients in seeing its meaning and applying it to the clinical situation. Whereas patients' evaluation of their quality of life was reflective and sometimes profound, many therapists' responses were perfunctory. Therapists' definitions often included a reference to holistic care and seldom were they as comprehensive as those given by patients.

It is important to note that a crucial aspect of quality of life for patients was 'being able to do what I did before'. The use of standardized measures, therefore, may not be appropriate, as baseline data for each individual will be different. It is of interest to note that this crucial element, that is loss of former activities, in quality of life was highlighted by Calman over a decade ago (Calman, 1984).

Vogel has contended that PD is not socially acceptable, and the concomitant uncertainty causes problems, such as isolation (Vogel, 1992). Vogel concluded that the psychological aspects of the disease are worse than the physical and that patients feel alienated by society's lack of understanding of the condition. We found numerous instances in both studies where patients reported that they turned inward and avoided situations expected to be stressful. This avoidance of social situations was particularly poignant since patients wanted to be able to get out and about, and a change of scene was all important. This gradual withdrawal must be seen also within the context of people wanting to be part of the outside world and not wishing to wait for the world to come to them.

The studies highlight the importance of social interaction to the participants. Shindler *et al.* (1993), in their study of PD, found 40% of respondents felt lonely and experienced mobility problems outside the home, and that these represented areas where help was most needed. Lee *et al.* (1994), following the identification of the main social problems of PD as loss of social contact, recommended that advice be given to patients on lifestyle management as well as aids to help overcome disability and improve quality of life. Our study supports the need for such help, and indicates that patients could be encouraged to overcome fears and anxieties and need to be discouraged from retreating to their homes. Counselling may be needed to help manage feelings of embarrassment.

The vital contribution of family to interviewees' quality of life emerged from our second study and, in general, the greater the disability the more significant were family members. They were a source of psychological support, as well as providing practical help with everyday activities.

Those patients without family contact emerged as having the highest levels of distress. Indeed, the need for social support was revealed in both studies.

3. The local and national picture

In this chapter two Scottish studies have been reported but is it possible to generalize to other parts of the UK? First, it must be acknowledged that the response rate to our membership survey was lower than might have been hoped (38% of the questionnaires sent were not returned), and our second study was qualitative and involved a relatively small numbers of patients and therapists, although the people with PD were of different ages and social backgrounds. Secondly, from both projects a picture of variable service provision emerged. For example, specialist clinics were available in Dundee and Glasgow but not Aberdeen, and it was apparent from our questionnaire survey that individual experience varied considerably with, for example, variables such as the general practitioner's interest in PD and the length of waiting lists for occupational therapy. We have no reason to believe that this would not also be true of other parts of the UK and pre-existing research would support this.

Nearly half of the members with PD who completed the questionnaire had received therapy, which suggests that a higher proportion of people with the disease are receiving therapy than in previous decades. Nevertheless, caution is necessary in interpreting our findings since Oxtoby's study (Oxtoby, 1982) was carried out 15 years before our own, and Mutch's figures were based on presenting cases and not PDS members (Mutch *et al.*, 1986). It seems likely also that, as 63% of our respondents were home owners, they were more likely to be better informed and more confident in requesting services than other socio-economic groups.

Furthermore, our findings consistently demonstrate different rates of referral between medical practitioners, as have previous studies. Only 6.3% of therapists indicated neurologists as the main source of referral and, of our 15 consultant respondents, 13 were geriatricians and two neurologists. Notably, one consultant reported that patients were rarely referred for therapy.

Although the majority of general practitioner respondents were able to refer directly to all three therapies, few therapists identified general practitioners as a main source of referral and, in fact, they were described as 'poor referrers'. Yet 61.9% of member respondents stated that they would approach their general practitioner if therapy were required. Clearly, we need to understand better why consultants and general practitioners refer patients for therapy.

4. The role of therapy: what are the benefits?

The fact that approximately half of our survey respondents had not had therapy, and that we had difficulty recruiting to the second survey, needs to be considered in the light of respondents' reports of their difficulties. Therapists' and practitioners' replies indicate that referral to therapy is not automatic or standardized throughout Scotland, even when functional problems are apparent.

Differential patterns of referral to physiotherapy, occupational therapy and speech and language therapy were also evident, which, given the nature of problems described, might suggest under-referral, especially to occupational therapy and speech and language therapy.

Respondents in both studies voiced fears about medication dosage and its likely future effectiveness. Since worries detract from quality of life, it would seem important to consider likely strategies. Patients may need to be better informed regarding drug regimens and discussion is needed on who should assume this role – nurse, doctor or community pharmacist?

Both therapists and patients in the quality-of-life study commonly saw a major benefit of therapy in the social aspects of treatment. The role of therapy for people with PD needs to be further examined. Since social aspects are to the fore, and the effectiveness of treatment may be open to doubt, is referral to an occupational therapist, physiotherapist or speech and language therapist appropriate? Fundamentally, is there a need for a new role to emerge – part therapist, part counsellor, part psychologist – or does therapy education and training need to place greater emphasis on the psychological aspects of disability, advice and information giving, and patients' self-management strategies? At the same time, it needs to be established whether social needs currently met by attendance at day hospitals could be equally well fulfilled by attendance at day or social centres, or community leisure facilities. A crucial question is the extent to which specialized health-related education and training are essential, if patients' needs are primarily social. Volunteers may be able to fulfil a social support role, given that health professionals are likely to become an increasingly scarce resource.

Although therapists often referred to a holistic approach when interviewed, the main emphasis was placed on physical problems and how these could be overcome from a functional point of view. Nevertheless, solutions were not always found. For instance, difficulties regarding sleep remained and would highlight the need for further research in this area. Many therapists did, indeed, acknowledge the psychosocial aspects of PD, but often expressed the opinion that either this was not their responsibility, or there was insufficient time to address such issues. Some mentioned that perhaps a nurse could help, but there was little overall agreement as to who should focus on such problems. Some therapists expressed a degree of helplessness, and felt unable to tackle the loneliness and isolation of many severely disabled people. For instance, one therapist said the extent of patients' problems 'make you feel inadequate. There's a huge feeling of inadequacy as to how you deal with these things.' Moreover, there was seen to be limited clinical psychology and social services provision. Therapists tended, therefore, to refer back to the general practitioner the problems which they felt they could not address. However, research to date on general practice and chronic illness, and specifically PD, indicates that general practitioners themselves often lack specialist knowledge and have insufficient time to discuss psychosocial problems.

The therapy profession may need to review their own roles regarding the management of psychosocial problems and may conclude that their part should be to screen and make onward referral, for example to clinical psychology. On the other hand, if it is regarded as undesirable and difficult in practice to separate the emotional from the physical, then both undergraduate and continuing professional education may need to be reviewed so that skills are extended.

In broad terms, it may be valuable to consider, given smaller families, the increasing numbers of composite families and the current rates of geographical mobility, whether social support for people with chronic disability should be provided by health and social care organizations. The precedent has already been established through, for example, support provided for mothers of low-birthweight babies. A volunteer network, organized by the PDS and extending the support already given, could make a valuable contribution.

For some people, e-mail may be an acceptable substitute for face-to-face meetings, especially since increasing numbers of households have access to the World Wide Web. This would be an option for relatively few people, but it is of interest to note that the PDS is currently investigating how televisions may be used in this context.

5. Educational needs
(patients, general public and health care professionals)

A need continues to exist for information for patients. Surprisingly, in the quality-of-life interviews at least two people appeared to lack basic information regarding the disease. Our interviews also revealed that when placed in the 'patient' role, people are often reluctant to express opinions or preferences. People may therefore not only require help and advice, but also advocates if they are to be empowered. Our work indicates that patients should be more involved in decisions regarding therapy, and be better informed regarding the purpose of treatment regimens.

At the same time, the general public needs to be better educated and have a better understanding of PD. A particular objective should be to remove fears which the lay person may have, and increase awareness of the social consequences of their response. The general public may need guidance so that, for example, they are able to cope with a person's tremor. Health professionals need both to contribute to this and to be more aware of patients' concerns in this respect and explore coping strategies. But to do this they may need further education themselves, including regarding appropriate referral. In our first survey, for example, it appeared that early referral to therapy was rare.

6. The role of the PDS

Throughout our projects, the work of the PDS was highlighted by members, therapists and doctors alike, and a wide-ranging role for the Society was described. Many respondents highly commended the Society, although none of our questions invited them to comment specifically. It was evident from accounts provided that pioneering work had been carried out by the Society regarding therapy, for instance the setting up of specialist clinics. Our survey revealed that therapists had diverse formal and informal links with the Society. Talks were given at local branch meetings and PDS-sponsored study days were attended. Over a third (37.5%) of practitioners said that they received training for treating patients through courses organized by the PDS. In addition, both members and therapists highly valued information provided by the Society. However, only a minority of members and therapists thought that the PDS should be a provider of therapy services. Ninety-one per cent of therapy managers, nevertheless, believed that the PDS should provide information about access to services.

The possibility would appear to exist, therefore, for the Society to extend its role, for example in the ways indicated in the quality-of-life study. Local branches already provide regular outings for members, but it may be that people would appreciate also one-to-one regular trips and visits, to shopping centres for example, to maintain social contact. More generally, the Society could investigate how social support might best be provided, especially for people with few friends and family. Further research may be needed to investigate alternative ways in which this provision might be made. Indeed, a significant role of the Society to date has been to fund non-medical research, and our research would not have been possible without its support.

Conclusions

During our research over recent years, we have asked a wide range of questions regarding therapy and quality of life. Unfortunately, several remain unanswered and our work has highlighted the complexity of several issues. For example, what are the functions of therapy for people with PD? Our studies would suggest that they are more diverse than previously thought. In order to meet people's needs, a first objective must remain to obtain as clear a picture of them as possible, and then to examine a range of alternative means by which their needs may be met. We conclude that, above all else, people with PD have psychosocial needs that are currently insufficiently met, and this may be the major challenge for the next millennium.

Acknowledgements

We are indebted to too many people to refer to them all by name, but our thanks are due to all those who gave up their time either to answer our questions or help in other ways. However, we wish in particular to thank Mrs Jean Couper and the Aberdeen branch of the PDS for their support. Finally, we are grateful to Mrs Lisa Stephen, who has managed to bring order and form to our writing and tables and who has helped in so many ways to ensure that our projects were completed successfully.

References

BAKER, M. and McCALL, B. (1991) The Parkinson's Disease Society. In F.I. Caird (Ed.) *Rehabilitation in Parkinson's Disease*. London: Chapman and Hall.

BEATTIE, A. (1991) Occupational therapy. In F.I. Caird (Ed.) *Rehabilitation in Parkinson's Disease*. London: Chapman and Hall.

CALMAN, K.C. (1984) Quality of life in cancer patients: an hypothesis. *Journal of Medical Ethics*, 10, 124–127.

CHESSON, R., COCKHEAD, D. and MAEHLE, D. (1996) *Availability of Therapy Services to People with Parkinson's Disease Living in the Community*. Aberdeen: Robert Gordon University (Report to the PDS).

CLARKE, C.E., ZOBKIW, R.M. and GULLAKSEN, E. (1995) Quality of life and care in Parkinson's disease. *British Journal of Community Practice*, 49, 288–293.

DEPARTMENT OF HEALTH (1997a) *Designed to Care*. London: DOH.

DEPARTMENT OF HEALTH (1997b) *The New NHS: Modern, Dependable*. London: DOH.

FALLOWFIELD, L. (1990) *The Quality of Life: The Missing Measurement in Health Care*. London: Souvenir Press.

FARQUHAR, M. (1991) Whose life is it anyway? The measurement of quality of life. Health and Society Conference. British Sociological Association.

HOEHN, H.M. and YAHR, M.D. (1967) Parkinsonism: onset, progression and mortality. *Neurology, 17*, 427–442.

JETTE, A.M. (1993) Using health related quality of life measures in physical therapy outcomes. *Physical Therapy, 73*, 528–537.

LEE, K.S., MERRIMAN, A., OWEN, A., CHEW, B. and TAN, T.C. (1994) The medical, social and functional profile of Parkinson's disease patients. *Singapore Medical Journal, 35*, 265–268.

MUTCH, W.J., DINGWALL-FORDYCE, I., DOWNIE, A.W., PATERSON, J.G. and ROY, S.K. (1986) Parkinson's disease in a Scottish city. *British Medical Journal, 292*, 534–536.

OXTOBY, M. (1982) *Parkinson's Disease Patients and Their Social Needs*. London: Parkinson's Disease Society.

SCOTT, S. and CAIRD, F. (1983) Speech therapy for Parkinson's disease. *Journal of Neurology, Neurosurgery and Psychiatry, 46*, 140–144.

SHINDLER, J.S., BROWN, R. WELBURN, P. and PARKES, J.D. (1993) Measuring the quality of life of patients with Parkinson's disease. In S.R. Walker and R.M. Rosser (Eds) *Quality of Life Assessment: Key Issues in the 1990s*. London: Kluwer Academic.

SLEVIN, M.L. (1992) Quality of life: philosophical question or clinical reality? *British Medical Journal, 305*, 466–469.

VOGEL, S.B. (1992) *The Quality of Life of Informal Carers for Cancer Patients and that of Informal Carers for Parkinson's Disease Patients – A Comparative Study*. London: Department of Social Sciences, City University.

WHITEHOUSE, C. (1994) A new source of support. *Professional Nurse*, April, 448–451.

Chapter 6

Children of parents with Parkinson's disease: families' perspectives

Roger Grimshaw

This research study was commissioned by the Parkinson's Disease Society (PDS) in 1988, when a younger persons' section was being formed within the Society. Younger people with the disease are likely to have specific needs, for example in relation to young families, and issues about the relationships between parents and children seemed ripe for investigation. On the one hand, there was an interest in how parents with disabilities could sustain and, if necessary, adapt their parenting role. At the same time, there were concerns about parents becoming dependent on their children, making them involuntary 'child carers'. Since the research report was published by the National Children's Bureau (Grimshaw, 1991), interest in carers and particularly children has grown markedly. Greater provision for their needs is now in evidence but unfortunately unmet need is still being documented (Becker *et al.*, 1998). By the same token, the rights of disabled people to become and remain parents still need to be championed. This chapter focuses on the multifaceted re-lationships among family members, which condition attitudes to services. The research offers a rare glimpse into the private family worlds into which Parkinson's disease (PD) gradually steals. Rather than establishing quantitative generalizations, the methodology of the case studies was qualitative, exploring perceptions and meanings (Yin, 1989). If the material gives some insight into the intricacies of family relationships affecting children, then it will have served a useful purpose.

Research objectives

A review suggested several areas of interest:

- children's knowledge about PD and their involvement in counselling and professional discussions;

- children's life at home and any help they give within the home;
- the contribution of external services and support in responding to children's needs;
- the care of infants and young children, and the advice given to adults with PD who may wish to have children;
- the effects of these changes on children's relationships with parents, such as the 'role reversal' of providing care for adults, possibly of an intimate kind, and children's contribution to the emotional climate of the home, which may be affected by the changed relationship of adult partners;
- the use of self-help and support networks.

It became clear that some previous work did not give an adequate basis for the study (e.g. Arnaud, 1959; Peters and Esses, 1985). Of more benefit were 'psychosocial' approaches, which looked at the individual in the context of the whole family's adaptation to the crisis of illness (Thurman, 1985; Rolland, 1988). These mainly theoretical studies examined the styles of communication and the resources which families could draw on in coping with change. They emphasized how changes affect particular stages in the lives of children and their parents.

Perhaps the priority was to see childhood as an active and responsive phase in people's social development. It was also essential to set the family in a wider social context, as a social institution concerned with dependence, whether dealing with the sick, the young or the very old. Children's sense of obligation to parents was to be understood as a foreseeable outcome of this social arrangement, as, indeed, was the reciprocal concern of parents not to be a burden on their children. In viewing families from this perspective, it was necessary not to overlook how the gender of parents and their children influences their responses. An account of the results of an initial, exploratory survey and family case studies will now be presented.

Exploratory survey

A brief survey of parents took place at three regional seminars for younger people with PD, held in 1989. It was explained that our interest was in parents with children, so this was a selective survey. There were in fact 45 responses (22 men and 23 women). All the people with PD chose to classify themselves as 'European' and their average age was 49 years (range 36–69 years).

Analysis of their marital status showed 38 were married, four divorced, two separated and one widowed. Of the people who replied, 42 had children and the total number of children was 99. Analysis showed that there were 38 households with children aged 0–19 at the time of

Table 6.1. *Ages of children at the time of their parent's diagnosis*

Years	0–4	5–9	10–14	15–19	20+	All
	18	25	20	17	19	99

diagnosis. The average number of children aged 0–19 per household was 2.1. It was revealed that the ages of children at diagnosis were spread more evenly than might have been assumed (Table 6.1).

As the parents were on average aged 41 years at diagnosis, it seemed that a number had started their families in their thirties. It therefore would be wrong to assume that people with PD have finished with the major burdens of child rearing.

At the time of the survey, there were more people retired (6) or permanently sick or disabled (20) than in work either full time (13) or part time (3). If this were to be the general position several years after the diagnosis, then children's prospects of living in a household with reduced income should be appreciated. Indeed, taking only those currently retired or permanently sick or disabled, it emerged that diagnosis was, on average, nine years earlier (range 3–14 years). These results were not clear-cut since they did not tell us how long was the interval between diagnosis and finishing work. Oxtoby (1982) gave figures for a comprehensive age sample of men with PD which imply that 13% were diagnosed before they were 45 years of age and 12% finished work before they were 55 years. While the figures were thus suggestive rather than conclusive, they did suggest the importance of that interval between diagnosis and finishing work.

The development of the case studies

After taking advice, it was decided to approach younger people with PD through neurologists and through the PDS in order to have access to a wider cross-section of people. The main qualitative research material was in the form of semistructured interviews, usually undertaken in the home, with 20 children and 20 parents, in a total of ten families. The age composition of the families varied: in two, for example, both preadolescent and older children were interviewed. In order to identify parental influences, details about the families are introduced in the separate sections concerning the two main age groups of children in the study – seven preadolescent children of school age and 13 young people. A further section concentrates on the perspectives of the ten parents with PD. None of the people with PD belonged to minority ethnic groups, despite several attempts to contact individuals with this background.

The perspective of preadolescent school children

A semistructured interview schedule was used to focus on key issues: children's understanding of PD, their ideas about health and illness, their perceptions of their parents in physical and emotional terms; their perceptions of parenting activity; and the daily routine at home and in school (Tamivaara and Enright, 1986). Since it was intended to explore broad themes, the seven children interviewed in depth (from four families) were sufficient to form a useful sample.

None of the four families were members of the PDS or its group for younger people. This should be borne in mind in considering the findings. The adults with PD ranged in age from 35 to 45 years and, on average, had been diagnosed five years previously, though this period ranged from about one to nine years. The group had representation from both sexes, and each of the parents had a regular partner.

The parents with PD had experience of several forms of impairment, each having a tremor, and most had experience of depression and tiredness. Speech difficulties were also encountered by two of the four parents. There were rather fewer disabilities, with writing the most common problem. Mobility problems tended to be subtle rather than obvious, with difficulties of balance and gait in evidence. Problems of handicap in such matters as employment and household work were not as frequent as the impairments stated above. One parent with PD was not working owing to disability but the others were generally working full time. Similarly, most of their partners were in either part-time or full-time employment. In terms of the Hoehn and Yahr scale of problems associated with the disease (see Chapter 1), the parents appeared to be at a mild or moderate stage (Hoehn and Yahr, 1967).

Their youngest children were four boys and three girls, ranging from five to twelve years of age. Two of the four families contained older brothers or sisters. In a preliminary questionnaire, most of the parents indicated that they had talked about the disease with their children. Two indicated that they had no difficulty at all in this, although others showed some concern, for example about discussing the idea of the children having the disease. Significantly, none had received any help in talking about the disease with their children.

PD – seen but not understood

In these four families, explanations of PD had been, in effect, rudimentary or non-existent. Most of the children, but by no means all, understood that the tremor – the most obvious of symptoms – was due to an illness, although one did not recognize it as PD. Only one of the parents with PD was acknowledged to have offered an explanation. Instead, explanations of the symptoms had come from a partner or neighbour. Other symptoms, such as the rigidity and difficulty of movement, had not been conclusively linked with an illness. The effect of PD on a person's inner feelings had not been established in these children's minds. They had generally not been made aware of the organic nature of the disease, its progression, or of its being (currently) incurable. Nor were the treatments generally well understood.

If we turn from explanations to observations, a rather different picture emerges. All the preadolescent children said they had observed the tremor and all but one – the youngest – said that they had noticed at least some difficulty of movement. Some children had become aware of specific feelings and states of mind in the affected parent such as sadness or anger. Observations of some difficulty in ordinary bodily activity were made by several of the group.

Instances of the parent's tiredness were cited by nearly all the children, connected with 'illness' or 'headache'. Occasions when the parent showed great energy were less frequently mentioned. In two instances, it was clear that children saw their parents as occasionally lazy or uninterested. Without adequate explanation it is understandable that such a perception can be maintained.

Talking about illness

Children's ideas about the source of illnesses in general were directly investigated in order to find out what 'baseline' knowledge they might use to make sense of their particular experiences. One important idea was of infection. A link between this idea and PD was made by one child who wanted to know how his father had caught the disease. An association with infection had been explicitly created by another parent, who had used it as a form of explanation for his illness.

Another central idea in children's thinking was the importance of good habits. Some children, in general discussions of diseases, referred to cancer and AIDS; the latter disease might also have moral connotations, connected with 'dirty needles' (i.e. drug abuse). Knowledge of such diseases could also influence reaction to PD. One child on first hearing his parent had a disease had asked if it was AIDS, only to be reassured by the partner of the parent with PD.

A further idea which may be available to younger children is the notion of inherited disease, but little evidence of it was found. However, the idea of children as sufferers from a disease did enter into a few interviews. One child, asked what the disease might be, appeared to fix attention on what the sound 'sons' in 'Parkinson's' implied.

Child: It's a disease for people that are going to have babies like that, I think
so.

It became evident that there was some discrepancy between what children had been told and what they observed. Above all, there was a veil
of mystery over any discussion of the parent's condition, which the parent (and partner) did little or nothing to remove. A similar rule of
silence was influential upon the children's own conversations. There was
no evidence that children in the same family engaged in discussion with
one another about the parent's illness. Silence was extended to conversations with friends. Other children might be told but trusted to keep
silent.

Sustaining normality

Family life and parenting are not straightforwardly affected by disease
and disability. Children showed an awareness of their parents' normal
activities, such as going to work, shopping and cleaning. It can be argued
that such visible activities may be important in confirming the children's
sense of their parents' normality as active household members. Parents'
leisure activities were also frequently mentioned.

Questions were asked about the parents' expressions of how special
the child was to them, about parental prohibitions and about praise
given to children. Generally, both parents were identified by children as
having a close personal involvement with them and, if anything, those
with PD were more easily associated with expressions of individual care.
Occasions when the parent had felt loving were identified by many of
the children. Asked to recall a particularly sad occasion, they did not,
on the whole, refer to PD, although one girl said her parent was sad
because of his shaking arm. Anger, too, was an emotion which children
mentioned. Some of these, predictably, were to do with naughtiness, but
one spoke about a parent's anger if the child did not help in the household.

Children's responses indicated that both parents showed some participation in developing their competence. Generally, the children said
that their parents with PD had talked about the children's major school
interest or about problems experienced at school. There was in fact no
evidence to suggest that the children's room to play was affected adversely. Constraints on play and friendships were indicated in just one
case, where it was perceived that the parent wanted to be on her own
when she was 'bad'.

Alterations to daily routines were not generally sufficient to require
a major overhaul of children's ideas of what was normal. Assistance was

given to both parents, but, in a number of cases, slightly more accounts of help to parents with PD were forthcoming than of help to partners without the disease. It seemed that help to parents was readily accepted as the norm in less affluent families. An 11-year-old girl, for example, made breakfast, usually made the tea and sometimes washed up. A number of difficulties in the relationship between the girl and the mother also emerged from the interview. Indeed, constraints on the children's freedom were produced by the parent's emotional state.

> Child (C): ... when we want to get something she gets annoyed and gets headaches.... She wants to be quiet on her own so we just go out to play...
> Interviewer (I): Does she take you out much?
> C: No.
> I: Why is that?
> C: She's not really bothered.

It needs to be pointed out that the partner in this family was obliged to work extremely long hours in order to maintain the household. Though the daughter said that she and her mother were able to 'cuddle each other and make up', such a family situation can lead to strains that are not easy to resolve.

Implications

It is possible that, when a parent's illness is represented to the children explicitly, their repertoire of illness knowledge is mobilized in ways that call upon the imagination. Unless this impulse towards knowledge is addressed by the provision of appropriate information, there is considerable scope for imaginative work, which brings in a varied stock of ideas. Ideas about infection, contamination, bad habits and terminal disease are current among children. The immediate question for them then becomes how their parent's condition relates to this set of ideas, some of which are frightening, others challenging to a parent's 'moral' status. Where disease itself is not regarded as responsible for what children see, they will call on ordinary explanations, which may be unflattering.

If the imagination is stimulated by discrepancies, it can also be satisfied by maintaining a good semblance of normality. We saw several ways in which normality, and active parenting in particular, were maintained. Continuing these ordinary activities, managing appearances where necessary, enables parents to reduce the scope for damaging speculation. Indeed, if adults are seen to receive care and attention, there is no reason in a child's eyes for regarding this as undesirable. It is more appropriate for children to conclude that such people are the holders of a privileged and possibly enviable position (Kirshbaum, 1988). It is important to emphasize how much society expects parents and children to relate to one another in active ways. Children's active relationships with parents who had PD were thus sustainable in large measure but were not invulnerable to strain.

It is clear that children's ordinary resources of understanding are likely to 'put them off the scent', since PD does not fit the standard profile of family illness available to children. However, the evidence of the interview does not imply that the parent's characteristics go unnoticed. Rather, the limited concepts available to these younger children reduce understanding of those features of the illness which are manifest to them. Thus a potential gap exists between their understanding and the realities of chronic illness. Family life tends to conceal and shore up this gap. What must be recognized is the absence of information strategies capable of bridging the gap or reducing the impact of recognition when it comes. 'Protected uncertainty' can, it appears, be sustained successfully but it may be a fragile structure.

It would be wrong to assume some natural urge in children to discuss issues and to find out more. The children held mixed opinions about whether they wanted to learn more about PD. Children who expressed an interest in further knowledge were also the ones who already knew that the illness was connected with the brain. These indications remind us of the importance of choice for children. While not every child will actively want to explore the ramifications of disease, it is essential to think about ways of allowing them to make that choice.

Obstacles to children's understanding of disability may be overcome if they are given the opportunity to talk in appropriate ways about what interests them. Talking with adults is a social process. Children learn through paying attention to the ways in which topics are discussed (Light, 1986). Children's competence may be more a question of how they are engaged in discussions and how they are encourage to see the 'point' of a particular statement. In considering 'what to tell' children about a disease, the issue may have more to do with *how* we talk with them than with *what* we say. If children are given the repeated opportunity to talk with adults about any aspect of a disease, there may be few limits to their understanding.

The perspectives of young people

The current attention given to young people who provide care for their parents has produced an interesting reversal of the 'generation gap' problem. Far from rebelling, young people became targets of concern and interest for the opposite reason: their devotion to dependent parents. For so many adults, the attitude of young carers is entirely laudable. But a very different view can be found among those who are concerned about the opportunities for personal development which young people may forego as a consequence of their care and support (Fallon, 1990). At the same time, it is argued that the extent of caring by young people reflects the failure of overstretched services to supply the necessary care.

The relevance of these arguments to the general situation of young people with chronically ill parents is not straightforward. Not all parents become dependent. Not all have only their children to turn to for help. Not all fall outside the network of services. However, the fundamental issues which the debate raises affect, in one form or another, all such families. They pose the problem of managing a transition into independence and adulthood at a time when the parents' condition creates a possible obstacle to this process. Perhaps, above all, the debate spotlights the family as a social institution responsible for the care of its members. Chronic illness in a parent puts a question mark on the transitions expected of both young people and their parents. While young people are drawn into closer involvement with their families, parents are faced with questions about their own capacity to promote or sustain young people's independence.

Young people's viewpoints were discovered by the use of a semistructured interview schedule which dealt with: their participation in discussions about the disease within the family or elsewhere; daily routines; their contributions to household activity and the care of the parent with the disease; their personal relationships with that parent; any consequences for the young people's health, education or career choices; possible consequences for friendships and leisure activities; young people's futures; and their contact with services and with networks of self-help. Most of these families were in touch with the PDS group for younger sufferers.

The eight adults with PD with children in this age category were on average 48 years old, the youngest being 38 years old. Most were between 40 and 50 years old, though the oldest was of pensionable age. On average, diagnosis of the disease had taken place seven and a half years previously, though that period varied from one to thirteen years. There were three women and five men, each with a regular partner.

The patients had experience of various forms of impairment associated with PD, some physical but others psychological, such as depression, confusion and anger. Some had difficulty with mobility while others lacked only hand dexterity. Some found it difficult to perform normal work or undertake social activities with children while others saw their activities as virtually unimpeded. Extensive disability and handicap were associated with no longer being employed.

Half of the parents with PD had ceased their employment, while the rest were in full-time or part-time employment. On the other hand, half of their partners were in full-time employment, while the others were in part-time employment, unemployed or looking after the home. Each of those who had ceased employment had partners who were in employment, usually full time. The main occupations of the adults with PD ranged from building work and child care to lecturing and management.

The young people consisted of five females and eight males, drawn from the eight families. Their average age was 20, the youngest being 16 and the oldest 24 years of age. Six of the families contained other children not included here; in two such families, other, younger children were also included in this study.

Learning about PD

Early awareness of the illness's effect on the parent was very difficult for most children to recall exactly. This may have been due to the creeping progression of the disease, and to a delay in informing the children. Most of the young people had first noticed the parents' health problems when they were between 10 and 18 years of age. At the beginning, while the disease was slowly advancing, physical changes in the parent were ambiguous. The emotional impact of realizing the nature of the disease was in several cases significant. Worry about the future emerged as an important aspect of these feelings. Strong emotions such as panic and shock were also described in a few cases. For some, however, negative emotions were said not to have been experienced.

Children's access to information about PD seemed to be a crucial influence. In general, what the parent with PD chose to say was pivotal. In cases where only one partner talked about the disease, there seemed to be difficulties in broaching the topic and uncomfortable feelings were left unresolved. In one case, information had come solely from a neighbour and the young person said that no discussion took place in the family. Engagement in discussions, while not a panacea, seemed to open up some possibilities for addressing issues. However, children's information sources were largely limited by what parents could provide, which was sometimes negligible. Nevertheless, some of the young people belonged to families in which the person with PD had an expert knowledge of the disease. Young people with access to sophisticated accounts of PD's effects were able to discern a great deal about their parents' day-to-day behaviour. But this knowledge – sometimes almost because of its sophistication and complexity – did not exclude them from experiencing uncertainty, insecurity or error.

Those young people who were asked for detailed accounts of their parents' health were usually able to give a discriminating picture not only of apparent symptoms but of the reasons for the problems they observed. Thus, they could see how activities became more difficult despite the fact that they were accomplished. There was awareness of variations in the parents' health and of the part which drugs played in governing the parents' levels of activity. At the same time, the adults' inner states were regarded as observable – 'thought block', tiredness, loss of temper, impatience and so on – and these could be linked to health problems.

> Young person: ... I am aware of the quiet storm of difficulty that he did have with medication.... There were different selves, there were different fathers.

It was evident that the idea of disease as contagious is a significant one for young people. The notion of a 'contagious disease' has an ominous ring to it. Other bleak prospects came into young people's minds. Visions of parents unable to walk, turned into 'cabbages' or prematurely senile were conjured up. Without clear information, young people who know about the progressive nature of the disease can be left with areas of speculation. The assumption that PD would shorten the parent's life was found in more than one case, not necessarily among the least-informed. The word 'terminal' proved to be a slippery one, most marked in a statement that the disease was 'terminal' but nevertheless the parent would not die because of it.

Providing help

It was clear that some participation in maintaining the household was regarded as a normal feature of young people's lives, whether concerned with housework, errands, shopping or looking after siblings. Regular activities of this kind could be regarded as part of a reconstructed domestic routine, especially if a partner was unable to give the attention required. Nonetheless, the routines of family existence were not generally affected by PD. Help was usually more incidental and diffuse, concerned with small items of assistance that flowed easily into the day.

A significant question was whether young women or young men helped differently. General help was, in some degree, given by some young people of each gender. However, participation by young males was not universal, and gender played a part in the extension of routine help to embrace the needs of the parent with PD. Here it appeared that young women were drawn into the process of caring in a more direct sense than their male counterparts.

> Young person: ... the daughter tends to be the one that helps, more so than probably ... [my brother] did.

In general, help given by young people to parents with PD included forms of personal care, especially in dressing, and extended to help with feeding, using the toilet, assisting mobility and lifting the parent. Examining patterns of help among children in the same family, there were differences among the various children in the scope of help which they provided.

It was necessary to look at children's help in the context of the various sources of other help that may have been available. There was a strong impression that, whatever the provision of other help, children's assistance was significant both materially and subjectively for family members.

Importantly, it was hard to identify anything resembling family discussion of the help provided by young people. If anything, assistance was underpinned by a code of silence. Children also had learned to be tactful in recognizing the limits that parents wished to place on the help which was given.

> Young person: It helped, I think, to pretend that, if you were helping him, you were just doing it in a very matter of fact way.... You would just do it as if it were the most natural thing in the world, when perhaps it might not be.

However, there were instances where the relationship altered and the balancing of roles could not be preserved. One form of this change was a recognition by the young people of the parent's sexuality. This could occur when helping the parent to dress. One parent apparently recognized the problem and help with dressing was brought to an end. At its extreme, however, caring by young people took on a purely practical aspect and the personal relationship was relegated to second place. What kept the caring alive was the thread of family obligation.

> Young person: The [parent] role has been slipping and slipping and slipping, because you start to stop seeing your ... [parent], but see a lump of human need basically.

Negotiating tasks within the household was not always straightforward. Partners could take a significant role in indicating what help was needed. However, the indirect ways in which these processes occurred could leave a burden on personal feelings. A sense of obligation was present in the young people which commonly made them feel their efforts were insufficient.

> Young person: I really feel guilty. I suppose I should say, 'Mum, would you like me to go and do some shopping' ... but I'm too lazy really.

The family became therefore a network of complex feelings rather than a theatre for open discussion.

The privacy of the family in these situations was accepted by services. A crucial indication of its social acceptability was the lack of discussion between young people and services, even when their contribution became burdensome. The strength of the family's willingness to cope normally was thus a powerful constraint on discussion with people outside the family, despite the strains that coping produced. By accepting the situation at face value, the services were perpetuating these strains.

Relationships and personal feelings

The study compared the close personal relationships of the two parents and their offspring. Here there was generally little indication that the person with PD had become a secondary participant. However, a parent's dependence on children's help was reported to lead to indulgence of their unacceptable behaviour. Or children were said to have taken advantage of a parent's inability to control their behaviour. There was little sign that the feelings of parents with the disease were less understood than their partners'. Nor was it evident that they showed less understanding of young people's feelings. Communication difficulties associated with the disease were, however, seen as hindrance to the continuance of close relationships. These included speech difficulties, marked talkativeness (a side-effect of drugs) and blank expressions.

While communication processes within families were often strong enough to enable parents to function, there were still complex issues of emotional significance. Children's responses to the parent's situation could be sharply observant, involving feelings of both resentment and identification. One response was to react against the aggressiveness and impatience of the parent; an alternative response was one of total identification with the parent. For example, one young person had become the partner's confidant and supporter. When the partner heard about the diagnosis, she was heartbroken, according to the child, who felt a similar impact simultaneously. This case was remarkable, not for the reactions of the individuals, but for the intensity of the family's communal life and sense of mutual responsibility.

It is vital to recognize that PD was not the only aspect of family experience that could be seen as problematic. Young people talked about PD as part of a broader family experience which could have a negative dimension. Though some families had experienced periods of unhappiness for a variety of reasons, these were not straightforwardly linked to PD.

Multiple health difficulties which had caused significant disruption or loss to the family were important topics sometimes fraught with emotion. PD became one aspect of a family experience in which a range of health problems had been experienced. Children's own health problems in some cases prompted reflections on the relationship between parents' and children's situations.

Developing themes – education, careers and friendships

During the phase of youth, education assumes great importance and parents are often expected to promote their children's achievements. Most parents were said to have participated in such encouragement, by visiting the school, talking about the major school interest of their children or talking over problems. Conversations at school, with teachers or schoolmates, about PD were limited or non-existent, confined to polite enquiries, or shared with close friends. If anything, such conversations were regarded as embarrassing. The only young person who claimed that PD had had a detrimental educational effect spoke of the difficulty of doing homework when she was helping at home.

A significant part of young people's development is also formed by leisure interests. A number of parents had talked about young people's major interest outside school, usually in a helpful way. Meeting friends is also an important part of growing up. There was no substantial evidence that young people encountered problems in seeing friends where they wished. One young person was, however, clearly aware of a difficulty which the current accommodation caused. Little change in the nature of the friendships was reported, though where there were several difficulties in the relationship with parents, intimacy with friends increased. One difficulty in some cases was the problem of explaining the nature of PD or dealing with friends' fears about it.

A number of children also spoke of their embarrassment in talking with friends. The onset of obvious symptoms coincided in one case with the beginning of puberty. Having a parent with PD became a social embarrassment and produced fears that friends would be rejecting.

> Young person: You think they are not going to want you because ... they are going to feel embarrassed by this situation.

Talking with their children's friends was something that a number of parents did but some were said to do so rarely. However, it was not usual for friends to go out with the young person and the parent. While several young people initially saw their parents as embarrassing, it was possible for these feelings to be overcome.

Looking backwards, looking forwards

Young people were faced with complex issues in negotiating a transition to independence. It is important to recall that families and illnesses each have a history. Asked to compare their perceptions of the parent with PD before and after its onset, young people tended to refer to physical changes. Asked to assess changes in their own feelings as they grew older, the young people generally spoke of greater understanding and knowledge, more acceptance and less discomfort, although worry was also mentioned.

As well as a history, young people have a future to consider. Leaving home is considered a normal part of developing an independent status in society. Young people were generally clear that PD was not a factor in their thinking about leaving home. Some young people asserted an independent identity which reflected dissatisfaction with their parents' norms, separate from the problem of PD, but certainly contemporary with it.

> Young person: I go back to the way it crept into life, became our life, the way it was stitched into the daily difficulties of being a mixed-up kid who wanted to be somewhere else, who wanted to be independent.

However, one young person said that he would stay at home if it was necessary to provide care for the parent. Another spoke of not wanting to leave home and one emphasized how sensitive was the topic of the parent's future. In some cases, living in the household still retained attractions or spoke to the mutual concerns of parents and child. Looking forward did not necessarily mean a complete break, and continuities of relationship were clearly significant.

Becoming a major carer

While a relationship may have continuity, this does not always mean that the relationship exists on the same basis throughout. While some attention to the dilemma faced by such young people in negotiating their independence has emerged in the literature (Rolland, 1988), the consequences of these dilemmas need to be fully grasped in particular cases, where caring responsibilities are onerous.

The ground was prepared for the extension of young people's responsibilities if the parent's alternative resources in the family were diminished either by growing needs for care or by the unavailability of a partner. The solidarity of the family as a communal unit was an important resource for parents in stressful and deprived circumstances, even if that meant increasing calls upon children's aid. But that could lead to a major reconstruction of relationships in which 'role reversal' became a possibility. A young person would then take on a qualitatively new role in the family, for example defending the partner from what were seen as the demands of the parent with PD. A further step was for the young person to uphold the needs of a sibling against the insistent calls of the parent with PD. PD then became only one claim on the family's diminished resources.

The apparent general attitude of external services to children's assistance could best be summarized as 'out of sight, out of mind'. No account was taken of the complex changes in relationship or of questions surrounding children's competence to provide care.

Implications

In examining the implications of young people's situations, their attitude to self-help networks and services must be taken into account. In general, few of the young people had experienced contact with other children of disabled parents or those specifically with PD. This was despite the membership of most parents of a self-help group organized by the PDS. Some had knowledge of the group's magazine, to which attitudes were generally favourable, while a few had experienced contact with the PDS, usually by attending its meetings. The attitudes of young people to make contact with others in the same situation were not generally positive. There was no great demand for counselling about family feelings, although a small minority would have welcomed some form of counselling had it been available. It can be suggested that, unless the home situation is one that young people feel unable to influence, they are unlikely to want to go outside the family in exploring the realities of PD. At the same time, they are likely to want to have some control over any service initiatives made in their name.

Parents with PD

Parental perspectives were derived from interviews with ten adults (four females, six males). Perhaps above all, their concern was to identify the signs of normality in family existence and in their children. The struggle to be normal was a pervasive goal.

Experiencing PD

Parents described how PD had initially affected them. The diagnosis tended to have been received negatively, as a shock. Lack of tact in disclosing the diagnosis was also a significant topic of complaint. Parents gave accounts of difficult health experiences which went beyond the classical signs of PD, such as tremor. These included adverse reactions to medication, such as cramps, hallucinations, tension, bad temper and volubility of speech. It is important to recognize that both disease and treatment influence the physical and social reality of the PD experience.

Social embarrassment was a problem. As one put it, 'if everyone else around me was blind, then I could handle it'. The variability of the disease posed a problem in suddenly revealing to outsiders what might otherwise be masked by treatment. One person described getting off a train before reaching the stop required, in order to avoid passengers' stares. Lack of confidence in social situations had been one result; communicating about the disease to strangers could be especially trying. In some cases parents felt a need to be accompanied, which was in itself restricting. Slowness in movement and even in thought could also be disadvantageous in public places. Overcoming such feelings presented a particular challenge.

A further insight into the psychological reality of PD was given by some parents who talked of unhappy states of mind, including depression, disinterest and hopelessness. Depression following the diagnosis could be exacerbated by other family adversities, including the responsibility of caring for young children.

Parent: That was in the very early stages, with a young baby my daughter just starting school, hubby out of work. It just all came down on me, sort of thing.

Communication

A few parents indicated that information given to children had been minimal or non-existent. Others confirmed that any information about the disease had been communicated informally and led to little discussion with the children. Though some parents had a good knowledge of the disease, lack of knowledge could be a handicap. While some parents took initiatives to explain points and make information available, others had not seen this as appropriate. In one case, the curiosity of a child relative had been passed off. In some cases the partner, not the parent, had talked with the children. While younger children might be seen as unaware of the disease or too young to understand, young people were reported to have posed a few questions. Some were said to have been 'unimpressed' or to have made jokes. One spontaneous question emerging from several young people was said to have concerned inheritance of the disease. Parents' accounts thus tended to emphasize the 'low-key' aspects of the communication process, perhaps even more than partners. A need for specific help was identified in a few cases, involving a booklet or contact with other children in the same situation. One parent reported an incident where a pupil had insisted to one of the children that PD was 'terminal' and life-threatening, causing considerable distress.

Work and income

Control over their material circumstances was also a significant concern. In a few cases parents described how they had tried at first to conceal their PD from work colleagues. It was clear that adjustments were sometimes necessary to patterns of work, although some people were continuing much as before. Nonetheless, concerns about the future were expressed. Several of the parents had ceased or reduced their employment and in a few cases this led to guilt at the load placed upon partners. Inability to continue work was felt as a particular blow when it resulted in confinement at home. The resulting drop in income led sometimes to hardship, especially when the financial costs of disability began to appear. Expenditure on children's needs could form an additional call on stretched resources. Other families had not mentioned this pressure. Accommodation difficulties were found to affect a minority of the sample, although their implications for children were significant.

> Parent: ... [my daughter] should really have a bedroom of her own. But with the council housing lists the way they are at the moment....

Accepting help

Attitudes to help have crucial implications for understanding the social meanings of illness and disability. Where those with illness and disability are felt to be misunderstood and patronized, people with health problems face acute difficulties in receiving appropriate help. Where help is perceived to be unnecessary or unsuitable, it may be rejected. Not feeling a need to call on help was an important part of maintaining normality for some people. Indeed, refusing help was regarded as appropriate in more than one case precisely in order to avoid feelings of helplessness. Being fussed over was unlikely to be acceptable, as it suggested invalidity rather than disability. Accepting help was therefore a stage in itself, when it was necessary to 'put your pride in your pocket'. Perceptions of help need therefore to be set against the background of wishing to remain independent.

Help and support from relatives and friends were reported in a number of cases, although sometimes this contribution was seen as disappointing. Supportive attitudes were a particular benefit given by friends. However, it was surprising to learn that practical help might be penalized. One very helpful relative was apparently threatened with official repossession of her home because of the time she was spending with the parent.

Lack of systematic information about help available had been a commonplace experience. It posed a great difficulty, especially when the parent felt an isolated case. One general practitioner, however, won exceptional praise for quality of advice.

Disturbances to daily routine were normally seen as minimal. In general, men tended to point out their lack of involvement in housework in ways that were not so clear-cut in women's descriptions of their own domestic arrangements. This difference may be due to norms about gender.

Children's help

Descriptions of children's help generally corresponded with the accounts set out previously. One daughter was described as 'a second Mum'. Variations among the children in their level of help were also pointed out, although little family discussion was reported. But the idea that help from children should be minimal was also a significant theme. Despite these reservations, the level of need could make help from children unavoidable. So strong was the sense of family obligation in one family that the children were said to have rejected the possibility of outside help, wishing to do everything themselves. Problems in service provision were, however, identified by parents in cases where children's help had become the norm. In the instance mentioned, the parent had spoken to a sympathetic hospital social worker, who was said to have been 'horrified' by the amount of work expected of the children, and as a result more home help had been provided.

Being a parent

A number of parents detailed the active ways in which they pursued a personal relationship with their children. However, it was necessary to come to terms with the advantages and disadvantages of the situation. The value of time spent with children was enhanced by awareness of reduced opportunities for interaction with them. Having more time was seen as a compensation for ceasing employment but disability hindered parents' physical activity with children, especially outside the home.

In some families it was customary for women, in particular, to control the children. Where this type of responsibility fell on a mother with PD, it seemed to be stressful. It was noticeable also that mothers of young children felt a particular strain from their children. Children's special needs were an additional call on parental energy and patience. If it was difficult to meet children's needs, this could be seen as a source of unhappiness. On the other hand, having a young child could be seen as a stimulus to cope with PD.

Communication was said to have been affected in a number of cases. One cause was speech difficulties, which could be frustrating. Another was a reduction in smiling. This blankness of expression was subject to an imaginative strategy: one parent had put up a poster with a picture of an impassive eagle, captioned 'I *am* smiling!' There was some tendency to qualify statements about mutual understanding between the parent and the children. One parent argued that children were loath to express their true feelings to their parents. However, only one parent was somewhat negative about mutual understanding and one thought he understood his children's feelings better. None felt the children's attitudes to health had been adversely affected. Even the vicissitudes of illness and treatment – 'short-term shocks and surprises' – could be dealt with by taking initiatives, encouraging children to look at the problem calmly and objectively, becoming a source of fascination and interest.

Children's own areas of development were generally looked upon as not presenting insuperable problems. Two parents, however, had found difficulties in supporting their children's education, a point that wider research has highlighted, at least for mothers (Pilling, 1990). Two parents referred to problems that may have affected children's friendships. Children's leisure was generally felt to have been positively affected. Although family holidays were not generally curtailed, one parent felt that others in the family needed a respite. In reflecting on age differences, there was a feeling that growing up with a parent's PD from an early age was preferable. A younger child who had always known the person as someone with PD was felt to have accepted the situation more than another who had first encountered it when beginning school. However, older children were not necessarily seen as responding poorly. In looking at their whole history, it was rare for parents to express any negative feelings about what had happened. A number of parents had conceived children around the time PD appeared; one mother had planned to have a baby in full knowledge of her diagnosis. Family fertility had not been curtailed by PD as such. It therefore seems that the family commitments of people with PD are unlikely to be reduced for this reason, although other difficulties did have an influence on decisions not to have more children.

Contacting other parents

Finally, attitudes to group contacts were explored. Those who had experience of the self-help group were more positive about contact with other people with PD than those who had not. One strand of feeling was that PDS meetings had a dull and passive atmosphere – 'stick-in-the-muds' – as one put it. Scones and raffle tickets summed up the impression of a similar group for older people. A more extreme position was the desire not to see a reflected mirror image, thus projecting uncomfortably the person's own problems. A desire for avoidance here contrasted with the benefits which a number of other parents had found from their contacts with the self-help group. However, not all felt that it was as helpful as it might have been; needs for counselling and for education in disability were also expressed. One problem was having the energy to participate in group organization.

Conclusions

Living with the disease can be summarized as a process of change in which there is a struggle to control problematic experiences and hold them back from others, especially children. Much can be done to achieve these aims but some part of those changes will impinge on the children. It needs to be recognized how people struggle to turn the extraordinary into the ordinary and how children's presence in the family can be an incentive to that normalization. But children's participation in the family emphasizes that they are not passive or unaware, but active contributors.

Implications of the study for services and networks of self-help

The points covered by this study obviously cannot provide definitive guidance to those concerned with children and young people. However, it is possible to formulate principles related to key aspects of their situation. These may serve as guidelines for the development of policy and practice among services and self-help networks.

From the evidence of the exploratory surveys, it should not be assumed that younger people with PD have ended their major responsibilities for bringing up children, including those in early childhood. Coping with parenthood is likely to be a significant issue for those in their forties and fifties, as well as in their twenties and thirties. The formation of second families can also occur at a considerable age.

Children have a right to a suitable explanation when a chronic illness in a parent impinges on their normal way of life. This explanation must relieve them of responsibility for those changes which are due to parental illness. Children should normally have a choice about when they receive information and how much. Their existing knowledge of disease and disability should be taken into account, as well as the ideas current in society.

Children's access to information is dependent on the access of parents and this is likely to be variable. Information designed for children themselves may be of assistance both to them and to their parents. Children's conceptions of disease are rooted in a common-sense knowledge of illness, which leaves room for uncertainties and errors. Discussion within the family is a potential instrument for clarifying their understanding and knowledge. Services have a responsibility to make information and counselling available to those who request it.

Children's contributions to maintaining the household and providing care tend not to be openly discussed within the family or with services. When children are asked to help their parents, they should be given an explanation which accounts for the role and consequences of parental illness. Where help is given by children, this should be openly regarded as part of a fair and reciprocal relationship and not as a simple duty.

Services have a responsibility to make clear the level and types of help they can provide to families, taking into full account the potential demands on young people and the consequences of those demands for their welfare. Services, in addition, should be obliged to ensure that young people are consulted about decisions concerning help which may affect them. Social embarrassment associated with PD represents a problem for adolescents in particular, and communication strategies which address this difficulty should be encouraged. The promotion of positive images of disability could make a contribution here. The personal development of young people having a parent with PD is influenced by a range of experiences and the disease may not be the only adverse element that they may confront. Services which become concerned with children's personal development should ensure they are capable of identifying those various difficulties. Initiatives designed to meet young people's needs must present clear objectives that address young people's aspirations to influence and control their personal futures.

Acknowledgements

This study would not have been carried out without concerted help from various organizations and individuals. These include: the National Children's Bureau, in particular David Berridge and Philippa Russell; the Parkinson's Disease Society, and Mary Baker in particular; the Carers' National Association, especially Huw Meredith and Anne Clarke; and members of the medical profession, notably T.H.M. El-Debas, Leslie Findley, Niall Quinn and Adrian Williams. The contribution of the families interviewed was greatly appreciated.

References

ARNAUD, S. (1959) Some psychological characteristics of children of multiple sclerotics. *Psychosomatic Medicine, 1,* 8–22.

BECKER, S., ALDRIDGE, J. and DEARDEN, C. (1998) *Young Carers and Their Families.* Oxford: Blackwell Science.

FALLON, K. (1990) An involuntary workforce. *Community Care,* 4 January, no. 795, 12–13.

GRIMSHAW, R. (1991) *Children of Parents with Parkinson's Disease. A Research Report for the Parkinson's Disease Society.* London: National Children's Bureau.

HOEHN, M.M. and YAHR, M.D. (1967) Parkinsonism: onset, progression and mortality. *Neurology, 17,* 427–442.

KIRSHBAUM, M. (1988) Parents with physical disabilities and their babies. *Zero to Three, 8,* 8–15.

LIGHT, P. (1986) Context, conservation and conversation. In M. Richards and P. Light (Eds) *Children of Social Worlds: Development in a Social Context.* Cambridge: Polity Press.

OXTOBY, M. (1982) *Parkinson's Disease Patients and Their Social Needs.* London: Parkinson's Disease Society.

PETERS, L.C. and ESSES, L.M. (1985) Family environment as perceived by children with a chronically ill parent. *Journal of Chronic Diseases, 38,* 301–308.

PILLING, D. (1990) *Escape from Disadvantage.* London: Falmer Press, in association with the National Children's Bureau.

ROLLAND, J.S. (1988) A conceptual model of chronic and life threatening illness and its impact on families. In C.S. Chilman, E.W. Nunnally and F.M. Cox (Eds) *Chronic Illness and Disability* (Families in Trouble Series, Vol. 2). London: Sage.

TAMIVAARA, J. and ENRIGHT, D.S. (1986) On eliciting information: dialogues with child informants. *Anthropology and Education Quarterly, 17,* 218–238.

THURMAN, S.K. (1985) Ecological congruence in the study of families with handicapped parents. In S.K. Thurman (Ed.) *Children of Handicapped Parents: Research and Clinical Perspectives.* London: Academic Press.

YIN, R.K. (1989) *Case Study Research: Design and Methods.* London: Sage.

Chapter 7

The experience of caring for people with Parkinson's disease

Anne D. M. Davies, Rossana Cousins, Christopher J. Turnbull, Jeremy R. Playfer and Dennis B. Bromley

Although there has been recent interest in the experiences of patients with Parkinson's disease (PD) (Brod *et al.*, 1998), there have been only a handful of studies of the morale and mood of their carers and very little is known of the day-to-day detail of their experiences. The few quantitative studies suggest that carers are at risk of psychiatric morbidity, reduced wellbeing, poor adjustment, depression and diminished social functioning (Dura *et al.*, 1990; Speer, 1993; Berry and Murphy, 1995; Miller *et al.*, 1996; O'Reilly *et al.*, 1996). As Hall (1990) points out, however, caring is an *interpersonal* process and its 'success' depends on the qualities and beliefs of both carer and care recipient. Carers vary greatly in personal and coping characteristics, such as optimism and emotionality, the one protecting, the other exacerbating expressed distress (Hooker *et al.*, 1998). Additionally, it must not be forgotten that PD is a progressive condition and the needs of patient and carer change over time. As the disease progresses, the relationship between carer and care recipient moves into uncharted waters and a new equilibrium may have to be achieved.

Psychological models of carer distress have generally been based on carers for patients with Alzheimer's disease, who typically suffer severe cognitive impairment but have little physical impairment until late in the disease (Morris *et al.*, 1988). As both a neuropsychological and a movement disorder, PD is very different and carers are faced with a wider range of challenges. The existing research on these carers provides little guidance because studies have not been designed to provide information about the *experience* of caring. It is also fragmented because studies have used a restricted range of outcome measures. To be effective, welfare provision needs to be based on knowledge of the actual day-to-day demands of caring. This chapter is based on the responses of a sample of PD carers to two semistructured interviews carried out at their carer home 14 months apart (phases 1 and 2). It also draws on care charts and diaries completed at each phase, together with carers' responses to the Motenko Frustration Scale, which assesses emotional response to the caring situation (Motenko, 1989).

Questions covered the onset of symptoms; the impact of diagnosis, the 'job demand' at different stages of the illness; the extent of discretion that carers had in delivering care; perceived change in the patient's personality and in the dyadic relationship, and concurrent life events. At phase 2, interviews covered not only the current situation but also changes that had occurred since phase 1.

Method

Recruitment

Recruitment was made by consultant geriatricians at outpatient clinics on Merseyside. Younger patients were not excluded from the study but only three such patients were referred from the three neurologists approached for cooperation. The study is thus more typical of the experience of caring for older PD patients. In order to sample caring at different stages, the definition of 'carer' did not require provision of any specified services. Instead, the concept of assuming 'responsibility' for the needs of the patient was seen as central (see Braithwaite, 1990, pp. 35–36). Thus, the definition of a 'PD carer' was 'someone who accepts the main responsibility for providing for the needs of a Parkinson's patient living at home'. Inclusion criteria were that the patient should: have a diagnosis of idiopathic PD; have an identifiable primary carer; be living at home; and be in receipt of informal care (rather than being totally dependent on professional care). Exclusion criteria were a history of other neurological illness or brain injury, or such poor health that the patient was judged unlikely to survive to one-year follow-up. The consultants also considered carer health and only where carer was also judged likely to survive to a one-year follow-up were the couple ('dyad') included. The research proposals were approved by the appropriate ethics committees and dyads were able to withdraw from the study at any time.

Sample details

Eighty-three patient–carer dyads were recruited. Sample details are shown in Table 7.1. In the presentation of results, code numbers are

Table 7.1. *Details of the sample of carers recruited to the study*

Variable		
Carer's gender	Male	21
	Female	62
Carer's age	Mean age	69.1
	s.d.	10.4
	Range	36–89
Relationship of carer to patient	Wife	53
	Husband	19
	Daughter	6
	Son	2
	Friend	2
	Daughter-in-law	1
Living arrangements	With patient	80
	Not with patient	3
Health status	Good	39
	Fair	24
	Poor	20

used to indicate dyads, with C and P to denote carer and patient, respectively.

The modal carer was an older woman caring for her husband at home. The health status of carers was determined on the basis of illnesses reported and current medication. While this is not as stringent a criterion as a physical examination, it is not to be regarded as a 'subjective health' measure. The criterion for 'good health' was that the carer had no existing diagnosed illnesses and had suffered acute conditions only (e.g. colds) in the previous 12 months. A rating of 'fair' health was made if there was a controlled presenting problem that was not currently disabling (e.g. angina, diabetes and irritable bowel syndrome). A rating of 'poor health' was given if the carer had a chronic disabling health problem (e.g. arthritis, cancer, emphysema, osteoporosis). Obviously, there is an overlap between the 'fair' and 'poor' health groups, based on the disabling nature of the underlying disease.

Details of the patients recruited to the study are shown in Table 7.2. It can be seen that the typical patient was a man. at Hoehn and Yahr stage III (bilateral disease with early impairment of postural stability; Hoehn and Yahr, 1967) (see Chapter 1), with moderate or advanced severity of motor symptoms (unified Parkinson's disease motor examination scores, Fahn *et al.*, 1987), who had developed PD in his mid-sixties and had had the disease for around eight years. Ten of the sample were seriously cognitively impaired, as indicated by a score on the Mini-Mental State Examination (MMSE) of under 24 (Folstein *et al.*, 1975).

Table 7.2. *Details of patients recruited to the study*

Variable		
Patient's gender	Male	55
	Female	28
Patient age	Mean	74.7
	s.d.	8.14
	Range	8–95
Illness onset	Early (<60)	14
	Typical (60–70)	36
	Late (>70)	33
Mean age of onset		66.55
	s.d.	9.77
Mean illness duration		8.22
	sd.. 5.11	
Severity of PD	Mild (UPD < 10)	11
	Moderate (UPD 10–24)	36
	Advanced (UPD 25+)	36
Hoehn and Yahr stage	Stage I	14
	Stage II	14
	Stage III	38
	Stage IV	13
	Stage V	4
Patients' MMSE score	24 or over	73
	Under 24	10
Current medication	Sinomet	44
	Madopar	31
	Benzhexol	2
	Anticholinergics only	3
	Apomorphine	4
	None	3

UPD = Unified Parkinson's disease motor examination scores (Fahn *et al.*, 1987).

Study design

The unit of the present study was the carer–patient dyad. Each was interviewed on two occasions a week apart (phase 1, visits 1 and 2) and then on a further two occasions, some 14 months later (phase 2, visits 3 and 4). In the first interviews, the patient was assessed and a history of symptoms taken, while the second were devoted to carer concerns. Between the first and second interviews at each phase, the carer was given a seven-day 'care chart' to fill in, detailing the actual hours of caring supplied each day and a diary was kept of any 'critical incidents' (e.g. falls, problems with medication). Additionally, carers completed a pack of questionnaires covering the effects of various aspects of caring on wellbeing. These were checked at the second interview.

Attrition

Of the participating 83 dyads at phase 1, 56 were also available at phase 2. In three cases the PD patient had entered a nursing home and so the dyad no longer matched the inclusion criteria, 12 patients had died, as had five carers, six carers withdrew from the study (of these, three carers had terminal cancer and were no longer caring). One carer was removed from the study on account of his communication difficulties. This was a son with Tourette's syndrome, caring at home for his mother who was at Hoehn and Yahr stage IV.

To examine possible attrition biases, the phase 1 characteristics of those who did not participate at phase 2 were compared with those who did. It was expected that they might be older, more severely ill and more cognitively impaired. Statistical analysis confirmed 'drop-outs' were indeed older and more cognitively impaired. However, there were no significant differences between the two groups in disease stage, severity or length of illness, or time since diagnosis.

Onset of PD and diagnosis

Patients and carers were seen together when details of PD onset were collected. Dyads were asked to describe the first symptoms from the time that they suspected that something unusual was happening. The pathway to receiving a diagnosis of PD was also explored. Table 7.3 shows the initial symptoms reported as being 'unusual'.

Since PD has an insidious onset and symptoms appear gradually, some degree of compensation and adaptation may be possible. Where

Table 7.3. *Initial symptoms among the PD patients*

Symptom	Percentage of patients
Tremor	45.0
Stiffness	8.4
Depression, or other psychiatric disturbance	7.0
Gait disturbance	5.6
Slowness	5.6
Could not lift feet off the floor	5.6
Fall	5.6
Handwriting disturbance	4.2
Muscle pain/cramp	2.8
Loss of coordination	2.8
General fatigue	2.8
Loss of arm swing	2.8
Permanently cold hand	1.4

the first symptoms were slowing or increased tiredness, these could be interpreted as part of the ageing process ('You expect that sort of thing at our age').

The predominant early symptom, however, was tremor. Carers tried to make sense of what was happening but PD was not recognized. For one dyad, tremor in one hand was attributed to 'a trapped nerve', and ignored by both patient and carer.

C113: I noticed him pulling his right leg whenever he used to worry, and it used to shake.

When asked how long it was before they sought medical advice, she replied:

C113: I can't say really, because when I used to tell him about it, he would deny it. But quite some time I suppose. It was only after he came in one night and said that he had fallen the full length of the pavement at Pier Head. The next thing I noticed him pulling his leg again to stop it shaking. I made some tea and asked him to pour it out, then I had to say 'Look at your hand! It's shaking! You should go to the doctor. I don't know if you have trapped a nerve or something, but you should go and get it sorted out'.
Interviewer: So you knew something was wrong. Did you know it was Parkinson's disease?
C113: No. No. Because I had never seen anybody with it. I mean I had seen people with shakes and things, but I never knew what it was.

A similar story was told by other carers:

C116: His hands started to shake a bit, and he got very tired and listless, whereas he used to be always on the go. And tasks that he would have done in five minutes were taking over an hour.... I said, 'You should see a doctor about that'. He went, but the doctor gave him nerve tablets, and he started to take them. But then he nearly fell over in the kitchen, so he came to me that morning and whispered, 'There is something wrong with me'.

Ignorance at onset of PD, of the cause of the symptoms, was the rule rather than the exception. C174 remarked, 'so between 1980 and 1983 we were wondering what was wrong'.

The modal period between onset of the first symptom and diagnosis was two years. Even when dyads saw a doctor, more than one in four came away without a diagnosis of PD initially. This was a particular problem in cases where there was no tremor.

C117: I thought he was having a nervous breakdown. The doctor thought it was just depression, and prescribed Prothiaden [dothiepin, an antidepressant]. He took them for a while and was able to carry on working. Then I noticed his handwriting! I thought he had had a stroke.

It was clear that, even before diagnosis, there was stress for many carers, because of the uncertainty. When the diagnosis of PD was made, carer's reactions were diverse.

> C126: [I was] upset for her. But at the time I didn't realize the full implications of it.

> C121: Well, I was shocked actually. Then I was very curious. I found out by listening to any programme on it on the telly. I would always listen intently to what they were saying.

> C120: I really didn't think of anything. To be honest I think I went round with a blindfold on. I think my trouble is that I can't accept it. And I think things are going to get right.

> C134: I said to him, 'Oh heavens, we are going to have a long, hard road to hoe.' I didn't know a lot, but I knew it was a very debilitating disease, and you could become a complete invalid.

> C150: I have followed my mother around hospitals for a great many years. It was just another thing.

> C167: I was obviously upset. But we tried to keep our lives as normal as possible.

> C127: Astounded. And realizing what Parkinson's is, I would say frightened. I knew there were problems ahead.

> C119: C. is so positive in everything, and it makes me positive as well. So we said we would go on as normal.

Despite the often long wait for diagnosis, there was rarely relief from knowing the reason for the manifest symptoms. The vow to 'carry on as normal' was frequently mentioned, but not always in the sense of trying to rise above problems seen as enduring. Rather, there was sometimes denial that there was anything wrong. Where trepidation was expressed, it was usually because the carer had some knowledge of the condition. Those who were completely ignorant of PD tended to be less concerned, and expected that medication would solve the problem. For some time it often did:

> C119: As soon as C. got on those pills that were prescribed, the difference was incredible.

> C141: I can't say life changed at all for some time after the diagnosis, except that we kept going to the hospital every six months, and he kept taking the tablets.

The 'honeymoon period', however, sometimes came to an abrupt end:

> C107: When she was eventually diagnosed as having PD, I was not concerned, because I knew so little about it. Things were all right for a while. I had no idea of the agony I would go through watching her wriggle and squirm.

Extent of caring

The sample represented the full range of patient severity of illness. In consequence, there were carers who regarded themselves as doing little for the patient and carers who saw themselves as giving care full time. To examine the relationship between severity of the patient's motor symptoms and 'job demand' in terms of time, carers filled in a care chart over seven days, marking off each half hour period during which care was delivered. Hours of caring per week were computed for each carer. Forty-five carers completed the chart completely enough for the data to be coded at phase 1 and 37 at phase 2. Figure 7.1 shows the distribution of hours of caring.

At phase 1, the duration of care ranged from 0 to 119 hours (median 34 hours; mean 39.5, s.d. 31.8). Forty per cent gave fewer than 21 hours a week of care but 13.3% gave over 75 hours. At phase 2, the range was 0 to 112 hours (median 35.0 hours, mean 40.84, s.d. 30.9). Thirty-two per cent gave fewer than 21 hours care and 13.5% more than 75 hours. For the 25 dyads completing usable care charts at *both* phases, there was a modest rise in the number of hours' caring between phases, from a median of 32 to a median of 35.2 hours per week.

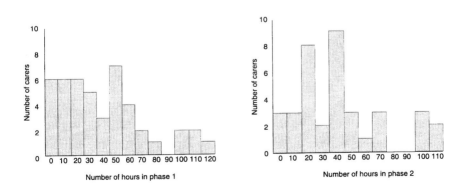

Figure 7.1. *Hours of caring per week at phases 1 and 2*

   Hours of caring were examined in relation to severity of PD based on the Unified Parkinson's Disease (UPD) rating scale (Fahn *et al.*, 1987). The UPD score is based on an assessment of motor functioning and inter-rater reliability is high (Lang and Fahn, 1989). Patients were categorized into three groups based on UPD score: 'mild' (UPD scores < 10); 'moderate' (10–24) or 'advanced PD' (scores 25 or more).

Mild PD

Eleven PD patients fitted this category. Most were able to do nearly everything for themselves and only five carers completed a care chart. The hours of care given differed markedly (0, 2, 5, 11 and 50 at phase 1, and 0, 5, 21, 24 and 67 at phase 2). Time demands for 'mild' patients are low. Carers who had a job at onset were able to continue working, so life did not change dramatically. For some carers, the situation was better relative to the pre-diagnosis period because the patient was now on medication.

   To investigate job demand, carers were asked a single specific question: 'What do you actually do regularly for ...?'

C119: Nothing ... oh yes I do! Fasten those little teeny weeny buttons. That is the only thing. And it is only that he gets impatient with them.

C161 (Works full-time): I don't do a lot. I perhaps do a little more around the house. During the week she will do the cooking, but at weekends I do it. She does need help putting on an awkward item of clothing, or her necklace. Very occasionally she might be ironing and I will have to carry on for her. Perhaps I am a bit more attentive and do more washing up than I used to. Things like that. Well she won't let me do anything. She is very good in the house because she really tries. When she feels she needs help with anything, she asks me, and I will do it. That is basically what it is.

C163: Although we have always shared the driving, I drive the car more now. If he wants to put his tie on, button things, or undo a belt, or even pick things up, I will usually help. Sometimes he will struggle and do it himself, but it is slower. I have to do all his correspondence for him because he can't write now.

   Of interest is the fact that some carers devoted so much time to caring, while others, whose patients were of the same severity, took mild PD in their stride. C133, aged 76, cared for her 78-year-old husband who had a UPD score of 6 and suffered depression.

C133: [I] get him up of course. And help him, if he needs help, with bathing. He can *always* manage to shave, although I will help him with the bits that he can't get to. Then I help him get dressed. And everything else really. I mean it's not so hard for me as it could be for other people, because D. has never done anything. You know he is of the age when [gentle]men didn't. But then I always have....

Throughout their married life this wife had got her husband's clothes out of the wardrobe for him. Observation during the motor examination revealed that he could button his shirt cuffs, usually a very difficult task for PD patients. In spite of this, he was dressed by his wife.

In contrast, C149 , aged 75, gave two hours of care a week to his wife, aged 73, whose UPD score was also 6 at phase 1. He was more physically disabled than his wife, suffering bronchitis and from the consequences of surgery for a tubercular spine.

> C149: I don't do a thing for her because I'm not able. The only thing is – she would moan if I didn't take her to bingo.

By phase 2, however, P149 had had a sudden decline following the withdrawal of selegiline and emergency treatment with apomorphine. Her UPD score was 12 and she had became withdrawn and frightened to go out. C149, who did not complete a care chart at phase 2, now felt he was a 24-hour-a-day carer – 'I am with her all the time now'. This change in the demands of caring had caused tensions. The examples of C133 and C149 make it clear that in mild PD the amount of time devoted to caring depends not just on severity but also on the temperament and circumstances of the carer and on habitual patterns of interaction.

Moderate PD

The amount that the 36 carers in this group did for the patient was influenced both by the amount patients could do for themselves and by the use of formal services. Twenty carers completed a care chart. Their median amount of caring was 21 hours at both phases. The distribution of hours of caring is shown in Figure 7.2.

Even at this 'moderate' severity level, there was one carer giving 95 hours of care a week. Comments from this group are given below.

> C114: I give him some assistance getting dressed – with buttons and his hearing aid. He needs help getting in and out the car. Chairs – we changed the suite because he had difficulty getting out of the other one because it was too floppy. Even this one, I've had to put a bit of extra foam in that one where he usually sits, behind him, to help him get out. The only other change we have made is the two banister rails because he came down the stairs, backwards of course, and knocked himself out at midnight one night. I ran him over to Arrowe Park [Hospital] for a quick check. He is up in the night

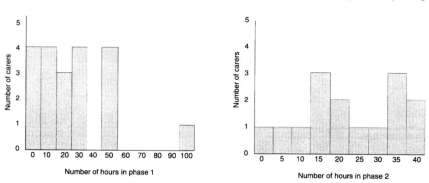

Figure 7.2 *Hours of caring for moderate PD patients at phases 1 and 2*

most nights, and we now sleep in separate beds because he sleeps so badly. I have to keep my dressing gown handy. The one thing that is demanding is that I always liked to be in the kitchen on my own. But unless he is asleep this is no longer possible because he is there at my side *all* the time.

C175: Most mornings I help him out of bed, because he is pretty stiff. He showers himself, but I help him get dry, then help him get dressed. He can do it on his own, but it takes forever. I mean last Saturday, I was working and I didn't wake him until just as I was going out. Because he was fast asleep I thought I would let him lie in. So I left at a quarter to nine. He probably didn't get down until a quarter to twelve. It would have taken him that long. He used to do a lot of cooking, but now it takes forever. He does try. The days I am at work, he will often have started to get the meal ready, but I have to take over. Peeling the potatoes and that sort of thing he can't manage now.

C118: Every day is the same. I have to help him out of bed in the morning and twice in the night. He washes himself, but I help him to shave and if he has a bath. I help him get dressed, then get the breakfast. I make sure he takes his tablets. I do everything in the house, all the gardening, and I do the decorating. I have certain jobs to do on certain days and I get them done in the morning. I spend the afternoon with him. Sometimes we go for a walk; I hang on to him all the time. When he falls he goes forwards on to his hands. I make all the meals. He just needs a little help getting undressed for bed. He is not bad really. He is all right at the moment.

At this stage of PD, most carers needed to provide some assistance with getting out of bed, bathing and dressing. Some dyads started to make adaptations to their home to increase the independence of the patient. Most assistance was required first thing in the morning, particularly for patients with early morning dystonia. These patients could not do anything for themselves until the first dose of medication of the day had been metabolized, but after that they required less assistance. Patients could eat by themselves, although some needed food to be cut up, and there might be some mess. Some carers had to get up in the night to attend to the patient, but this was not the norm. Some carers reported that patients would get distressed if they went out. Those caring for patients who were prone to falling increased their vigilance with each successive fall.

Advanced PD

Giving care to someone with advanced PD is often a 24-hour job. In this sample there were (originally) 36 advanced PD dyads. There were full care charts for 20. The median weekly amount of care given was 56 hours at phase 1 and 51 hours at phase 2. Figure 7.3 shows the distributions.

At phase 1, a fifth of the group provided over 100 hours a week. At first sight it may seem surprising that the median number of hours of care per week at phase 2 was (marginally) lower than at phase 1, but this probably reflected increased use of formal care services such as day care, home helps and care aides. Even at this 'advanced' disease stage, two patients managed to live alone. This was achieved through well organized formal care to supplement care provided by daughters. Some of this group of patients were mentally alert, but hallucinations and dementia were frequent. To provide a flavour of advanced PD caring, excerpts from the interviews of four carers follow: two were wives (C105, C120), one a husband (C106), and one a non-resident daughter (C126).

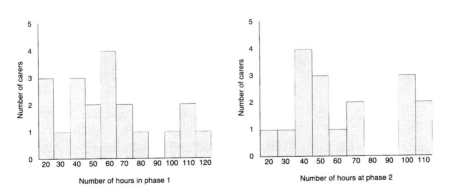

Figure 7.3. *Hours of caring for advanced PD patients at phases 1 and 2*

In the interview, carers were asked a single specific question: What do you actually do regularly for ...?

> C105: Everything. I do literally everything. I wash him, I shave him, I dress him, I catheterize him every four hours. I give him enemas. I see to all his medication. He does *nothing* for himself. I write cheques, I sort out all his finances. I never knew before how much money he had in the bank. I *try* to get him to do things, but then he says he cannot do it. I would like him to do more because it is stimulation. I mean I never used to consult him about what we are going to eat. Now I ask him, 'What shall we have for dinner?,' to stimulate him. I think he draws on me. I mean he uses my strength. He is that dependent now that if anything happened to me.... I have got to be in good health. I can never leave him.
> Interviewer: Do you have anyone to help you? Do you have a home help?
> C105: I would not have one. I would rather live in dirt. I had a home help with my mother and they let me down very badly. My son helps with the garden and if I ever need anything doing in the house. We rely very much on our son.
> Interviewer: Is there any help you would like?
> C105: Oh there are times when I do feel like I am going under, and it is too much. There are dark areas, but I don't tell J., and I don't tell D., but I have got a very good GP. She is marvellous. She thinks I am better off without medication, and I manage to pull myself round, and get on until the next time.

At phase 2, P105 was receiving even more personal care after a bowel infection. He had also started having periods of confusion and hallucinations. In response to the ever increasing demands on his mother, their son and family moved into their (large) house, taking over the upstairs. Nevertheless:

> C105: The minute he opens his eyes I am on call. No matter how much I tell him, he is oblivious to my needs.

The next case to be considered is a lady who had a similar level of disability to P105 above in phase 1, although she was continent. They had moved from a large house to a warden-assisted flat to make life easier.

> C106: I do virtually everything. I *have* to help her to dress. I do all the cooking, the shopping, the laundry. I fetch and carry. I organize everything. I have to watch to make sure she doesn't fall, and I have to support her if we go out. We sometimes go out for a drive; I do all the driving, but then I always have. She likes to do things for herself when she can. But sometimes she takes too much out of herself trying to do things that are a struggle and take her a long time. But I like to help her too. I often feel on edge when I watch her struggling to do a simple task.

Interviewer: Do you have anyone to help you? Do you have a home help?
C106: Yes. We have a cleaner. She comes for three hours on a Wednesday morning. You see Wednesday is wash day, so I am busy, and not here all the time.

In phase 2, P106 was much weaker and now needed support even to go to the toilet. In addition, she had recently begun to have early morning periods of confusion. There was no additional help. The cleaner had been sacked for stealing and C106 was visibly tired during the visit. Nevertheless, he felt that caring had given him something to do in his retirement, and he seemed pleased with his ability to cope.

The next case was the youngest man in the sample, who had been aged 36 years at the onset of PD and whose duration of illness was 14 years at phase 1. His caring wife was four years younger. Two of their three children were still at home. P120 was also dementing.

C120: I help him get dressed. He used to be able to do that a little bit, not long ago. Everything really.
Interviewer: Everything?
C120: Well yes. Help him get round, help him in and out the car. I mean he can walk around a bit, but you have to watch him because he falls. He has been falling a lot more lately. His legs just seem to give way – especially on the stairs. On Wednesday night I went to the front door and, as usual, J. followed me. The next thing I heard a smash. I couldn't believe it! J. had fallen backwards into the side porch window and the glass had gone right through. He was covered with glass, and I just can't believe that he wasn't seriously hurt. I mean, one of the pieces of glass cut my foot and it was bleeding quite heavily. I don't know what to do about the window. Do I get it replaced, or do I have it blocked up with wood, and lose a lot of light in the hallway? J. didn't seem bothered at all, and the trouble now is watching that he doesn't go near the glass until it is repaired.

Our eldest son and his wife come and sit with him while I go to get the weekly shopping. He likes it when people visit, but he is not keen on me going. He likes to go out in the car. But I can't leave him outside Asda for an hour. He does like to go out. My friend W. rang up on Friday and asked if we would like to for a walk in [the] park. I said no, because I didn't think I could cope with supporting him. J. heard the conversation and seemed to want to go, so I thought about it and rang her back and said we'd decided we would go. I started to get us ready. I can't stand all the hassle of getting J. ready – it just wears me out. And to make matters worse he had wet his trousers which meant all clean clothes. We got there, and had a short walk and J. wasn't too bad. Then we went back to W.'s for a cup of tea. J. just fell asleep. He was worn out.
Interviewer: Is there any help you would like?
C120: We are waiting to have a downstairs toilet put in. We have got the grant and everything, but that was 18 months ago, and it has still not been done. When J. wants to go to the toilet I have to help him a lot more now

because he doesn't seem to be managing the stairs as well. And it is very tiring standing behind him and pushing him up.

Interviewer: Do you have any formal help?

C120: No. The neurologist says that J. is in the advanced stages of PD and medically there is nothing else that could be done, so the only help he can give is to ask for a social worker to see me and advise on what help is available. He thinks that all the extra work I have with J. is going to make me ill. He also suggested respite care or a nursing home. I said categorically 'No' to a nursing home, and he looked at me as though 'well it will come to that in the end'. So I've got to decide now what to do next, not an easy decision. Everybody keeps telling me I've got to think of my own life, but my life is with J. and I think I will have to carry on as best as I can. Perhaps I will accept more help.

At phase 2, C120 had done just that. She was having respite care in the house two afternoons a week.

C120: I have been having this service for the past six months and it really has made a great difference to me. I can go shopping in peace and know that J. is being cared for.

The long-awaited downstairs toilet was built as an extension with a shower, so C120 did not have to struggle up and down stairs with him several times a day. J. could no longer get out of the chair without help so this prevented him from following her everywhere and cut down on the number of falls. Nevertheless, she reported:

C120: I really hate bedtimes now though. I have to get him upstairs and it is really tiring. Helping him come downstairs in the morning is a hard task these days too. I think that is why I have rather a lot of shoulder pain at the moment. I seem to be really tired at the end of the day lately, and I think that over the last year I have had to do much more for J. than I used to.

The fourth case in this section illustrates the way of life for a daughter caring for her mother who has advanced PD with severe dyskinesia. P126 was intelligent, very articulate and had lost none of her previous sharpness. She was widowed before the onset of PD. C126 spent most days at her mother's. She did not drive and a single journey would usually take her over an hour. Ideally, she would have liked to go by taxi but, having no income, could not afford to.

C126: The problem is that she still wants to be independent, and it is a struggle for her to have to accept that I have to do some things for her now. So it has all been very gradual. The first thing was the shopping. She couldn't get to the shops on her own, so we used to take her in the car. Then one day I discovered, quite by chance, that the effort of preparing her midday meal would render her too exhausted, or having too many movements to actually sit down and eat it. So I started to filter help in. It was when my son first went to college, about nine years ago, I would pretend I had been absent minded and had cooked for my son as well, 'So could you eat it up', and I brought it round, and she did enjoy the food. Over a period of a few months she came to accept me cooking her dinners and freezing them. It was easy enough. I'd just cook for five instead of four. Now we have reached the stage where I have to leave her something for her tea too. She can manage a piece of bread and butter, and to put the meals in the microwave. I also do her laundry; she can't hang things out now. The cleaner changes her bed. She comes once a week for three hours. And the gardener always comes on a Friday for four hours. When Mum was capable, she got into the habit of making him sandwiches and tea. When she couldn't do that I started coming on a Friday just to feed the gardener.

Interviewer: Do you get her up in the morning?

C126: Not at the moment. Although I have noticed the problem is increasing, so I think that before long I will be. But then I can get dropped off at 7.45 in the morning.

C126 was right. In phase 2, her mother's mobility, strength and dexterity had deteriorated dramatically. She refused to agree to a social services assessment, as she was convinced that things would improve with the medication change to apomorphine. As a result, C126 was at her mother's house seven days a week, from 7.45 a.m. until 6.30 p.m. for six months. In her diary she wrote:

C126: This caused tremendous strain for several reasons [including]: 1. No time for my own home, decent meal preparation, etc. 2. My husband had to contribute a lot of help on top of a demanding job and a lot of travelling. 3. My health deteriorated as I had so much back pain I lost sleep. 4. I became totally exhausted, mentally and physically.

In despair, C126 eventually arranged for a social worker to visit 'as routine'.

C126: He was able to make mother realize that she would be in a nursing home if I was ill, and it was coming to that. A home help started coming six hours a week. I still went seven days a week to give her tea and get her to bed. I was there all day at weekends and Wednesdays and Fridays. Once mother was used to people coming into the house, the care increased to the present level. Now carers are coping with the heavy work – bathing, dressing, bed-making, putting her to bed and getting her up. But I still feel that I am always on call. Now I don't go on Tuesdays, but I am preparing food for her at home. I try to let Mother know where I will be when I am not visiting her, in case she is so frozen that she is frightened. She has become totally reliant on me to make all phone calls and write all letters. She rarely answers the phone. She has lost all her confidence and relies on me to protect her from visitors. She will not agree to anyone, not even other relatives, visiting her unless I stay there all the time to protect her from their conversation if she is exhausted or frozen. She is still intelligent and still a decision maker, controlling her life, but she seems to want my opinions these days before making decisions.

The case of C126 illustrates how demanding the needs of an advanced PD patient can be. She was 50, a lot younger than most PD carers, yet admitted to total exhaustion. It was perhaps harder, she felt, because her mother was mentally sharp and understood the situation painfully well. An impossible workload had crept up on her, creating difficulties for her own family life, yet she found it difficult to withdraw.

Caring in advanced PD was invariably described as physically and mentally exhausting. In order to continue with reasonable equanimity, delegation of some responsibilities to formal services was crucial.

Carer discretion in delivering care

Carer discretion in providing care was predicted to affect wellbeing. It was expected that where the carer had some hours away from caring and was able to keep up his or her own activities, morale would be higher. Several aspects were explored, including use of respite care and the extent to which carers made time for their own leisure pursuits and personal care. Following Motenko (1989), carers were also asked: 'Do you feel obliged to comply with all the demands of caring?'

Respite care

Although each of the hospitals from which the sample was drawn had day centres providing respite care, and there were also social services day centres, in practice not all who wanted care were able to get it. One carer for an advanced-stage patient who would have liked National Health Service respite care was not offered it. She paid for private carers to look after her husband on a regular basis. A very independently minded patient living at home arranged for a rota of paid help overseen by her daughter.

The use of formal care was, in fact, uncommon: overall, only 14% of the sample used day care on a weekly basis. The need for respite depends of course on the severity of the PD patient's symptoms. Where PD was mild, there was no need: carers had considerable discretion as to how they spent their day. If carers could leave the patient for half a day without undue concern, respite was usually thought unnecessary.

With advanced PD, however, few carers felt able to be away from the caring situation for any length of time unless there was formal backup. Nevertheless, patients sometimes complained about a lack of care:

C201: He says 'You've been too long'. He gets worked up.... If I'm out an hour, he's at the window. I feel I've got to be there.

The availability of respite care could be very helpful. For instance, C120, giving care to a demented patient, Hoehn and Yahr stage V, re-marked in phase 1: 'I couldn't leave him on his own ever, not the way he is now.' Fourteen months later the patient was even more physically demanding, but respite care gave the carer two free afternoons each week. This changed her outlook because she now looked forward to her 'free' time.

Not all arrangements for respite care worked so satisfactorily. For some, it had been tried and rejected, because the care recipient became upset.

C127: Well the only time I can leave B. (and I do leave her) is between about 11 o'clock and 1 o'clock, when I go shopping. Then I leave her up-stairs, because of the toilet and facilities. Otherwise I do not leave her.
Interviewer: Would you like any respite from caring?
C127: Yes. We looked into all that recently. Social services arranged for B. to go to C. House [a day care centre] a couple of days a week. It didn't work out I'm afraid. B. didn't take kindly first of all to going at all. She wanted me to be there with her. Well, this defeats the object. The first time she went for about three hours and just had some lunch – some sandwiches. The next week she went for four hours. Before she came away she was speaking to the manager and trying to tell him something. There wasn't a problem, but be-cause of her speech, making herself clear, he thought that a problem had arisen and there was some criticism of his staff. There wasn't. Not at all. The other thing was that again she can't talk to the other people who were there, freely. She couldn't chatter to them very well so she got isolated, and more so because of her problems going to the toilet and this sort of thing. Again she felt a large sense of embarrassment more than anything. So the two things together introduced some state of trauma. So I thought if this is going on there is no point in her going. But this was instituted by our GP, because he thought that I should have a day, or two days a week, not just to rest, but to be able to have the time to go where I want to. For business reasons and that sort of thing. Because this didn't work out. I have to do things by dash-ing there and dashing back. As quickly as possible. If I need to go out for more than the two hours, then someone would probably have to come in.

Sometimes the PD patient simply did not want to go to the day care centre: inflexibility of transport arrangement exacerbated this type of problem and the carer was unwilling to use persuasion.

C164: When he came out of hospital, on each occasion, he was supposed to go to the day hospital. But when he comes home he doesn't want to go. Mind you, it might have been hard to get him ready, because the first Wednesday when he should have gone the ambulance men were ringing the bell at a quarter past eight. Another thing, which is a nuisance, is the water-works problem. So he hasn't wanted to go. People have said I should press him, but I haven't. It doesn't bother me that much, I probably would benefit, but I wouldn't press it.

In a further case the carer was unwilling to let the patient attend the day centre because she thought death was near. Asked if she could leave him at all, she replied:

C121: Yes. I could leave him for an hour if he was asleep in a chair. You are like a caged bird.
Interviewer: Is that how you feel?
C121: Yes.
Interviewer: Would you like some respite from caring?
C121: If I did get relieved I would go and get my hair done. But I wouldn't be happy leaving him now, because I actually think he is getting worse. And last night he didn't know me. I got a shock. The doctor doesn't say much. He didn't say it was the end, but he said it is the last part of Parkinson's when they get like this.

Even when informal caring was offered in the house by relatives, it was sometimes not welcome. C201 was Greek. It was difficult for her to make even occasional visits home:

C201: He won't have anyone come to stay in the house. M. [his sister] offered to stay ... but he refused.

Holidays were difficult or impossible for carers of advanced patients and sometimes the patient's doctor imposed a restriction.

C205: Dr B. said, 'I'd rather you did not go on holiday. Stay near your own doctor.'

In this sample, 43% of patients were classified as having 'advanced' PD but less than a third of these had a formal day care arrangements. This suggests that most carers sustained a 24-hour caring regimen, or that respite care, as in the examples above, was not seen as a viable option. While some carers used respite care successfully, others had a negative attitude to formal care. They did not think that the patient would be properly looked after, or would be happy there.

Table 7.4 tabulates carer responses to a question about their perceived obligations to the patient.

Table 7.4. *Perceived obligation of carers at phases 1 and 2 (percentage giving an affirmative answer to the question)*

	Phase 1	Phase 2
'Do you feel obliged to comply with all the demands of caring?'	63%	84%

At phase 1, nearly two-thirds felt they should always consider their care recipient's needs first; by phase 2, most took this point of view. Carers felt clearly obliged to their patient, even to the extent of neglecting their own needs. About a third (32%) said that this bothered them.

The phrase ' I don't like leaving [the patient]' was often used.

C202: I'm without choice. It's not a life. It's a job to be done.

Time for personal care

It is important that carers remain in good health to enable them to continue with the caring task. They should have enough time, to ensure their own personal care. To investigate this carers were asked: 'Do you have enough time to take care of yourself?'

The figures for the responses were very similar in phases 1 and 2. About three quarters said yes and 26% said no. Most of those who agreed that they did not have enough time for self-care said that this bothered them at least 'a little' of the time. But they did not seem to see a way round it. Their attitude was 'the patient comes first'. There was not always a realization that it might be in the patient's best long-term interests for the carer to attend to his or her own basic needs.

Time for own interests

Carers were asked what they did with their leisure time. It was found that 37% maintained or adapted previous leisure pursuits, 32% enjoyed a reduced range of leisure pursuits, and 31% had very little leisure time or social interaction. Whereas carers for mild and moderate patients were able to continue most previous leisure pursuits, the more active hobbies and pastimes would be dropped as the disease progressed, earlier when this was a shared interest, such as rambling.

A few advanced carers did make a particular effort to keep up some social activities by carefully considering the capabilities of the patient.

For example, P106, at Hoehn and Yahr stage IV, had limited mobility, yet enjoyed watching films. Besides spending time together selecting what to watch on the television, carer and patient went to the cinema, and theatre, together. C106 also managed to get out on his own for a limited period, with the patient's blessing.

> C106: We get the car and go to B., to those big cinemas, and select which film we are going to see. And we go to our old Amateur Dramatics Society. We get out, weather permitting. And yes, I am a season ticket holder for Tranmere Rovers. I used to play for them, as an amateur. H. has said to me, 'You love your football, and as long as you can get there, you are guaranteed your seat, so go. You are not to stay in.' I am away for three hours, sometimes three and a half hours, and that concerns me more than anything. I come out of the game, *always,* five minutes before the end, so that I can get into the car and away. It enables me to beat the traffic. That causes anxiety. H. usually watches the television while I am out, but once or twice she has fallen. I have bought her one of those personal alarms now though, which has helped me. I put it around her neck before I go out. She hasn't had to use it, but if she were in distress the warden would be here very quickly, and I would not be long after. That has helped me to feel comfortable enough to carry on going.

As this example shows, it is not only severity of PD but also the patient's attitudes and carer's characteristics which determined whether the carer had a social life.

The financial situation

Chronic illness has the potential to cause financial worries if it prevents the sufferer from working. Only 18% of patients were working at onset of PD and all these continued to work for some time, enabling some preparation for the drop in income. At time of interview, just one patient was still employed and he was over 65. Given that the majority of the sample were already pensioners at onset, it was perhaps not surprising that when carers were asked 'Has ...'s disability put a strain on your financial situation?' only 17.3% percent said yes at phase 1 and 25% at phase 2. It is possible that this is a cohort effect, for, as pointed out by C167, many had lived through rationing during and after the war and were used to 'managing'.

> C167: No. I have never been the sort of person to waste money. I still make all my own jam, and do all my own cooking. The way one did. I still say I had the best training because when we got married everything was on rationing, so you had to learn to cope. And you go on that way.

A younger carer whose husband had had PD for 15 years felt she had to continue working full time until she was 65 so she could draw a pension. Her husband lived on disability benefit. She pointed out that although they had no money worries at the time of interview, they would have them if she stopped working.

When carers were also asked whether the financial situation bothered them, 79% responded 'none of the time', 9% were bothered 'a little of the time', 6% were bothered 'some of the time', and 6% were bothered 'all the time'. Together, this information suggests that finances are not a major concern in PD caring.

Personality change

During the interview, carers were asked at both phases whether they considered that their care recipient had changed since PD onset. Fifty-one per cent considered it had and 49% considered that there had been no change. There was no pattern to the presence of perceived personality change with respect to illness severity or duration. P169 had stage III PD, with a duration of illness of eight years. Her husband reported:

C169: Not personally no. Just her physical movements. In herself she is exactly the same as she was before. With people, family, everybody.

Where personality change was reported, carers were asked about it:

C160: He doesn't laugh anymore. He said to me last week that his chuckle muscles have gone. He used to have a real hearty laugh. And we used to go to the Empire [theatre] a lot because he likes the shows. We don't go now. He doesn't want to go. It is not the same. He has no interest.

C151: She has gone a lot quieter and won't let anybody in the house.

C105: Joe has changed completely. He won't speak, he won't go out, he won't do anything. He is very depressed. Right from the time he was told he had this illness [14 years ago] he has been negative. I can't seem to reason with him at all now.

Certain themes recurred in carers' descriptions of patient personality change. Apathy, withdrawal and deterioration in communication, together with a lack of appreciation, were mentioned. There were also reports of a reduction in confidence, and an increase in worrying and agitation. Sometimes the change was in the direction of irritability or aggression in patients who had previously been even-tempered.

C156: I suppose a lot of it is frustration. He used to be very placid and easy going. But he is not the same now. He is different altogether. He is much more difficult and his temper is quick.

C205: He's a completely different person. He was always very quiet, very gentlemanly. Now he wants to assert himself. He says 'Why have I got to do it this way? Why? Why?' He keeps questioning. But it's the simplest way.

Increased depression was noted in many of those reporting changes. However, some of the 'no change' carers recalled that the patient had been depressed early on (perhaps as a reaction to diagnosis) but had subsequently recovered. In the 'change' group, carers' descriptions of their patients were virtually the same at phases 1 and 2. This suggests that where there is perceived change, it is enduring.

Where patients suffered hallucinations, both carer and care receiver could become very distressed. At phase 1, 29 patients (35%) had experienced hallucinations, mostly visual in nature, and carers were then more likely to think that their patient had changed. Vivid dreams were sometimes a precursor of hallucinations. A retired teacher of science would dream that he had been out at night and would awake confused, lost in his own home, unable to find the toilet.

C205: He gets lost and says 'Where is the toilet?', 'Is there a toilet?' When he gets there he can't recognize it. He sees balls attached to the cross-members of his Zimmer frame. He thinks it's quite normal. And he sees people. He says, 'Is that little man still with us?' He calls him Fred and thinks he walks behind his shoulder. Sometimes he sees children sitting on the sofa and says 'Aren't we inviting all those children [to tea]?' At other times he sees full sized people, dressed in countrified dress from the early days of the century. We just accept them. They are not unpleasant. Dr B. says leave the drugs as they are.

However, not all this patient's hallucinations were pleasant. They ranged from relatively innocuous visual hallucinations (inanimate swirling patterns on the carpet and on the lawn) to frightening episodes when he would go to the toilet but be afraid to use it because he thought the bathroom was full of people watching him.

C205: Which is the real world for him? He seems to have some insight. Sometimes he feels ants or spiders. He wakes and thinks the bed is full of insects. At least that's what I suppose it is. I have to change the sheets. He can feel them. There are both kinds and some of them bite. He says that some of them could be real ants and some are 'hypothetical'. Sometimes it's humorous.

This patient was very independent by nature, yet had had several falls. His wife, who herself suffered from a hereditary muscular disorder, had a bad neck and was losing the use of both hands. She found it increasingly difficult to cope with him. In the week up to the second visit he had had two falls, one behind the bedroom door, and she could not reach him. She had a well developed system of sending for help, first telephoning her son-in-law, then neighbours and finally using the security alarm panic button which rang in the police station. This carer was very depressed and pessimistic about the future.

The dyadic relationship

Carers were asked if the personality change had affected the dyadic relationship at any time. Most carers agreed that it had.

C133: I still love him deeply. I hope it will soon pass.

C156: It is not the same at all. I don't feel we are as close.

C125: The fact that communication has somehow ground to a halt has made things difficult. He doesn't complain, he never does, he is long-suffering and patient. The problem is that nothing is ever said.

C175: Everybody says to me 'I think he is wonderful because he doesn't complain'. No, he doesn't moan, because I am sure I would. And he is quite grateful for anything that I do. This makes it a lot easier. The sexual side has gone. Completely. He is impotent now. That is not something that bothers me. At my age it is not worrying me.

C176: Oh yes. I mean we are just like strangers really. It is like me looking after a stranger.

C202: I try to be tolerant but sometimes it slips a bit. She can be very demanding. Maybe I shout, she shouts too. There's a bit of tension occasionally.... She sits there and wants something. You have to get it. She can't just jump up.

C205: Sometimes he's hurtful. He says 'I don't really care for you'. I know he doesn't mean it. I couldn't really live if I thought he did mean it.

Reductions in a sexual relationship were deeply troublesome to some carers, even when the reduction was on account of their own illness rather than the PD. C203 spoke of sexual tensions which he felt made him irritable. He suffered from prostate cancer and was impotent. He had also recently had shingles. Asked whether his wife had changed he said:

C203: She's not her own self but quieter and slower. She's cool, calm and collected. It's not her, it's me. I'm impatient and don't give her time to say or think. I push her instead of treating her, because I'm fed up. The Parkinson's taken my life over. It's top of the agenda. It's difficult to restrain my temper. Not violence, but I tend to shout, get in a twist. I'm not the same person.... It's lack of self control.... I used to be happy-go-lucky and back horses. The circumstances have been forced on me. I'm very affectionate. I need to be loved. M. is not physically affectionate, not sloppy. I'm frustrated when I get no response. Sexually. It's worse since the twin beds. Before, I knew how far I could go.... I didn't want the change [from a double to twin beds]. It's almost totally fallen. It's made me niggly. I didn't feel wanted. I like my feelings to be expressed. M. is very shy. Sex and personal relations. I say, 'You've gone off me. I'm useless.' Mr P. [his cancer surgeon] said, 'Now you're impotent, you're like a little boy again'. That's not how I feel! If I mention sex M. thinks it's dirty. It's a totally different outlook. She knows I will never perform again. She needs strength. I don't know if she gets it. M. is not a very vociferous person. I say things and shout. I go out of the room and slam the door. I go in the garden and dig a hole. It's frustrating. I'm not patient. I go for a bath and shut the door.

It was clear that a lack of communication was seen as one of the most damaging aspect of personality change on the relationship. It had the potential to make carers frustrated and lonely. But this was more of a problem for some carers than others. It seemed that if the patient expressed some gratitude, the carer was more likely to accept that 'it's not him, it's the Parkinson's'.

Some dyads insisted that the PD had made them closer and drew upon joint religious belief for strength. C204 cared for his wife, who not only had advanced PD but also had a long history of depression and severe arthritis which had deformed her hands. Her drug regimen necessitated 27 separate doses of medicine per day (13 separate pills between 7.30 and 8.00 a.m. alone). He himself had suffered seizures 12 months before phase 1 of the study and had had his driving licence withdrawn. This had led to considerable hardship. He had refused offers of formal services but reluctantly accepted offers of transport from neighbours when there were hospital appointments.

C204: I'm a sharer not just a carer. It's astonishing that the Parkinson's Disease Society have never produced a paper on love and spirituality. To us, love has been more deeply enhanced and more real since the PD. That depth of love would never have been reached if it were not for the PD.
Interviewer: Are you thinking about the uniqueness of your relationship?
C204: It's spirituality. If you want to believe, you do believe. Faith has sustained us. Like Christ. I see these crucifixions. Executions on hill sides and all the agony. He knew someone would knife Him and He would end up on the Cross. But He faced it. The fact that someone faced it inspires us.... There is not enough emphasis and encouragement on how love sustains. Some of our

friends at … [the local branch of the Society] are of the same view. But we don't talk deeply at branch meetings. It's acceptance. I can't do anything. Because of our lovingness, I know others find something in our handling of it. They felt stronger. It helps others to see us together. We are showing others. It is a positive act of love between man and wife. I'm on call all the time.
Interviewer: Do you ever get out on your own?
C204: I did try it once. My son encouraged it. But it's no value at all to walk in the woods alone. Since then we have done everything together.

Throughout the interview this carer emphasized the positive aspects of caring as an almost religious duty. He wanted his story to be told to the Parkinson's Disease Society, which he felt gave an unduly negative picture of the illness. P204 wrote religious poetry and C204 sent examples of this to the research team. At phase 2, however, the situation was very different. There was no mention of religious belief and the carer was facing the possibility of having to find residential care for his wife.

Emotions in PD caring

Emotional responses are an integral part of the stress process, and so to explore carers' feelings about their situation, they were asked to consider the nine emotions on Motenko's Frustration Scale (MFS) at each phase. For each emotion, carers were asked 'How … [*angry* or one of the other eight emotions] do you feel about the fact that … has got PD, and its subsequent effect on you?' The coded responses are presented in Table 7.5, which suggests that, at each phase, the predominant emotion

Table 7.5. *PD carers' expression of the nine MFS emotions in phases 1 (n = 81) and 2 (n = 56) (% of sample)*[a]

Emotion	Phase 1		Phase 2	
	'Not at all' or 'a little'	'Quite a lot' or 'very much'	'Not at all' or 'a little'	'Quite a lot' or 'very much'
Angry	87.7	12.3	85.8	14.2
Resentful	86.5	13.5	89.2	10.8
Ashamed	98.8	1.2	98.2	1.8
Resigned	47.0	53.0	39.3	60.7
Regretful	51.9	48.1	46.5	53.5
Overwhelmed	84.0	16.0	87.5	12.5
Fearful	79.0	21.0	87.5	12.5
Hopeful	65.5	34.5	58.9	41.1
Guilty	97.6	2.4	100.0	0

[a]The original Motenko scale was a four-category Likert scale. For this study, frequency data are used combining frequencies in the two categories shown.

expressed was resignation, followed by regret. At phase 1, only a third expressed hope for the future, more than a fifth felt fearful and one in six felt overwhelmed. A further breakdown of the figures for the two-thirds of those without much hope revealed that, at phase 1, 48% felt the situation 'not at all hopeful'. At phase 2, the situation seemed a little brighter, with 40% felt hopeful and only one in eight felt fearful and overwhelmed. This is probably because the phase 1 data included the older, more cognitively impaired patients who were lost to the study between phases 1 and 2. One in seven, however, felt angry about the PD at phase 2. Very few carers reacted to the caring situation with emotions of guilt or shame.

Medication

Quality of life is compromised by PD, but the medication enables a degree of normality to be maintained. Drugs, however, are two-edged weapon, in that continued use eventually reduces their potency, and they also have side-effects. In PD, unlike many other chronic illness, compliance to medication regimens is very high. Indeed, there seemed to be great faith in 'the tablets'. One patient set an alarm clock to ensure that she never missed getting her medication at the right time. A young-onset patient reported that 'I live watching the clock, because my life revolves around the tablets'.

Many of the older patients, however, had given responsibility for their medication to their carer. Usually, carers adopted formal methods to remember to keep to what were often complex drug schedules. Many carers bought daily or weekly pillboxes into which the tablets were sorted at a regular time. One carer had a diary in which she had written down every tablet and every apomorphine injection her mother had and the exact time at which they were taken/administered. She had done this for over three years. However, some carers had made their own decisions about the medication, especially if confidence in the doctors had been lost.

> C202: I don't feel any confidence. It's just 'Keep on with the tablets'. But it's not doing anything for her. I get down at times.

This carer had withdrawn co-careldopa (Sinemet LS) from the patient without the doctor's knowledge and tried to justified this:

> C202: The consultant says it's just trial and error. I've studied the pamphlets. If I find she's missing it I will put it back. There was too much writhing. She still gets a bit.

Surgery

This sample of PD patients contained three patients who had had surgery for the condition. All three were under 60, and had severe tremor/dyskinesias, which were much worse on one side than the other. P109 was currently waiting for his third thalamotomy.

> C109: At the moment R. is pretty poorly, because it [violent tremor] has started on the other side now. I never thought that would happen after the operations.
> Interviewer: Why did he have to have the second?
> C109: The [effects of the] first one only lasted three weeks. We thought it had been a success because the tremor stopped, and then it came back. It was roughly 11 months before he had the next one. R. didn't want to go through it all again, obviously, because it is not a nice operation. It is not like getting a tooth out because he is awake while it is all going on. But we encouraged him. I didn't think it wouldn't work. It was the only hope he had, put it that way. And it turned out brilliantly. The second time his arm was left completely normal. He still had to take the tablets, of course, but he was virtually normal. And then this started on the other side [dyskinesias], which is, I must admit, a lot worse than the first. It is more violent. When we went six months ago, they said they didn't operate on both sides. So we thought there was no hope. But between us going for the next appointment, the surgeon said he will do both sides, and he asked R. whether he would be willing to have it done. I was waiting for him to refuse, but he said yes.
> Interviewer: Do you want him to have the operation?
> C109: Oh yes, yes. He can't go on like this, can he?

The improvement in P109 following the second thalamotomy enabled him to stay at work for another six years and they had a relatively normal life. He was still under retirement age and the carer was working part time. C109 was very keen to seize the opportunity to have a normal life again. At phase 2, however, the third operation still had not been done. Drugs were not helping his dyskinesias at all, but C109 remained hopeful that surgery would still go ahead.

In phase 1, C140 mentioned that her mother, who had a severe unilateral tremor and dyskinesia, had been offered surgery.

> C140: She is worried about being a guinea pig. Perhaps they need to be tried and tested a bit. I also worry about her brain. I don't think she has any memory loss at all; I feel she is quite on the ball. I don't know. It will have to be her decision.

Before phase 2, P140 went ahead with the thalamotomy.

> C140: I was surprised that she was so poorly after the operation. She was confused for a couple of days, and I slept beside her in the hospital because

I was so concerned. But it has turned out marvellously. Her movements are much, much better and she is just the same mentally.

This was true. P140 was tested on the neuropsychological tests included in the study two weeks after the operation, and again two months later. There was no reduction in her previously very high scores.

The third patient who had this operation was also improved. His carer regarded it as 'great', and although it was winter, they had been out walking much more than they had done for some time. All three carers regarded their experience of caring to have been greatly improved by surgery. Surgery does not appear to be widespread for PD. It appears that it is suitable only for patients who are relatively young, and who have severe unilateral disease. Not one of the older patients in this sample was offered surgery as a means of controlling symptoms.

Life events

A diagnosis of PD provides a chronic difficulty for patients and carers. Critical incidents are likely to have an effect on the PD and the caring. There were carers who were aware of this:

P101: Life is very smooth at the moment. We've had no major catastrophes. I try to keep it that way. That's the secret with this illness. If you keep things running smoothly it is all right. But if it isn't then it just makes them [the PD patient] more agitated and that upsets their thinking, so it is no good.

Sometimes, though, accidents happened. In other cases, positive events occurred which improved life. Carers believed that major negative life events, accelerated progression of the disease. Positive events were not seen to occasion any remission of motor or cognitive symptoms but the patient's mood was reported to be brighter in the presence of a positive life event.

In this section, four short illustrations will be given of the effect of a life event on the experience of caring.

Carer accident

In phase 2, P104 had tremor, but his main complaints were slowness and tiredness. He was aged 80. Much of C104's caring, by her own admission, was doing things for him to save time.

C104: When he takes the car out, I open the garage doors and the gates, things like that. Sometimes he starts a job and he gets tired, so I finish jobs.

But C104 had not worked outside the home for a long time, so she was already completely running the house. She was perfectly fit and healthy. Then their circumstances changed quite dramatically. C104 fell over a workman's brick in the street against steel railings and broke her hip and pelvis. She was in hospital a fortnight for a hip replacement, and then had a long recovery period. Ten months later she was still on penicillin because her hip had become infected. The accident had a great impact on both of them. P104 admitted that it frightened him and upset him a lot. His tremor had increased noticeably. His balance was affected. He had several falls. Twelve months after the initial visit he was struggling to get out of the chair, despite the fact that his levodopa intake had been doubled. When C104 came home, he accepted that she could not do as much for him, and he struggled to do what he could for himself. They have no children.

> C104: For the first two weeks after my accident, it was absolute hell. I was so worried about S. while I was in hospital that the doctor gave me some tranquillizers. But not now. He knows I wouldn't take them. I am fed up of it all though. We had some help from the social services for six weeks, but that was terminated and there was nothing I could do about it. I was crying because I was so upset and worrying about S. And how we were going to manage. How can I put it? I can't alter what has happened. So I just live with it. One thing is that I talk about it [PD and caring] to S. I never used to. But I sometimes think of how life could have been. S. says to me that I am bitter, but I am not.

C104 thought that her accident had affected P104's PD symptoms, increasing job demand at a time when she could not respond to his needs. This compounded the stress of the situation for her, and at phase 2, ten months after the accident, she had changed from a confident woman who was only slightly affected by PD caring to being frustrated because she could not continue the way she would have liked. She also remarked that as well as the accelerated physical deterioration in her husband, he got depressed.

Death in the family

P171 had had a long duration of illness, but had deteriorated to the advanced state only in the two years before the interview. Now he was also dementing. He and his wife had moved into a warden-assisted retirement complex eight years previously. They were very close to their daughter, their only child, who lived in Germany. They spoke every day on the telephone, stayed with her for a month each year, and she also came home for frequent visits. Six months before the interview, she had been run over and killed by a drunken driver, the day before she was due home for a visit. At interview, C171 still felt devastated. Her daughter's belongings had been just been delivered.

> C171: The light has gone out of our lives now that D. has gone. She was the hope. What is there now?

During the interview, C171 recounted a series of problems that P171 had experienced and her desperation about coping with them. This had been the case only since her daughter's death. She was not even sure whether her husband appreciated that their daughter had died. He had, however, got worse since that time and was falling every day. She remarked, 'I only keep the car for the convenience of getting to A. [hospital] to get him stitched up'. He began having 'accidents' before getting to the toilet, and he began hallucinating. This was the worse change for C171 because he frequently 'saw' their dead daughter.

> C171: Now I haven't got a shoulder to cry on. He is quite immune to any emotion. He has never shed a tear about D. because he doesn't understand. He has receded and keeps referring to what time is she coming home. I say, 'She is not coming home anymore. She is in God's presence,' and he will say, 'She is sitting by you there'.
>
> He should be in hospital. He must be looked after and cared for all the time. He has to be watched around the clock whatever he is doing. I have to get up at 6 a.m. just to see to him, and I have all D.'s things to sort out and I just have no time to do it.

It seemed that C171 was not able to find time to grieve because of the demands of caring for her husband.

> C171: Sometimes I feel like packing a bag and clearing out, and then the thought comes 'It is not his fault. He can't help it'. It bothers me that I am not well enough to look after him now, when he needs me most, to the best of my ability.

Although it was not possible to verify whether P171's symptoms had worsened objectively, his wife was convinced that this was so. By phase 2 he was dead.

Birth in the family

Several carers noted that seeing the grandchildren was a highlight for both them and the care recipient. There was also some delight that young children readily accept disability. One patient, who had recently had a birthday, had been delighted to receive a card 'To my wibbly-wobbly grandma'. It did not depress her but gave her a real uplift.

A birth in the family was also perceived as a positive life event for both patients and carers. C113 reported that her husband's mood was better, and his previous apathy gone since the birth of their first grandchild, seven months previously.

> C113: This was marvellous for B. It really has picked him up a lot. It has made him more confident. He used to try and lift her to the child seat in the car. My daughter said, 'I am not saying anything Mum, but I am terrified in case he falls with the baby'. He wants to do it to help, and he still tries to do it. I say to him, 'Just take it easy'. He really looks forward to P. coming, so that he can play with the baby. It has helped him a lot.

Bankruptcy

C172 and her husband had three children, but had lived alone for over 20 years. P172 was diagnosed with PD 11 years before interview. A year before phase 1, her unmarried son became bankrupt. He lost everything and turned to his parents for help, moving back in with them.

> C172: P. had a good job four years ago, and he gave it up to go into business. He hired out hats and ball gowns. But it did not work out. He tried not to go bankrupt, but in the end he had to. That was 12 months ago. It worried me, and it worried his dad. He came back here, and well, it is good knowing he is safe. But, well, I have still got about 90 hats upstairs. He has got rid of the ball gowns – I had them all up hanging around, as if I haven't got enough to do.
> Interviewer: So P. is around a lot now during the day. Does he help you and his dad?
> C172: Not really. We gave him the lounge you see. His choice of music and television are not ours, so it saved a lot of hassle. So really we see him mostly at mealtimes. But if there is any football on, he will come in and discuss it with J. They will talk football. But if I said to him, 'I am going out, please keep an eye on your Dad,' he does. I can rely on him for that. He is trying to get work, but he is 44, and they all want younger people.

Although her son's circumstances worried both patient and carer, C172 was unable to say whether her husband's symptoms had changed. There were extra costs in terms of housework but also some benefits, in that C172 was now able to go out more. This was to prove more important by phase 2, when J. began having periods of confusion.

Ethical issues in PD caring

Carers were questioned about whether they ever felt caught in situations where there were ethical conflicts, in which for example the interests of patient and carer differed. This followed Hasselkus and Stetson's (1991) work on the *meaning* of caring to carers. The question was: 'I am sure you find that sometimes you are pleased with the way you care for ... but that sometimes you may think you should be doing things differently. Is this true for you?'

One theme was the carer's sense of frustration and irritation with the patient.

> C120: I do lose my patience with him. So I could be a little more patient. I am not very good in the morning, you know when you first wake up. And when you to think about getting someone else ready and not just yourself. Sometimes I think, oh, I can't cope with all this.

For C128, her mother's expectation that she would attend to her needs immediately, even when she only wanted something to be passed to her, was a source of frustration. Requests were sometimes ignored.

Irritations of caring posed ethical dilemmas where the carer felt that he or she had departed from a personal inner standard of 'beneficence' (doing 'good' and avoiding 'harm'). Even small departures were interpreted as failings by some.

> C156: In a way. I have to make it a matter of prayer, to give me more patience. That is what I am lacking. Because it is so frustrating for me as well as for him when he is trying to tell me something and he can't get the words out. Then he tries to write it, and I can't understand his writing.

> C150 (a non-resident caring daughter): I could be spending more time with her. I mean we have been invited to go away for three days after Christmas, and I would like to do this. We will go down Wednesday morning before we go and we will be back Friday lunch time. So there is only Thursday.... Why I feel I have to do this I don't know. I still feel guilty about going away when she can't.

Some carers attempted to justify their actions.

> C202: You've got to be cruel to be kind.

A further dilemma centred on when to foster the patient's autonomy. Most carers realized that doing things *for* the patient that he or she could do alone might be harmful in the long term. However, slowness is a characteristic of PD and most carers were busy.

> C203: I'm impatient and I don't give her time to say or think. She's independent, but I do the baking and dinners. If we shared it out, there would be rows.

C119: Sometimes I do want [to do] things for C., you know, just help him because he might be struggling a bit, then I think no, it helps him if he can do it himself.

Autonomy issues sometimes merged with issues of fairness. Carers with other family responsibilities had to decide how much time it was reasonable to devote to the patient. P140 was a widow who made the decision to move across the country to be near her youngest daughter, who had three children and did not work outside the house.

C140: We talked about it very openly, because I think a tension could have arisen. She had made a few comments about plated meals and microwaving them and it set a few alarm bells going in me really. I asked her to write down exactly what she expected of me if she came to live in W.... The last thing I wanted her to do was to move from S. where she was with all her friends, and expect things from me that I did not feel it was right to be giving at this point. My youngest one has gone to school now, so I do have a bit more time, but I mean I just did not think it was good for her. And that is a continual process really. I mean: how much should I be doing and how much should I be standing back? So I don't see her every day. I think the day-to-day, and having to get out and get her shopping, and having to do her washing and her ironing and her cooking is very good for her to keep her mobility going. I think that if she were to expect meals to be cooked, washing done, and shopping done for her, then she would just sit in the flat and vegetate.

In contrast, some carers went beyond what was strictly necessary.

C171: I cannot possibly do any more for him than I do. He is waited on hand and foot. Three good cooked meals a day. Midmorning coffee, afternoon tea. How can I do less for him when he has to be followed round?

This patient had exactly the same UPD severity score (15) as P140, yet the responses of the carers in dealing with the uncomfortable feelings arising from ethical dilemmas was very different (although both in their way entailed a prioritizing of activities).

C127, whose wife not only had PD but had an independent mental impairment, had consciously let 'standards' slip.

C127: I try to avoid all unnecessary things, naturally. Lots of days, if I don't feel like it, I think to myself – is that really essential today? And if it isn't, then I don't do it. I am not a perfectionist. The case is that sometimes things are left undone or unsaid just to keep things normal.

Violations of the patient's autonomy are seen in their starkest form when carers manipulate medication to further their own ends. No cases of deliberate elder abuse or neglect were admitted. Nevertheless, medication was occasionally used as an instrument of control. In PD, medication can have a substantial and rapid effect upon the patient's capacity to move. Drug regimens were often complex and time consuming, and the patient's need for the drugs in advanced PD gave the carer considerable power. Although, as discussed, most carers followed the recommended drug dosages to the letter, two examples will be quoted where carers manipulated the medication to lighten the load. In both, the carer was troubled by the patient's dyskinesias. C120 completely removed her husband's co-careldopa (Sinemet) after he became demented because:

> C120: He didn't know where he was. It was frightening. He was flinging himself all over the room and he had absolutely no awareness. He would only have to have one [tablet] and he was off. Now he sits happily, and he is no worse off. He is not going to get any better. I couldn't cope with it. Occasionally I will give him one if he is frozen.

For C112, the manipulation was more subtle. Following a very distressing period of hallucinations, her husband's sole medicine was apomorphine, self-administered via a syringe driver, during the day. P112 could only do this, however, after his wife had set the driver up for him. During a training period, nurses came at 9 a.m. to do this, but later responsibility was passed to C112. She would get her husband up at the same time but she would wait up to three hours before injecting him, gaining a few hours of 'respite', because he doesn't need it'.

> Interviewer: When do you know it is time to inject T. with the syringe driver?
> C112: He starts to look unwell. And it is an effort for him to talk. I will then put the syringe driver in, and he is soon benefiting.

Hasselkus and Stetson (1991) draw attention to one further ethical concern of carers, namely a sense of justice regarding the balance of needs between carer and care recipient. They suggest that carers may subjugate their own needs to those of the patient in the belief that patients who are disadvantaged 'deserve' the greater part of available resources. However, paradoxically, this very subservience of carer to patients makes carers feel that their situation is unjust. This was the case for C133 (P133's UPD score was 6), whose case was discussed above.

> C133: He does very little for himself: it does not even occur to him that he can get himself a drink now. He used to do that, though he has never done very much for himself. That is the way we were, and it is what he was brought up to expect.... I am still waiting for the cup of tea that D. was going to make me when I was ill.

That carer blamed herself.

> C133: I certainly think D. could help himself more. But I think that I'm almost 100% to blame for that. Having had a handicapped child you tend to rush in, whereas perhaps sitting back and letting D. try might be better.

Because most of the sample of carers in this study were spouses, there was not much sharing of caring round family members in this study. If a spouse is available, he or she will normally provide care. Next, daughters, daughters-in-law or sons assume the caring role, then siblings, followed by other family members or friends (Qureshi and Walker, 1989). Violations of a sense of justice are most likely to be felt where care is provided mainly by one from a number of children, especially if others are felt not to be pulling their weight. Later on in the disease a lack of justice can also be felt if medical or social services which had been are expected to share the caring at this stage are found wanting.

Reason for caring

There are several reasons for taking on a carer role. Carers were asked 'What is the *most important* reason why you care for...?' The four qualitatively different categories mentioned are shown in Table 7.6.

It was interesting that carers rarely hesitated before answering. Love was the principal reason given. Although the majority of the carer sample were spouses, daughters also gave love as their main reason. Examples of the four respective categories are given below:

> C133: Because we love each other, and love overcomes all other things.

> C126: Because she is my mum and she needs me.

> C165: I just care about him. He's always been good to me. And if it were the other way round, he would look after me.

> C128: Really I have no choice in these matters. I do feel trapped.

Table 7.6. *Reasons for caring*

Reason	Percentage responses
Love	71
Feeling of responsibility	19
Feeling of reciprocity	6
Feeling trapped	4

Most stressful aspects of PD caring

In phase 1, carers were asked a single question to determine what the one most stressful aspect of PD caring was for them: 'What aspect of looking after ... do you find most stressful?' There was surprising variety in the responses. Nineteen per cent of carers said that they did not find anything stressful, but 81% described a particular aspect of their caring that caused them concern. The responses are shown in Table 7.7.
Examples of responses were:

C113: That I can't drop off to sleep because I am listening for him all the time.

C129: The need to provide cover *all* the time.

C133: The depression. I feel that I should be able to get him motivated, and I can't.

C140: The unpredictability of the disease. Not knowing how she is going to be from one day to the next, let alone one year to the next.

Table 7.7. *Aspects of PD caring that were the most stressful for individual carers at phase 1 (n = 77)*

Most stressful aspect	Number of carers
Watching the patient deteriorating	10
Patient personality change	8
Fear of being ill oneself	6
Patient falls	6
The need for patient cover	3
Relationship change	3
Patient forgetfulness	2
Dressing patient	2
Having no spare time	2
Being patient with patient's slowness	2
Toileting	2
Not getting enough sleep	2
Lifting patient	2
Leaving patient alone	2
Dying first	2
The unpredictability of the illness	2
Feeding patient	1
Having to learn to drive	1
Hallucinations	1
Dyskinesias	1
Money problems	1
Totally resigned to situation	1
Nothing stressful	15

There were some surprises in the responses. First, not one carer mentioned dementia, either in the sense of dealing with it, or fearing it. Two carers, however, mentioned the patient's forgetfulness as being what was most stressful: both these patients were cognitively impaired. Secondly, only one carer picked out hallucinations as the most stressful phenomenon, even though many carers indicated that they found these distressing. This may be because the hallucinating patients had more advanced PD, where there were more salient ongoing concerns, whereas hallucinations occurred sporadically. Thirdly, lack of communication was not explicitly commented on, even though the reports of personality and relationship changes already discussed make it clear that communication difficulties were indeed prominent.

Satisfaction in PD caring

Carers find satisfaction in their role (Stone *et al.,* 1987). In phase 2, they were asked: 'Can you tell me if there are things which you enjoy, or find satisfying in your role as carer to ...?' Of the sample, 78% did get some satisfaction from their caring efforts. The responses are shown Table 7.8.

Table 7.8. *Aspects of satisfaction from PD caring at phase 2 (n = 56)*

Source of satisfaction	Number of carers
Satisfaction from accomplishing a duty	30
The sense of acting from love	25
The company of the relative	12
Preventing institutionalization	6
Learning new skills	2
Nothing enjoyable	12

Carers who gained some satisfaction from PD caring mentioned an average of 1.7 sources.

As in the study of Reis *et al.* (1994), there were essentially six qualitatively different categories of source of satisfaction. Several carers mentioned more than one aspect but almost 22% found nothing enjoyable.

C142: Dear me. Well I don't mind shopping. That part doesn't worry me. I can spend money all right.
Interviewer: Anything else?
C142: Not really. Even the cooking side, well you have got to do that because you have to eat yourself, haven't you.

Increased emotional closeness was enjoyed by some.

> C162: It is not what I would have chosen at all, but yes, I do enjoy his company and being with him more.

Some regarded caring as a task to be accomplished with greater or lesser job satisfaction.

> C123: You just get on with things.

> C112: I always wanted to be a nurse, and especially since I learnt to do the syringe driver and inject T., I have felt like I have become one.

The most frequently mentioned satisfactions, however, were the sense of giving care out of love and of fulfilling a duty successfully. Six carers mentioned that they were preventing institutionalization, but each also gave one of the two main responses. Although many carers qualified their answer by pointing out that it was not something that they would have done by choice, nevertheless, the vast majority did get some satisfaction from their role.

Discussion

The interviews provided information about carers' experience from the time of initial presentation of symptoms. These data may have been subject to memory distortions. In contrast, the data on caring duties and emotional experiences were prospective.

The insidious onset of PD often meant a period of around two years of worry and uncertainty before a diagnosis was made. But since levels of knowledge of PD were low, the diagnosis, when made, did little to resolve uncertainty.

Responses to a direct question indicated that over 80% of carers found the caring task stressful; however, around the same proportion also found some source of satisfaction in supplying care.

Braithwaite (1992) has asked why the experience of caring for an older person should be more stressful than, for example, the experiences of normal child care. She identified five 'crises of decline': awareness of degeneration, unpredictability, time constraints, the carer–receiver relationship and lack of choice. There are echoes of all these 'crises' in the present study. The most stressful single experience mentioned by carers was watching the patient deteriorate. Most carers felt that they had to impose a routine on their life to get through the day, but unpredictability of response to medication, including 'on–off' phenomena, and the side-effects (see Chapter 1) meant this was difficult, especially for those whose standards had always been high. Hallucinations in the patient led to further unpredictability and a need for flexibility of management.

The care charts demonstrated the demands on carers. Overall, those who completed the charts gave around 35 hours a week, equivalent to a full-time job. Time demands were related to illness severity. In interpreting the care charts for patients whose motor symptoms were mild, however, it must be remembered that carers tended not to define their role as a 'carer' and six did not complete a chart (though in principle they accepted responsibility for caring). More generally, as severity of PD increased, so did the number of hours that carers devoted. For patients with moderate PD (UPD score 10–24) the median duration of caring was 21 hours a week at phase 1, but for advanced patients (UPD score 25 or more) it was 56 hours and a fifth of all carers were giving over 100 hours a week. In this context it may be pointed out that PD caring is unlike that with Alzheimer's disease, where the demands on the carer diminish as the patient becomes less capable of independent action. In PD, the demands become greater as the disease progresses.

Carers were asked about changes in their care recipient's personality. Half the carers reported that there had been such changes and these were almost always viewed negatively. Increased apathy and withdrawal were the major changes noted and usually led to a change in the dyadic relationship. However, some patients became irritable and aggressive. Depression was also a salient feature of advancing PD. These changes must be taken seriously, both because they placed strain on carers and because it is possible that this study actually underestimates the extent of distress. This is because it is possible that those with very poor dyadic relationships might be unwilling to undergo the scrutiny that participation in a longitudinal study of caring implies. It is clear that research on methods of helping carers 'manage' episodes of challenging behaviour is needed. Some carers were skilled at recognizing the emotions this aroused and distanced themselves by engaging in tasks such vigorous gardening or going out. This was not open to some carers who were themselves ill. Some saw respite care even for a few hours as a lifeline. Others resolutely refused help.

When asked about the emotion that the caring task aroused in them, the most frequently endorsed emotions were resignation and regret. There was also a degree of acceptance. In this predominately elderly sample, however, a chronic disabling disease may have been seen as 'on time' for the stage of life. Neugarten (1970) has emphasized the role of social expectations in adaptation. If events or situations are seen as being appropriate to the life span developmental stage, they will require less adaptation than if they are seen as untimely. Coping strategies may have been rehearsed, role models for appropriate coping may exist and there is a sense of completion about shared experiences in the time *before* the illness. Taking both phases together, only around one carer in eight admitted to anger and resentment focused on the caring task. In a group of younger dyads (where PD is 'off-time'), these hostile emotions would be predicted to be more prevalent. Nevertheless, the fact that around half the carers felt not at all hopeful and nearly a fifth felt overwhelmed and fearful is a cause for concern.

Ethical dilemmas in caring were recognized by some carers, including violation of principles of 'doing good', especially as far as the patient's autonomy was concerned. Few carers, however, felt that it was 'unjust' that they should have to care. This, too, is probably because of the nature of the sample. In our culture, spousal caring is expected ('on-time') in late life. The situation could be very different both in a group of younger patients with PD or in samples where most carers were children, where issues of 'unfairness' would be expected to be greater. The extent to which ethical dilemmas are related to the quality of the dyadic relationship has not yet been examined, but one would predict that the worse the premorbid relationship, the more ethical dilemmas and the more distressed the carer would be. Such dyads may need specific help.

There are very few sources of professional emotional support for PD carers. Although the majority may be able to cope, there was a core of demoralized carers. Development of quick and reliable methods of screening for 'carer demoralization' might allow services to be more effectively targeted. Not all dyads need emotional support, of course, but existing services are clearly not sufficient for the emotionally most needy.

Carers brought their own personality characteristics to the caring task and their circumstances in terms of health and of other life problems also differed. These influenced the carer's capacity to cope. Patients with a similar severity of illness could be treated as being fairly independent or being almost totally dependent, according to the carer's outlook. There was also some evidence to support the view that major life events affected not only the carer's but also the patient's mood, though this has not been tested systematically.

Despite the stresses of PD caring, the majority of this sample were able to say that they got some satisfaction from the experience of caring. This largely stemmed from a sense of successfully performing a duty and as an expression of love.

Finally, it must be stressed that the data reported here are illustrative rather than exhaustive. More detailed analysis of the patients' neuropsychological and personality characteristics and of their relationship to carer experience remain to be reported.

Acknowledgements

The study was part of a larger investigation into perceived psychological change and carer distress in PD. It was funded by the Welfare Committee of the Parkinson's Disease Society of the United Kingdom, to whom grateful thanks are extended, in grant N10 to Dr A.D.M. Davies, Department of Psychology, University of Liverpool.

References

BERRY, R.A. and MURPHY, J.F. (1995) Well-being of caregivers of spouses with Parkinson's disease. *Clinical Nursing Research, 4*, 373–386.

BRAITHWAITE, V.A. (1990) *Bound to Care.* London: Unwin Hyman.

BRAITHWAITE, V.A. (1992) Caregiving burden: making the concept scientifically useful and policy relevant. *Research on Aging, 14*, 3–27

BROD, M., MENDELSOHN, G.A. and ROBERTS, B. (1998) Patients' experiences of Parkinson's disease. *Journal of Gerontology, Psychological Sciences, 53B*, 213–222.

DURA, J. R., HAYWOOD-NILER, E. and KIECOLT-GLASER, J.K. (1990) Spousal caregivers of person's with Parkinson's disease dementia: a preliminary comparison. *Gerontologist, 30*, 332–336.

FAHN, S., ELTON, R.L. and UPDRS Development Committee (1987) Unified Parkinson's disease rating scale. In S. Fahn, C.D. Marsden, D. Calne and M. Goldstein (Eds), *Recent Developments in Parkinson's Disease* (Vol. 2, pp. 153–163 and 293–304). Forham Park, New York: McMillan Healthcare Information.

FOLSTEIN, M.F., FOLSTEIN, S.E. and McHUGH, P.R. (1975) Mini-Mental State: a practical method for grading the cognitive state of patients for the clinician. *Journal of Psychiatric Research, 12*, 189–198.

HALL, J. N. (1990) Towards a psychology of caring. *British Journal of Clinical Psychology, 29*, 129–144.

HASSELKUS, B.R. and STETSON S.A. (1991) Ethical dilemmas: the organization of family caregiving for the elderly. *Journal of Aging Studies, 5*, 99–110.

HOEHN, M.M. and YAHR, M.D. (1967) Parkinsonism: onset, progression and mortality. *Neurology , 17*, 427–442.

HOOKER, K., MONAHAN, D.J., BOWMAN, S.R., FRAZIER, L.D. and Shifren, K. (1998) Personality counts for a lot. *Journal of Gerontology, Psychological Sciences, 53B*, 73–85.

LANG, A.E.T. and FAHN, S. (1989) Assessment of Parkinson's disease. In T.L. Munsat (Ed.), *Quantification of Neurologic Deficit* (pp. 285–309). London: Butterworth.

MILLER, E., BERRIOS, G. and POLITYNSKA, B.E. (1996) Caring for someone with Parkinson's disease: factors that contribute to distress. *International Journal of Geriatric Psychiatry, 11*, 263–268.

MORRIS, L.W., MORRIS, R.G. and BRITTON, P.G. (1988) The relationship between marital intimacy, perceived strain and depression in spouse caregivers of dementia patients. *British Journal of Medical Psychology, 61*, 231–236.

MOTENKO, A.K. (1989) The frustrations, gratifications, and well-being of dementia caregivers. *Gerontologist, 29,* 166–172.

NEUGARTEN, B.L. (1970) Dynamics of transition of middle age to old age: adaptation and the life cycle. *Journal of Geriatric Psychiatry, 4,* 71–87.

O'REILLY, F., FINNAN, F., ALLWRIGHT S., SMITH, G.D. and BEN-SHLOMO, Y. (1996) The effects of caring for a spouse with Parkinson's disease on social, psychological and physical well-being. *British Journal of General Practice, 46,* 507–512.

QURESHI, H. and WALKER, A. (1989) *The Caring Relationship: Elderly People and their Families.* London: Macmillan.

REIS, M.F., ANDRES, D., GOLD, D.P. and MARKIEWICZ, D. (1994) Personality traits as determinants of burden and health complaints in caregiving. *International Journal of Aging and Human Development, 39,* 257–271.

SPEER, D.C. (1993) Predicting Parkinson's disease patient and caregiver adjustment: preliminary findings. *Behavior, Health and Aging, 3,* 139–146.

STONE, R., CAFFERATA, G. and SANGL, J. (1987) Caregivers of the frail elderly: a national profile. *Gerontologist, 27,* 616–626.

Part II
Assessments and interventions

Chapter 8

A psychological group approach to meeting the needs of people with Parkinson's disease and carers

Sue Watts, Polly Kaiser, Justine Porter, Nina Cockton and Mike Morley

A number of factors influenced both our decision to approach the Parkinson's Disease Society (PDS) for a research award and the plan of the proposed project. Broadly speaking, these factors fall into three categories: first, the psychological research literature on people with Parkinson's disease (PD) and their carers; secondly, the clinical experience of Salford psychologists of work with people with PD; and finally, specific discussions arising from a session with a local PDS branch undertaken by one of the service psychologists. The following three sections outline the influence of each of these on the development of the study, which involved interviewing patients and carers, and its findings are described in the remainder of the chapter.

Literature on psychological adjustment in PD

Adjustment in people with PD

It has long been recognized that chronic illness can have a major impact on emotional wellbeing. Studies have mostly focused on depression and anxiety, and how these relate to physical disability in people with PD. There are practical problems in estimating the rate of, for example, depression in PD, due to an overlap between some symptoms of depression and of PD. Although the proportion of people with PD who have depression is probably between 10% and 25%, up to 70% of sufferers may have some depressive symptoms (Ring, 1993). Researchers have suggested that there are common biochemical factors underlying PD and depression, but it is also likely that the impact of illness on lifestyle, social stress and support is the major explanation. Physical disability in PD does not appear to be the only factor influencing depression. MacCarthy and Brown (1989) found a complex pattern of interacting factors, with adjustment to disability a continually evolving process.

Dakof and Mendelsohn (1986) reviewed the psychological research on PD, noting that a stongly medical model had dominated investigation and treatment of this condition. They argued for a new approach, combining the psychosocial investigation of people's adaptation to their illness with the prevailing biomedical approach to research. This seems a logical way forward, as psychological factors and PD probably interact in a complex way. For example, Marsden (1982) observed that stress has a marked effect on the motor (physical) symptoms of PD, as well as vice versa, thus disabling the client further. This can become a 'vicious circle' and in addition can interact further with any family stress.

Adjustment in carers

Caring for a disabled relative can impose a physical, social and psychological burden. Research on conditions such as coronary heart disease and oncology has indicated the need to integrate psychological ideas into care plans, but relatively little work has been done on the needs of PD carers. The combination of physical and mental/emotional effects of the condition would suggest that input with this group is strongly indicated. Miller *et al.* (1996) reported that 40% of carers show some signs of strain. There are suggestions from this and other studies that there is a complex relationship between distress and disability in the person with PD, and with the carer's perceptions of these.

Psychological interventions

Theories which help to explain the different ways in which people with chronic illnesses and their carers cope are still in the process of development. An individual's personality, social circumstances, relationships and practical supports can all influence the response to stress and ways of coping. However, there is evidence that some coping strategies are associated with psychological wellbeing. Most of these involve good problem solving, using a limited range of helpful strategies, positive thinking and self-adaptation (McCrae and Costa, 1986). The interaction of personal characteristics and environmental factors with stressors such as illness has led various researchers to recommend that psychological interventions should reflect this complexity of issues in chronic ill-health and caring, rather than focusing on a single aspect of stress.

To date, there have been few studies looking at the effects of psychological or educational interventions, either with people with PD or their carers. Ellgring *et al.* (1993) described a German service which provided people with PD and their relatives with psychological counselling and help in applying effective coping strategies in everyday situations. They found that participants benefited, and were able to apply the skills they had learned to practical situations. Relaxation and positive self-instruction were particularly successful strategies.

Clinical experience

In Salford, a small team of psychologists specialize in work with older people, including using psychological ideas to contribute to the care of people with physical illnesses. As a result, members of the service were already working occasionally with people with PD, for example when a consultant recognized that a psychological problem had arisen and made a referral. The following fictionalized case example gives an indication of this type of involvement.

Case example
George has PD, but his consultant reports that George's mobility sometimes appears rather worse than anticipated on purely physical grounds. George has noticed that his PD is particularly bad 'in public'. His wife still works part time and has a very active social life, from which George is tending to withdraw. She would like him to go out more, but George feels that he's too much of a nuisance if his PD symptoms become particularly bad.

George was worrying in advance about his PD creating problems when he went out and of spoiling things for others. This was leading to anxiety and occasional panic. The physical symptoms of these were compounding the motor difficulties from his PD. He was given information about anxiety, taught a combination of relaxation and thinking strategies and helped to plan ways of coping in public situations in conjunction with his wife, using approaches adapted from standard cognitive behavioural therapy.

From a pragmatic perspective, this individual clinical input has its limitations. Psychology is a relatively small resource, particularly in the specialisms dealing with the needs of older people and those with long-term health problems. As a result, only small numbers of people can be seen and, in general, work is concentrated on those whose mental health is more severely affected. There was no regular psychological advice to PD services, and no 'preventative' approaches offering psychological information before individuals' difficulties become 'clinically significant'.

Contacts with a local PDS branch

The final impetus for the study originated with Polly Kaiser, a Salford clinical psychologist who was asked to talk to a local PDS branch about depression. She chose to undertake this as a participatory exercise for the members, looking at issues for carers and people with PD separately. As is often the case, the issues raised proved broader than the topic originally envisaged.

The key themes which emerged from the session were:

- Participants found the opportunity for carers and people with PD to talk separately particularly valuable. The usual joint branch sessions offered little opportunity to consider their different perspectives.
- Both carers and people with PD had similar concerns, of which, in many cases, they were mutually unaware. For example, people with PD had concerns about overprotectiveness, 'carers doing too much', while the carers reported feeling 'exhausted' and 'doing too much'.
- Communication about these types of issues was often a problem, with each being concerned about upsetting the other.
- Some superficially mild stressors and communication problems could become a major source of frustration and, indeed, anger in the already stressful context of chronic ill-health.
- As a group, participants were able to be creative in generating and sharing coping strategies, such as their use of humour in describing ways of getting around awkward day-to-day practical problems.

As a result, the idea of developing a group approach to share psychological knowledge with people with PD and their carers was generated.

Aims of the study

Encouraged by the success of other researchers, and taking into account the research literature, knowledge based on clinical experience and the opinions and concerns of the local PDS branch, a group approach to the provision of information about psychological approaches to communication and anxiety was developed. The group, supported by psychologists, could provide an environment which carers and people with PD would experience as safe enough to enable them to address their potentially sensitive concerns. The study had therefore sought, first, to investigate the perceptions of people with PD and carers about their circumstances, using a semistructured interview, and second, to find out how helpful they would find a regular group providing education about how psychological factors can interact with PD. There were two aspects to the latter:

1 to investigate the impact of the group on psychological stress and coping;
2 to investigate participants' satisfaction with the group.

Factors influencing choice of study methodology

There are recognized benefits of group approaches:

- A group is a good medium in which to address communication needs.
- A group can provide peer support and helps confirm the 'normality' of issues.
- A group approach would build on the strengths of the PDS branch meetings with little disruption to routine.
- To stimulate improved communication and joint problem solving, the *system* in which the individual lives should be taken into account. A group approach with people with PD and carers gave the opportunity to address both their separate and joint perspectives, and could also help people generalize new ways of coping.
- Although the focus was on people with PD and their carers, the intervention was designed to be relevant to a person attending alone, by providing information about others' perspectives and ideas which individuals could use alone or share with others in their network.
- The group made effective use of the limited resources of the psychology service.
- A successful group could be used to develop an outline protocol for psychological approaches to PD which could be used more widely.

Since the project was inspired by a Greater Manchester PDS branch, which had already requested psychological information, the study concentrated on this group. Neighbouring groups were invited to participate on the basis of their proximity to the research base, size, non-participation in any other major research, and likely similarity of the group in terms of age, sex, living circumstances and so on.

The needs of younger individuals with PD presented something of a dilemma. Clearly, communication, anxiety and psychological issues in general are as relevant to these as to others with PD. However, there can be difficulties in running a successful group if individual members have very heterogeneous characteristics and needs (Stock-Whittiker, 1985). For example, a younger person with PD, small children and work commitments would need to address different issues from a retired individual. As a result, a decision was taken to offer a restricted group in the first instance, targeted at the needs of members aged 55 years and over.

To assess the impact of the group, it was necessary to separate any effects of this psychological intervention from the benefits to participants of having an increased opportunity to meet and gain support and advice in general. This meant developing a parallel programme of 'placebo' sessions for a control group, which would offer the same frequency and duration of sessions, but covering 'non-psychological' topics as far as possible.

Method

Interviews and instruments

Two parallel forms of a semistructured interview were developed for people with PD and carers. The content was informed by pilot interviews undertaken with a sample of people with PD and carers by the researchers, information from the original PDS branch sessions, and from the research base covering both PD and stress in other health conditions. The final interview included some standardized, published questionnaires, Likert scales and open questions which could be analysed quantitatively or qualitatively. Areas covered:

- background details/demographic characteristics;
- clinical details (e.g. medication, mobility, history of illness);
- general health status and psychological wellbeing;
- lifestyle and financial changes;
- emotional and relationship changes;
- methods of coping;
- cognitive status;
- service support.

Measures for people with PD were:

- McCarthy and Brown's (1989) adaptation of the Folkman and Lazarus (1985) Ways of Coping Checklist;
- the 28-item General Health Questionnaire (GHQ-28) (Goldberg, 1979);
- the Beck Depression Inventory (BDI) (Beck *et al.*, 1979);
- the Symptom Rating Test (SRT) (Kellner and Sheffield, 1973);
- MacCarthy and Brown's (1989) adaptation of the Hoehn and Yahr (1967) rating of stage of illness;
- Mini-Mental State Examination (MMSE) (Folstein *et al.*, 1975).

Measures for carers were:

- the GHQ, BDI and SRT (see above);

- the CAPE Behaviour Rating Scale (Pattie and Gilleard, 1979), included as Calder *et al.* (1991) had reported this scale to be the best predictor of a relative's stress;
- the Machin Strain Scale (Gilleard, 1987);
- Ways of Coping with Caring, Matson's (1994) adaptation of the Ways of Coping Checklist.

Subjects

The mailing lists of two PDS branches were used to contact people with PD and their carers. The following exclusion criteria were applied:

- caregivers not living with or in daily face-to-face contact with person with PD;
- those with current mental illness severe enough to preclude participation in a group;
- people with PD diagnosed for less than six months;
- those with probable dementia (as identified by a score of 20 or less on the MMSE);
- persons under 55 years of age.

Contact procedures followed a protocol agreed with the local research ethics committees. Invitations to participate in the initial interviews were made by post. Of the 150 people approached, 40% agreed to participate. (This is comparable with the percentage routinely attending branch meetings, although some people not currently attending groups chose to join, suggesting that psychological issues met a perceived need.) Of the respondents, 36 (60%) were people with PD and the remaining 24 (40%) cared for someone with PD.

Procedure

Participants were visited at home and asked to complete the initial interview. They were then invited to participate in the groups.

Branch A   the psychological treatment group – members in this area were invited to take part in eight fortnightly psychological group sessions;

Branch B   the control group – members in this area were invited to take part in eight fortnightly group sessions covering other practical approaches to managing PD. (At the end of the follow-up period, branch B were also offered the psychological group sessions.)

Structure of the sessions

The sessions for both treatment and control groups followed the same pattern:

- Opportunity for group members to chat and meet informally (this allowed time for staggered arrivals, recovery from the journey, and to address PDS branch business);
- short talk/presentation on week's theme;
- further discussion;
- participants asked to complete standard questionnaires by a researcher – the SRT (to measure changes in distress levels) and a feedback questionnaire (designed by the team).

All sessions were facilitated by the psychology team and lasted about 1.5 hours. After the final session and three months later, a trained interviewer visited participants at home to reassess them and collect completed questionnaires.

Psychological sessions

The aim was to provide participants with information about psychological ideas, with emphasis on the normal psychological responses to illness. The key topics covered were anxiety, problem solving and communication. After the initial presentation, the group split into smaller discussion groups to consider the issues separately, as they applied to carers and people with PD. These then gave feedback to a final discussion. The sessions covered:

1 'Introduction' – group rules (e.g. confidentiality), hopes and concerns of participants;
2 'Psychological responses to illness, I' – normal responses to stressful events;
3 'Psychological responses to illness, II' – models of anxiety and complication of PD symptoms, and relaxation strategies using guided imagery and breathing techniques;
4 'Problem solving' – brainstorming, solution selection and evaluation;
5 'Pressures' – personal, social and practical resources and an interactional model of stress (see Cox, 1978);
6 'The impact of thoughts on communication' (see Ellis, 1990) – examples of miscommunication and effective alternatives (an outline of this session is given in the box on pages 208–209);
7 'Follow-up' – progress with new strategies;
8 'Ending' – feedback, reflection on the group sessions and moving on.

Control group sessions

Each session consisted of a presentation on a practical topic relevant to the general management of PD. Presentations were undertaken by professional staff involved in the care of people with PD, while the sessions and group discussions were facilitated by the psychologists. Topics included: benefits/welfare advice, aids and adaptations, diet, physiotherapy and shiatsu massage.

Results of semistructured interviews

Background details about participants and scores on the various standardized measures are shown in Table 8.1.

Table 8.1. *Mean and standard deviations for age, physical symptoms, psychological distress and strain*

| | People with PD (n = 36) | | Carers (n = 24) | |
	Mean	s.d.	Mean	s.d.
Age (years)	72.4	6.9	69	7.2
Hoehn and Yahr score	4.0	–	–	–
Duration of illness	7.3	7.5		
CAPE Behaviour Rating Scale	–	–	8.9	5.3
GHQ	8	5	3	3.3
BDI	13	11	6	3.1
SRT	24	13.7	11.5	7.5
Machin Strain Scale	–	–	10	4.3

People with PD

The Hoehn and Yahr rating of stage of illness indicated that:

- 11% of the sample were minimally or mildly disabled;
- 31% had moderate levels of disability;
- 58% had severe or very severe levels of disability.

The GHQ and BDI, respectively, showed that:

- 78% showed significant psychological distress;
- 31% were at least moderately depressed.

Session example: notes summarizing session content

'The impact of thoughts on communication'

Aim
- To look at the demands that people with PD and their carers can experience as a result of their own or others' expectations.
- To discuss some examples of self-imposed (or 'internal') demands identified by people with PD and carers in the previous session.

Main points for presentation
- Review the importance of issues about dependency and loss of independence with the group.

Question: *How do we decide how much help to give* (as carers), *or how much help is acceptable from others* (for people with PD)?

Generally we *don't* decide. Often we do what we *think* the other person wants us to do, not because we want to or because they've made a request, but because we think we *should* or *ought* to. (See cartoon for illustration.)

- Explain the idea of 'internal' demands and negative thoughts. Consider the example of the internal demands the couple in the cartoon are placing on themselves and point out how this causes an increase in tension between them. Consider examples of the internal demands they may be making on themselves:

Her: 'I should do everything for him – he has a lot to put up with'.
     'I must keep the house tidy'.
     'I ought to keep him happy'.
Him: 'I ought to do what she wants – she does so much for me'.
     'I should keep the peace and I shouldn't upset her'.

Small groups
1 Ask group members what are the shoulds and oughts they tell themselves everyday. Go round the group asking them to provide specific examples if possible.
(Example from facilitator: *'I should have more patience with my friend'*.)
2 Ask group members to try to change these shoulds and oughts into coulds. (Example from facilitator: *'I could have more patience with my friends, but I don't because I'm too tired all the time'*.)
3 Explain that by changing these into coulds, and arriving at a reason why we don't do something all the time, can provide us with the key to what needs remedying, or to help us get our thoughts into proportion. (Example from facilitator: *remedy the tiredness.*)

'Homework'
- Ask group members to look out for negative thoughts, and to make notes if they are able.
- Ask them if they can think of more helpful things they could say to themselves and to make notes of these if possible.

Handout
'Things to ask yourself when you are thinking negatively'.

As expected, there were significant correlations between the different measures of psychological distress. There were also significant correlations between these and the 'maladaptive coping' score from the Coping with PD Scale and others with the total amount and number of coping techniques used. There were also associations with perceived changes in relationship with the carer, which is comparable with findings by Seiler *et al.* (1992). However, as with Ellgring *et al.*'s (1993) report, there were no significant correlations between the person's level of impairment or duration of disability and psychological distress in this group.

Carers

Questionnaire results showed that:

- 66% were caring for relatives with moderate–severe levels of dependency;
- 31% showed significant psychological distress (on the GHQ);
- 13% were at least mildly depressed (as measured by BDI).

On the basis of previously published data, the average level of strain in carers indicated by the Machin Strain Scale scores was considerable.

There were no significant correlations between the various measures of carers' psychological distress and duration of illness or level of disability in the person with PD. Level of disability was positively correlated with scores on the Strain Scale, which would be expected as this scale lays greater emphasis on the physical burden of care. The duration of the illness, while not correlating significantly with any other variable, was strongly correlated with carers' scores on the BDI scale.

Some additional analyses indicated that the total amount of time spent coping was the strongest determinant of psychological distress and strain, and that carers who felt that their relationship with the person with PD had changed were most distressed.

Comparison of group interventions

Some participants were lost to follow-up, due to a deterioration in health during the course of the study, and some were unable to attend all sessions (see Table 8.2).

The two groups were compared to investigate how well they were matched at the outset of the study, in terms of demographic characteristics and scores on standardized tests. Despite efforts to

Table 8.2. *Number of subjects participating in the project and at follow-up*

| Assessment | Psychological group | | Control group | |
	People with PD	Carers	People with PD	Carers
Initial interviews	23	14	13	10
Included in group	15	8	11	9
Three-month follow-up	15	7	10	9

achieve satisfactory matching, there were some statistically and clinically noticeable differences between the groups, particularly in the participants with PD:

- The psychological group had higher levels of distress at the outset, as measured by the BDI and SRT.
- There were differences in the living arrangements between groups.
- Although not statistically significant, members of the control group were more likely to have a higher socio-economic status.

Due to the small size of the groups, which restricts options to use statistical methods to control for these differences, the above place some limitations on the interpretation of results.

The largest changes were seen in the carers attending the psychological group sessions. Carers showed a decrease in psychological distress, as measured by the SRT, in comparison with their initial scores, after the group. This was maintained at three-month follow-up. This also applied to control group members attending the psychological intervention *after* completion of the control phase. GHQ-28 scores decreased (but not significantly) among carers in the psychological group.

There was a trend for people with PD to make less use of maladaptive coping strategies after the group intervention.

There was a downward trend in psychological distress, as measured by the GHQ-28, in people with PD attending the psychological group, in contrast with an upward trend in the control group.

The carers in both groups showed a decrease in the use of 'value coping' on the Coping with Caring scale. This means that they were less likely to report reminding themselves of the importance of the caring role as a coping strategy. Possibly this reflects a natural trend in carers over a period of time, rather than any effect of the intervention.

There were no other significant changes in the control group.

Feedback about the group content was generally very positive. The responses to standard questions are summarized in Table 8.3.

Table 8.3. *Percentages of people with PD and carers selecting each rating,* *based on mean scores of ratings for all eight sessions*

	Very/Quite		Don't know		Not very/at all	
	Patients	Carers	Patients	Carers	Patients	Carers
How helpful did you find the sessions?	87.5	88.4	5	5	7.5	6.6
How interesting were the sessions?	96	98	2	2	2	0
How easy was it to understand the sessions?	94	96	2	4	4	0
How much opportunity to talk was there?[a]	14	3.5	85	84.5	1	2

[a]Responses to this question were in respective categories 'Too little', 'About right', 'Too much'.

Specific comments

The vast majority of comments were very positive, especially in relation to the opportunity to talk openly, to express thoughts and fears, to feel they were not alone with problems and to develop supportive relationships with others. Specifically, members appreciated: 'the questions that asked about how we felt'; 'finding out about helpful ways to cope'; topics [that] were close to the real problems'; 'the variation in content – covered everything'; 'learning how to relax'; I feel this course has made us a stronger group. It has forged a bond and led to a better understanding of all our problems'.

A few negative comments related to difficulties in hearing, finding it difficult to relate to older or less able people in the group, and finding some sessions not interesting.

Difficulties encountered

Methodological issues

Problems were experienced in identifying a well matched control group. Although both participating PDS branches covered a combination of inner-city areas and suburbs, there were larger psychological and social/economic differences between the treatment and control groups than anticipated. It would have required more resources and the participation of more PDS branches to control for this.

It was difficult to identify psychological measures appropriate for older people, and especially for those with PD, as there can be some overlap in the presentation of symptoms, as discussed earlier. In consequence, they afford indications of general distress levels, not of formal mental health problems. Also, measures designed to assess psychological distress may not adequately reflect aspects of the process of adjustment to chronic illness.

There were some difficulties in providing a satisfactory 'placebo' control group. It was necessary to provide a realistic alternative intervention, but it could not be presumed that the sessions would be without effect. Also, it is not possible to separate completely psychological issues from other topics. For example, a presentation on massage also provided a relaxation method, and information about management of the physical and financial impact of PD increased people's practical coping strategies. Further, the presence of psychologists as facilitators and the repeated use of psychological assessments may have led the control group to reflect on psychological matters. A number of individuals did ask specific psychological questions during the control sessions.

The local research ethics committee required that the research team notify participants' general practitioners if they took part. Some PDS members felt this was inappropriate and that it pathologized their situation. It is not possible to give numbers for those who withdrew as a result, as the process was explained as an introduction to recruitment to the project.

Practical issues

There are considerable practical obstacles to running this kind of group, as any PDS branch coordinator will be well aware. Appropriate transport, access and facilities are essential if sessions are to run smoothly, and timings needed adjustment to allow for mobility problems. Sensory impairments in participants presented difficulties for which access to appropriate technology would have helped – such as loop systems for the hearing impaired. A communication assistant to help individuals with particular sensory deficits to participate effectively might also be a useful innovation. Also, sadly, some people's health deteriorated sharply during the course of group, changing their needs as sessions progressed.

Clinical issues

Psychologists have developed a broad range of relevant strategies over the years, which provided a rather full menu of ideas from which the group participants could pick. Also, even within one group, different members worked at different paces on a given idea and some ideas suited one person's style more than others. As a result, it was necessary to adapt the content as sessions progressed.

Comments and future directions

Research

The findings of this small-scale piece of research support those of Ellgring *et al.* (1993), who found that psychological approaches have a useful role to play within the range of strategies available to people with PD. The sessions showed most benefit for the carers, although this may have been a function of the measures used. Further studies are needed to clarify which components of a psychological approach may be of most benefit.

There are a whole range of complex questions about how chronic illness in general, and PD in particular, affects sufferers and carers. The theme of perceived change in the relationship between the person with PD and carer and its relation to emotional wellbeing is important. In other areas of caring, the physical burden has often not been a key issue. A sense of 'loss' of the other is often important. The problems of PD for communication, both verbal and non-verbal, make this an important area to address.

This project focused on the needs of older people. It is likely that for younger people with PD there will be some differences in the relevant psychological factors. However, a supportive group could be more valuable, because the condition is less common in younger people and can lead to increased isolation. Thus, it would be interesting to adapt and evaluate a psychological approach with this group.

On a final note, it may also be interesting to look at the impact of this type of approach on the physical management of PD. Ways of dealing with stress and communication can only be beneficial for interactions with medics and other professions.

Clinical perspectives

Generally, the results obtained in this study support psychological approaches as potentially useful strategies to add to the services offered to people with PD and their families. First, though, it is important to 'debunk' the notion that psychological needs equate with mental illness, so that psychological knowledge can benefit people without any trace of stigma.

Psychological ideas and information could be integrated into a multidisciplinary approach to PD. For example, relaxation and anxiety management could fit in with physiotherapy information and advice. Likewise, communication issues can overlap with aspects of speech therapy. Some elements of this approach could be learned and sessions facilitated by other disciplines, such as PD nurse specialists, providing that they have suitable back-up. Occasionally, more severe mental health or relationship problems may be identified through this kind of work. As long as the facilitator has access to a skilled therapist for advice and referral, this should not prove a major problem.

The Salford team has developed some guidelines and information which could help other people working with PD address some psychological issues as part of their clinical practice. Groups need to be fairly small in size – our experience would suggest a maximum of about eight people. Clinically, the ideal format for one group might not be appropriate for another, meaning that facilitators need to be flexible. A 'psychologically minded' or longer-running group might want to examine some ideas in more depth. Equally, psychological approaches can be applied to work with families or individuals, rather than groups. Similarly, some psychological information could be provided in the form of leaflets tailored to the needs of people with PD and carers. The authors plan to complete the development of a handbook outlining ideas and session strategies that could prove useful, together with a description of the intervention process and other options for treatment.

Acknowledgements

Special thanks are owed to all the members of the Salford and Trafford PDS branches who contributed to the organization and development of the project and gave their time to take part in the research; and to Gillian Stanley, social worker, who contributed a great deal to this project in terms of advice, experience and support.

References

BECK, A.T., RUSH, A.J., SHAW, B.P. and EMERY, G. (1979) *Cognitive Therapy of Depression*. New York: Guilford.
CALDER, S.A., EBMEIER, K.P., STEWART, L., CRAWFORD, J.R. and Besson, J.A.O. (1991) The prediction of stress in carers: the role of behaviour, reported self-care and dementia in patients with idiopathic Parkinson's disease. *International Journal of Geriatric Psychiatry*, 6, 737–742.
COX, T. (1978) *Stress*. Basingstoke: Macmillan Education.
DAKOF, G.A. and MENDELSOHN, G.A. (1989) Patterns of adaptation to Parkinson's disease. *Health Psychology*, 8, 355–372.

ELLGRING, H., SEILER, S., FRINGS, W., GASSER, T. and OERTEL, W. (1993). Psychosocial aspects of Parkinson's disease. *Neurology, 43*, 41–44.

ELLIS, A. (1990) Rational–emotive therapy. In I.L. Kutash and A. Wolf (Eds), *The Group Psychotherapist's Handbook*. New York: Columbia.

FOLKMAN, S. and LAZARUS, R.S. (1985) If it changes it must be a process: study of emotion and coping during three stages of a college examination. *Journal of Personality and Social Psychology, 48,* 150–170.

FOLSTEIN, M.F., FOLSTEIN, S.E. and McHUGH, P.R. (1975) Mini-Mental State: a practical method for grading the mental state of patients for the clinician. *Journal of Psychiatric Research, 12*, 189–198.

GILLEARD, C.J. (1987) Influence of emotional distress among supporters on the outcome of psychogeriatric day care. *British Journal of Psychiatry, 150*, 219–223.

GOLDBERG, D. (1979) A scaled version of the General Health Questionnaire. *Psychological Medicine, 9,* 139–145.

HOEHN, M.M. and YAHR, M.D. (1967) Onset, progression and mortality. *Neurology, 17*, 427–442.

KELLNER, R. and SHEFFIELD, B.F. (1973) A self-rating scale of distress. *Psychological Medicine, 3*, 88–100.

MacCARTHY, B. and BROWN, R. (1989) Psychosocial factors in Parkinson's disease. *British Journal of Clinical Psychology,. 28*, 41–52.

MARSDEN, C.D. (1982) Emotion and movement. In D. Garlick (Ed.), *Proprioception, Posture and Emotion.* Sydney: Committee in Postgraduate Medical Education, University of New South Wales.

MATSON, N. (1994) Coping, caring and stress: a study of stroke carers and carers of older confused people. *British Journal of Clinical Psychology, 33*, 333–344.

McCRAE, R.R. and COSTA, P.T. (1986) Personality, coping and coping effectiveness in an adult sample. *Journal of Personality, 54*, 385–405.

MILLER, E., BERRIOS, G.E. and POLITYNSKA, B.E. (1996) Caring for someone with Parkinson's disease: factors that contribute to distress. *International Journal of Geriatric Psychiatry, 11*, 263–268.

PATTIE, A.H. and GILLEARD, C.J. (1979). *Manual of the Clifton Assessment Procedures for the Elderly (CAPE).* Sevenoaks, Kent: Hodder and Stoughton Educational.

RING, H. (1993) Psychological and social problems of Parkinson's disease. *British Journal of Hospital Medicine, 49*, 111–116.

SEILER, S., PERLETH, B., GASSER, T., ULM, G., OERTEL, W.H. and ELLGRING, H. (1992) Partnership and depression in Parkinson's disease. *Behavioural Neurology, 5*, 75–81.

STOCK-WHITTIKER, D. (1985) *Using Groups to Help People*. London: Routledge.

Chapter 9

Coping and support networks for people with Parkinson's disease

Peter Hobson and Jolyon Meara

The physical impairments often associated with chronic illness are also likely to affect many other areas of a person's life – social relationships, social support, mental health and quality of life. Some or all of these are likely to be powerful predictors of how a patient or carer may adapt to an illness. The acceptance of a chronic illness for both patient and carer is, accordingly, potentially demanding, which may lead to the development emotional and psychological distress for both (Gilleard *et al.*, 1984; Whittick 1988; Baumgarten *et al.*, 1992; Saad *et al.*, 1995, Draper *et al.*, 1995). After the initial diagnosis of a serious illness, it is often the carers who are left to meet the emotional and physical needs of the patient. This assumes that the partner is able and willing to provide this support. The course and progression of an illness may make this role more difficult or even impossible to fulfil.

An individual's disposition to adjust to a chronic illness is likely to be influenced by many variables and the determination of these is of great importance in the management and understanding of any chronic illness, for patients, carers, medical professionals and service providers.

Coping with stress and learning how to reduce it involve both changing a stressful situation and managing or coming to terms with their thoughts or emotions. Thus, coping strategies may be categorized as problem-solving or emotion-focused coping (Folkman and Lazarus, 1990; Lazarus and Folkman, 1994). Problem-solving or problem-focused coping is where the individual moderates and adjusts to a stressful situation such as chronic illness and in a number of studies it has been found that it tends to be associated with a better prognosis. In contrast, emotion-focused coping, where the individual's attempt to manage the emotional consequences of a chronic illness or stressful situation, tends to be associated with a poor prognosis (Folkman and Lazarus, 1990; Lazarus and Folkman, 1994).

Informal social networks are often used by patients and carers when they are faced with problems, as a source of physical and emotional support, advice, help or buffering from their problems. Chronic illness will influence the ability of an individual's social network to provide care or help – formally or informally (Cohen, 1988; Wenger, 1991; Berkman *et al.*, 1992). These social networks may also act positively or negatively in terms of the access an individual may have to resources. It has been found that some social networks appear to be more able to adjust as support needs change (Walker *et al.*, 1977; Wenger, 1990). There is also evidence to suggest that certain support networks are associated with increased health risk factors, such as cardiovascular disease (Olsen, 1993).

One of the most frequently reported neurological disorders is Parkinson's disease (PD), which is estimated to affect around 100,000 people in the United Kingdom (see Chapter 1). In common with others with progressive chronic illnesses, PD patients rely on formal and informal services. With the onset of PD there will inevitably be demands placed upon not only the patient but also their partners, carers and family. Although caring for any disabled person is likely to pose a major challenge for the carer, there has been little research on the effects of caring for a person with PD. Consequently, in addition to the physical symptoms of PD, psychological and social factors are also likely to be of considerable influence in the management of PD. The role of coping strategies in PD has, however, been investigated in a few studies. MacCarthy and Brown (1989) investigated the psychological factors in PD and found that patients employed both problem-focused and emotion-focused coping strategies and that these were independent of depression. A study assessing coping, by Ehmann *et al.* (1990), found that active coping (where patients attempt to modify the problem by, for example, finding out more about it) appeared to offer protection from depressive symptoms, compared with those who employed avoidance coping strategies. A more recent study investigating coping in PD and stroke survivors, by Herrmann *et al.* (1997), found no significant correlates with depression or disease severity and the coping strategies employed by patients. They suggested that depression in PD is more likely to have physiological, rather than psychological, causes.

This chapter will draw on two studies investigating the influence of coping, social support and social networks on PD. The first will describe the coping strategies used by both patients and their carers and the influence of disease-specific, generic and health-related quality-of-life (HRQL) measures. The second study is an investigation of the role social networks play in the management of PD. It employs the support network typology developed by Wenger (1990), which has found a number of independent risk factors that are specific to five types of networks (see Appendix). This study will describe the support networks of PD patients, the predictive factors for use of formal services and the frequency of contact with family, friends and neighbours, by support network type.

Coping with Parkinson's disease: a patient and carer perspective

The patients in this study were all drawn from a community-based PD register held in North Wales. All fulfilled the Parkinson's Disease Brain Bank Clinical Criteria for probable PD (Gibb and Lees, 1988) and all were residing in their own homes and were identified as having a main carer.

Patients' physical, psychological and social functioning were assessed with the following self-report measures. Depression was assessed using the 15-item Geriatric Depression Scale (GDS-15), where a score of 5 or more indicates depression (Sheikh and Yesavage, 1986). Cognition was assessed with the CAMCOG examination, were a score of less than 80 (out of 106) indicates dementia (Roth *et al.*, 1986). The PD-specific Webster rating scale was used to determine the severity of PD: a score of 1–10 is early illness, 11–20 moderate illness and 21–30 severe illness (Webster, 1968). The 19-item Self-report Coping Questionnaire (Billings and Moos, 1981) consists of three main scales: active cognition, behavioural and avoidance coping. From these, two further scales are constructed, rating problem-focused and emotion-focused coping. The anglicized version of the 37-item self-report Parkinson's Disease Quality of Life (PDQL) questionnaire (De Boer *et al.*, 1996; Hobson *et al.*, 1998) was also mailed to patients. This scales provides an overall total score and four subscale scores (PD symptoms; systemic functioning; social functioning; emotional functioning), where higher scores indicate better HRQL. The GDS, Coping Questionnaire and PDQL are self-report instruments, while the other assessments were completed by the research team.

The carers in the study provided demographic details and completed the self-report GDS-15 and Coping Questionnaire.

Results

A total of 79 PD patients and their carers (Table 9.1) where identified. Carers were significantly younger, tended to be female, a spouse (68 of the 79) and were less depressed than patients (as measured by the GDS-15). The PDQL was returned by 61 of the 79 patients (77%); the results are shown in Table 9.2.

Table 9.1. *Patients' and carers' age, sex and GDS-15 scores (n = 79)*

	Mean (s.d.)	Range
Patients		
Age (years)	70.9 (9.5)	46–89
Gender (% female)	37%	
GDS-15 score	5.0 (3.5)	0–13
CAMCOG score	81.5 (13.4)	54–97
Webster score	16.4 (5.4)	6–28
Carers		
Age (years)	68.8 (9.5)*	44–87
Gender (% female)	63%*	
GDS-15 score	3.4 (2.7)*	0–14

* Non-parametric Wilcoxon *t*-test, *p* < 0.05.

Table 9.2. *Patients' scores on the PDQL and subscales (n = 60)*

	Mean (s.d.)
Age (years)	70.5 (9.8)
CAMCOG score	82.3 (12.9)
Webster score	16.2 (4.5)
GDS-15 score	5.4 (3.3)
PDQL total score	110.1 (8.6)
PDQL subscale scores	
PD symptoms	42.1 (11.8)
Systemic functioning	21.1 (6.1)
Social functioning	18.2 (8.4)
Emotional functioning	28.8 (8.6)

Table 9.3. *Mean (s.d.) scores on the Coping Questionnaire of patients and carers group (each n = 79)*

Coping item	Patient	Carer
Active cognitive	64.0 (24.5)	68.9 (21.2)
Behavioural	62.4 (27.1)	59.9 (23.7)
Avoidance	67.2 (22.1)	33.9 (21.9)*
Problem-focused	68.9 (28.0)	65.5 (24.5)
Emotion-focused	46.2 (14.3)	49.9 (13.2)

* Non-parametric Wilcoxon *t*-test *p* < 0.001.

The PD patients reported significantly more avoidance as a coping strategy than did carers (Table 9.3). Within the PD group, depression correlated with increased emotional coping and increased disease severity. Depression was also associated with higher PDQL total scores, social functioning and emotional functioning. Avoidance coping strategies employed by patients were associated with greater overall PDQL scores and with the subscales of PD symptoms and social functioning. However, depression was the most predictive variable associated with poorer social functioning. Problem-focused coping was found to be associated with PDQL total scores and PD symptoms.

Carers who reported more depression were found to use more avoidance coping strategies. Increased avoidance coping and depression were found with those caring for patients with poorer cognition. Better cognitive coping was predictive of less depression in carers.

Discussion

Coping strategies perform an important role in the patients' and carers' adaptation to and management of PD. The association between emotional coping and depressive symptoms is to be expected, given that patients used significantly more avoidance coping strategies than did carers. The PDQL results may indicate that patients use greater avoidance in a positive way, because they are aware that their illness is progressive with a poor prognosis.

Carers' ability to cope appears to exert considerable influence on their own and their partners' psychological wellbeing. In this study and others it was found that patients who were depressed were also significantly more likely to have depressed carers (Miller *et al.*, 1996; Meara *et al.*, 1999). There is also some evidence from O'Reilley *et al.* (1996) that those caring for people with PD have an increased likelihood of poor social, psychological and physical functioning. This study highlights the importance of collecting information on both patients and their carers, because both will influence the management of the disease.

In order to reduce the burden of PD for patients and carers, adequate provision of community services, psychological, pharmacological and alternative interventions needs to be explored through more focused research. The physical problems of the illness cannot be investigated in isolation from the psychosocial variables.

Support networks of elderly people with Parkinson's disease

A total of 110 subjects with PD participated in this study (mean age 72.3 years, s.d. 9.5). PD patients' network types were identified using the

Practitioner Assessment of Network Type (PANT). A brief description of the network types is given in the Appendix. The PANT instrument determines the person's network from eight questions and the highest score indicates the respondent's network type. The Webster scale, the CAMCOG and the GDS-15 were also completed. Carers were again identified, their demographic details recorded and they also completed the GDS-15.

Results

The demographic profiles, performance and clinical data for the patients are presented in Tables 9.4 and 9.5. Carers' age and GDS-15 scores are presented in Table 9.6. The individual network types, demographic profiles and their disease characteristics are given in Table 9.7.

The family-dependent support network. The family-dependent support network patients were found typically to be older, to have higher than average levels of disease severity and to have higher levels of cognitive impairment. This support network was predictive of specialist consultant care, district nurse inputs and occupational therapy inputs (Table 9.8). In this network, around 50% of the patients were living with and being cared for by a family member (usually female); it appears that this high level of family caring increases carer depression.

Locally integrated support network. The patients in this network were younger, their PD was not as severe and generally their cognitive functioning was better than that of patients in the other networks. Since this network is associated with close relationships with local family, friends, neighbours and high community involvement, these patients consequently have a number of sources from which to seek help. Overall, patients and carers in this network had the lowest levels of reported depressive symptoms.

Locally self-contained support network. Most help here was provided by a carer rather than by more formal services. This high level of carer involvement, however, results in high levels of depression in both patients and carers, which is commonly reported in other chronic conditions where carers are attempting to provide care alone. It is also important to note that, with increasing dependency and limited contacts with friends, family or neighbours, patients in this network are more likely to move to residential care in the absence of an informal carer.

The wider community-focused support network. The patients here had lower levels of reported disability and cognitive impairment. This network was the smallest. Since these patients do not have a large pool of local family, friends or neighbours from which to seek help, as they become more dependent they either move into residential accommodation or move closer to, for example, their families.

Table 9.4. *Demographic profile of patients (n =110)*

	Number	%
Gender (female)	47	42.7%
Residential status:		
living alone	20	18.2%
living with partner	80	72.7%
living with family	10	9.1%
Marital status:		
single	1	0.9%
married	80	72.2%
divorced/separated	6	5.4%
widowed	23	20.9%

Table 9.5. *Disease characteristics (n = 110)*

	Mean (s.d.)	Median
Age at onset of PD (years)	64.9 (11.7)	67
Duration of PD (years)	7.3 (6.9)	5
Webster score	15.9 (5.2)	15
CAMCOG score	82.3 (13.6)	85
GDS-15 scroe	5.4 (3.2)	5
Disability score	2.8 (1.1)	3

Table 9.6. *Carer's age and depression scores (n = 79)*

	Mean (s.d.)	Median
Age	69.7 (9.4)	71
GDS-15	3.5 (3.3)	2

Table 9.7. *Sociodemographic and disease characteristics by network types*

	Family-dependent (n = 16)	Locally integrated (n = 35)	Local self-contained (n = 33)	Wider community (n = 11)	Private (n = 15)
Mean age (years)	72.2	67.9	72.7	79.2	76.4
Percentage female	37%	54%	42%	27%	33%
Mean Webster score	16.5	14.9	15.3	14.6	20.1
Mean GDS-15 score	5.9	4.4	6.1	5.7	6.1
Mean CAMCOG score	78.6	86.7	81.9	87.1	72.1

Table 9.8. Service utilization frequencies in a 12-month period by support network type

	Family-dependent (n = 16, 14%)		Locally integrated (n = 35, 32%)		Local self-contained (n = 33, 30%)		Wider community (n = 11, 10%)		Private restricted (n = 15, 14%)	
Occupational therapy	8	(50%)	8	(23%)	9	(27%)	3	(27%)	4	(26%)
Physiotherapy	6	(37%)	11	(31%)	10	(30%)	2	(18%)	4	(29%)
Social worker	1	(6%)	3	(9%)	6	(18%)	1	(9%)	1	(7%)
Speech therapist	7	(44%)	11	(31%)	13	(39%)	3	(27%)	4	(26%)
Care attendant	1	(6%)	9	(26%)	3	(9%)	3	(27%)	4	(26%)
District nurse	6	(37%)	1	(3%)	4	(12%)	2	(18%)	5	(33%)
General practitioner	16	(100%)	33	(91%)	30	(91%)	11	(100%)	11	(73%)
Consultant	15	(94%)	19	(54%)	23	(70%)	7	(64%)	6	(40%)
Mow	0		1	(3%)	2	(6%)	3	(27%)	1	(7%)
Health visitor	0		0		0	(12%)	0		1	(7%)

Private restricted support network. The patients and carers in this group had much higher reported levels of depressive symptoms, and the patients had more severe disease symptoms and cognitive impairments compared with the other networks. A distinctive feature of this network is the low level of contacts with friends or family. An important finding was that although they had the highest reported levels of disability, cognitive impairment and depression, their uptake of more formal services did not differ considerably from that of the other networks. Another study of elderly persons found that the individuals in this type of network were often admitted to hospital for social reasons and were reluctant to report medical problems to their general practitioner (Wenger, 1990).

Discussion

This study raises the important role that family, friends or neighbours have to play in the support of an individual with PD. The support networks of PD patients described here significantly influenced the uptake of formal services and the amount and type of informal support from family or friends. It is important to understand that these networks are not fixed and individuals may move from one network to another because of illness or death of a partner or the carer's inability to cope with the progression of the illness. The assessment of support networks allows clinicians to have a greater understanding of the psychological and social processes involved in living with an illness such as PD. Instruments such as the PANT will be useful in identifying those who are at risk and may well assist in the design of more appropriate services. It also highlights the need that treating only the physical symptoms of PD patients is not sufficient, given the other psychological processes that influence the management of PD.

Conclusions

These studies examined the coping and social support network types of elderly PD patients and their carers, all of whom were residing in the community. More focused research is still needed to establish whether the needs and expectations of carers of PD patients are being met. We need to listen to both patients and carers to organise interventions that will be of value to them. The use of instruments like the PANT network typology needs to be evaluated in clinical practice to determine how effective they are in identifying those at risk and in the design of appropriate interventions.

Appendix. Network typology

Family-dependent support network

Families-centred, where the majority of support needs are met usually by an adult child, with little community involvement. Persons in this network tend to be widowed, elderly and have poorer health compared with the other networks.

Locally integrated support network

These individuals are characterized by their long-term residence in an area, which results in close ties with family, friends, neighbours and high levels of community involvement.

Local self-contained support network

The persons in this network tend to be more reserved and insular and are typified by having infrequent contacts with friends, neighbours and families.

Wider community-focused support network

The individuals in this network are often associated with middle-class retirement migration and are frequently involved in voluntary or community organizations. They have active relationships with relatives (usually their children), who often live a considerable distance away. A close-knit circle of friends rather than neighbours provides support in this network.

Private restricted support network

Often the individuals in this network have little or no community involvement, few family or friends locally, are socially isolated and independent.

References

BAUMGARTEN, M., BATTISTA, R.N., INFANTE-RIVARD, C. and HANLEY, J.A. (1992) The psychological and physical health of family members caring for persons with dementia. *Journal of Clinical Epidemiology, 42,* 61–70.

BERKMAN, L.F., OXMAN, T.E. and SEEMAN, T.E. (1992) Social networks and social support among the elderly: assessment issues. In R.B. Wallace and R.F. Woolson (Eds) *The Epidemiologic Study of the Elderly.* Oxford.

BILLINGS, A.G. and MOOS, R.H. (1981) The role of coping responses and social resources in attenuating the stress of life events. *Journal of Behavioral Medicine, 4,* 139–157.

COHEN, S. (1988) Psychosocial models of the role of social support in the etiology of physical disease. *Health Psychology, 7,* 269–297.

DE BOER, A.G.E.M., WIJKER, W., SPEELMAN, J.D. and DE HAES, J.C.J.M. (1996) Quality of life in patients with Parkinson's disease: development of a questionnaire. *Journal of Neurology, Neurosurgery and Psychiatry*, *61*, 70–74.

DRAPER, B.M., POULOS, R.G. and EHRLICH, F. (1995) Risk factors for stress in elderly caregivers. *International Journal of Geriatric Psychiatry*, *11*, 227–237.

EHMANN, T.S., BENINGER, R.J., GAWEL, M.J. and RIOPELLE, R.J. (1990) Coping, social support and depressive symptoms in Parkinson's disease. *Journal of Geriatric Psychiatry and Neurology*, *3*, 85–90.

FOLKMAN, S. and LAZARUS, R.S. (1990) An analysis of coping in a middle aged community sample. *Journal of Health and Social Behaviour*, *21*, 219–239.

GIBB, W.R.G. and LEES, A.J. (1988) The relevance of the Lewy body to the pathogenesis of idiopathic Parkinson's disease. *Journal of Neurology, Neurosurgery and Psychiatry*, *51*, 745–752.

GILLEARD, C.J., GILLEARD, E., GLEDHILL, K. and WHITTICK, J.E. (1984) Caring for elderly mentally infirm at home: a survey of the supporters. *Journal of Epidemiology and Community Health*, *38*, 319–325.

HERRMANN, M., FREYHOLDT, U., FUCHS, G. and WALLESCH, C.-W. (1997) Coping with chronic impairment: a contrastive analysis of Parkinson's disease and stroke. *Disability and Rehabilitation*, *19*, 6–12.

HOBSON, J.P., HOLDEN, A. and MEARA, R.J. (1999) Measuring the impact of Parkinson's disease with the Parkinson's Disease Quality of Life questionnaire (PDQL). *Age and Ageing* (in press).

LAZARUS, R.S. and FOLKMAN, S. (1994) *Stress Appraisal and Coping*. New York: Springer.

MacCARTHY, B. and BROWN, R. (1989) Psychosocial factors in Parkinson's disease. *British Journal of Clinical Psychology*, *28*, 41–52.

MEARA, R.J., MITCHELMORE, E. and HOBSON, J.P. (1999) Use of the GDS-15 as a screening instrument for depressive symptomatology in Parkinson's disease sufferers and their carers: a community-based study. *Age and Ageing*, *28*, 35–38.

MILLER, E., BERRIOS, G.E. and POLITYNSKA, B.E. (1996) Caring for someone with Parkinson's disease: factors that contribute to distress. *International Journal of Geriatric Psychiatry*, *11*, 263–268.

OLSEN, O. (1993) Impact of social network on cardiovascular mortality in middle aged Danish men. *Journal of Epidemiology and Community Health*, *47*, 176–180.

O'REILLY, F., FINNAN, F., ALLWRIGHT, S., SMITH, G.D. and BEN-SHLOMO, Y. (1996) The effects of caring for a spouse with Parkinson's disease on social, psychological and physical well-being. *British Journal of General Practice*, *46*, 507–512.

ROTH, M., TYM, E., MOUNTJOY, C.Q., HUPPERT, F.A., HENDRIE, H., VERMA, S. and GODDARD, R. (1986) CAMDEX: a standardised instrument for the diagnosis of mental disorder in the elderly with special reference to elderly detection of dementia. *British Journal of Psychiatry*, *149*, 698–709.

SAAD, K., HARTMAN, C., BALLARD, C., KURIAN, M. and GRAHAM, C. (1995) Coping by the carers of dementia sufferers. *Age and Ageing*, *24*, 495–498.

SHEIKH, J.A. and YESAVAGE, J.A. (1986) Geriatric Depression Scale (GDS): recent findings and development of a shorter version. In T.L. Brink (Ed.) *Clinical Gerontology: A Guide to Assessment and Intervention*. New York: Howarth Press.

WALKER, K.N., MCBRIDE, A. and VACHAR, M.L.S. (1977) Social support networks and the crisis of bereavement. *Social Science Medicine, 11*, 35–44.

WEBSTER, D.D. (1968) Critical analysis of the disability in Parkinson's disease. *Modern Treatment, 5*, 87–85.

WENGER, G.C. (1990) Change and adaptation in informal support networks of elderly people in Wales 1979–1987. *Journal of Aging Studies, 5*, 147–162.

WENGER, G.C. (1991) A network typology: from theory to practice. *Journal of Aging Studies, 5*, 147–162.

WENGER, C.G. (1994) Support networks and dementia. *International Journal of Geriatric Psychiatry, 9*, 181–194.

WHITTICK, J.E. (1988) Dementia and mental handicap: emotional distress in supporters. *British Journal of Clinical Psychology, 27*, 167–172.

Chapter 10

Involving carers in communication groups for people with Parkinson's disease

Caroline Haw, Peter Trewhitt, Margaret Boddy and Jane Evans

The study by Oxtoby (1982) into the social needs of people with Parkinson's disease (PD) found that nearly half of them had some difficulty with their speech. Furthermore, a high proportion of PD sufferers do not receive speech and language therapy (Oxtoby, 1982; Mutch *et al.*, 1986), despite the fact that the positive effects of speech and language therapy in PD have been reported (Scott and Caird, 1981, 1983; Robertson and Thompson 1984; Johnson and Pring, 1990; de Angelis *et al.*, 1997).

The broader communication difficulties in PD have received little attention to date. It has been found that because of characteristic poor facial expression, professionals often respond to people with PD as if they were of low intelligence or depressed (Pentland *et al.*, 1988). Lister (1994) reported a self-help programme making use of a video and booklet to help improve facial animation. As Lister notes, those with reduced facial expression, while experiencing difficulties in communication, do not always have problems with their speech and are often not referred to speech and language therapy. However, having a 'mask-like expression' can have devastating effects on the person's quality of life.

The involvement of carers in therapy

The value of carers assisting with follow-up of speech and language therapy has been demonstrated in a few studies (e.g. Allen, 1970; Crozier and Hammill, 1988), but only one study has reported the inclusion of carers in the therapy process itself (Boddy *et al.*, 1992). Placing the communication problem solely with the client does not take into account the two-way nature of communication.

A group intervention with elderly people in nursing homes by Jordan *et al.* (1993) involved carers in the evaluation of individuals' 'communicative competence'. Carers were asked to rate the participants' ability to communicate in a variety of situations, but they were not asked to rate their own ability to communicate with the person. Thus, while this study went some way towards a broader view of communication, it did not address the question of sharing the responsibility for communication.

The bulk of the literature found relating to carers is concerned with the carers of people with dementia, such as Alzheimer's disease (AD). Knight (1992) proposed that 'the profile of people caring for AD sufferers is likely to be the same as for any other group of impaired elderly'. Dura *et al.*'s (1990) study comparing carers of people with AD with carers of people with PD reported that they did not differ significantly on measures of distress. They concluded that research with carers of people with AD could be extended to carers of people with PD. Knight (1992) reported that carers who received more social support had lower levels of stress. It would appear that, despite the role carers play in the management of PD, more information is needed to determine the types of support they require. None of the literature surveyed dealt with the needs of clients and carers together.

Zarit *et al.* (1987) compared two different interventions with carers supporting people with dementia and found no significant differences between a support group approach and an individual family counselling approach. They mentioned that 'significant numbers of caregivers do not believe management of their stress to be an appropriate or potentially effective intervention'. Even though therapists felt that carers were showing considerable change, carers' final evaluations did not reflect this. Haley *et al.* (1987) also compared different approaches to group intervention with carers' support groups, support and skills training groups and a waiting list control group, and found no differences between them. Chiverton and Caine's (1989) investigation of an educational programme for carers of people with AD, which measured coping, found a significant difference between the group receiving the educational programme and the control group. In particular, they identified the areas of 'therapeutic competence', 'knowledge' and 'emotional competence' as having changed. The authors stated that this type of approach is shown to have good short-term effects, but did not make any claims for its long-term benefits.

In conclusion, there is some evidence that working with carers in other client groups is beneficial. However, it is not clear how this can be applied in relation to PD, since much of the previous research with carers has tended to focus on them as a separate group from the clients.

Survey of speech and language therapists

In order to evaluate the role carers play in therapeutic groups, we asked therapists what they thought about working with this client group and what approaches they used with carers. We sent a questionnaire to therapists drawn from Sheffield and neighbouring health trusts. Forty-two therapists returned the questionnaire. Their experience of working with PD clients ranged from 1 to 32 years. The majority of respondents (33/42) reported that they worked with carers as part of their therapy process, because it was supportive for the client. Less carer involvement was found to be associated with less experienced therapists.

Involving carers in groups – the rationale

There are several reasons why we believed it to be important to evaluate ways of involving carers in communication therapy groups. First, the practice of therapists indicates that carers are important to the therapy process. Secondly, the value of carers, their role as partners in the multidisciplinary team and their needs as a group have long been recognized. Lastly, there is a need to establish how best to involve carers in communication therapy groups in a way that is of benefit to themselves, the clients and, indeed, the therapists. The benefits for clients may be improved communication with their carers, possibly associated with clearer speech. For carers, benefits may be improved communication with their partner, and support in terms of meeting other carers and information about PD and communication.

A study of group communication therapy with carers

Three groups were established, and compared in terms of efficacy. The first was the 'communication group'. Clients and carers stayed together for the whole session, working exclusively on communication (including non-verbal) activities.

The 'support group' entailed social contact with other carers, information and emotional support. Clients and carers remained separate for the whole session, clients working on communication and carers taking part in both communication and support-oriented activities. We decided to impose some structure on the carers' support group so that specific topics could be addressed, as well as free-flowing discussion.

In the 'mixed groups', clients and carers spent the first hour of the session working together on communication-related activities. After a break, clients worked together on communication, while carers met separately for their own support group, as above.

Inclusion for the groups was determined by the following criteria: the presence of a carer, motivation of a client to participate; communication concerns, and adequate cognitive skills. We hypothesized that when carers were involved in both the communication activities and their own carers' group, both clients and carers would benefit most.

Method

As no available standardized assessments were appropriate, we designed our own. Comparing three similar types of intervention required an evaluation procedure which was sensitive to small but potentially significant changes.

Assessments took the form of video recordings and questionnaires (available from the authors), which were completed by both clients and carers. For the communication assessment, key areas covered were: speech, conversational communication, body language and communication changes since diagnosis of PD. For the support assessment, key areas were information, meeting other carers and how carers manage. For the video recordings, each couple was recorded before and after the group interventions. The client was asked to describe a complex picture to the carer and to have a conversation. These recordings were analysed by two therapists, one involved in the groups and one not involved with PD work at all. Speech characteristics and body language on the recordings were rated.

An evaluation questionnaire administered after the interventions dealt with both process (what happened) and participants' perceptions of that process (what people thought of what happened). Clients, carers and therapists completed the questionnaire independently.

Two experienced therapists ran each of the groups with the assistance of one inexperienced therapist (so that the third therapist could be 'lead therapist' in later groups).

The communication programme comprised the following activities:

* group cohesiveness (saying names, what you've learned so far, etc.);
* group discussion (e.g. sharing histories of PD);
* information (e.g. what goes wrong with speech in PD?)
* communication issues (e.g. what helps and what hinders communication);
* communication tasks/activities (e.g. describing line drawings)
* speech work (e.g. volume).

The support programme comprised:

* sharing experiences;
* information about communication;
* information about resources, from both therapists and other carers;
* developing strategies (e.g. relaxation techniques).

The groups ran once a week for two hours over a period of six weeks. Our plan was to recruit 36 PD clients, each with an accompanying carer. Clients and their carers were recruited via a variety of channels, including clinical referrals and the local branch of the Parkinson's Disease Society, via its newsletter. In the event, because of low referral rates, the project had to be extended and groups were also run in neighbouring health trusts under the supervision of the project therapists.

Results

In total 22 clients (12 men and 10 women) and their carers were recruited. Their ages ranged from 53 to 72. Onset of PD was from 2 years to about 20 years previously. No attempt was made to rate the severity of PD. The carers tended to be female. A sibling cared for one client and two had privately financed carers; all other carers were the spouse of the client.

Overall, the questionnaires showed that all participants benefited from the group interventions. However, there was no statistically significant difference between the mixed and communication group results. There were insufficient data to include the support group format in the statistical comparisons. Throughout the project, the support group format (client and carers spending all the group time apart) was the most difficult to administer and was least liked by participants and therapists.

The video recordings of clients' communication, rated by the therapists, showed general improvements (Table 10.1).

Findings from the evaluation questionnaires strongly indicated a preference from both clients and carers for the mixed group format.

Table 10.1. *Average difference in therapists' ratings of video-recordings*

	Average difference	T score	n
Articulation	+0.05	25	10
Volume	+0.55	17.5	12
Speed	+0.65	60	19
Intonation	+1.80*	1	15
Intelligibility	+0.20	39	14
Facial expression	-0.25	30.5	12
Body and hands	+0.20	30	11
Body language	+1.75*	6	3

*$p < 0.05$ (two-tailed Wilcoxon's signed rank test).

Conclusions

The difficulties of communication in PD impinge on every aspect of the individual's life and as a result therapists must try to reflect this in the types of intervention which they offer to people with PD and their carers. The therapy approach needs to take into account how couples are interacting and to help them develop skills to enable them to manage communication. The use of video recordings in identifying communication strategies is potentially a useful clinical tool – more research is needed in this area. This approach will also necessitate active involvement of carers in speech and language therapy, where they feel they become a partner, rather than a passive observer, in the therapeutic process. Carers in our study seemed to welcome the opportunity to meet regularly in a small, well supported group.

Of the three group formats explored, the support group was not liked by therapists or participants. It was not possible to confirm that the mixed group was more effective than the communication group; on some evaluations one group showed a tendency to be more effective and for other evaluations the other group. However, both clients and carers indicated a preference for a group format that involves both time apart addressing carers' issues, as well as time with clients and carers working together.

We feel that this study has highlighted the potential contribution carers have to make to the management of PD.

Recommendations

- Speech and language therapy should be holistic in its approach to communication in PD, and appropriate evaluation should focus upon strategies for coping with the variability of communication difficulties faced by PD patients and their carers.
- This approach to therapy needs to develop a partnership with clients and their carers. Carers should have greater access to support.

References

ALLEN, C. (1970) Treatment of non fluent speech resulting from neurological disease – treatment of dysarthria. *British Journal of Disorders of Communication*, 5, 3.

BODDY, M., EVANS, J. and LLOYD, C. (1992) Group communication – meeting the needs of clients and carers. *Bulletin of the College of Speech and Language Therapists*, 48, 6–7.

CHIVERTON, P. and CAINE, E.D. (1989) Education to assist spouses in coping with Alzheimer's disease. A controlled trial. *Journal of the American Geriatrics Society*, 37, 593–598.

CROZIER, E. and HAMMILL, R. (1988) The benefits of combining speech and music therapy. *Speech Therapy in Practice*, November 1988.

DE ANGELIS, E.C., MOURAC, L.F., FERRAZ, H.B., BENLAU, M.S., PONTEES, P.A. and ANDRADE, L.A. (1997) Effect of voice rehabilitation on oral communication of Parkinson's disease patients. *Acta Neurologica Scandinavica*, 96, 199 – 205.

DURA, J.R., HAYWOOD-NILER, M.A. and KILCOTT-Glasser, J.K. (1990) Spousal caregivers of persons with Alzheimer's and Parkinson's disease dementia: a preliminary comparison. *Gerontologist*, 303, 332.

HALEY, W.E., LEVINE, S.G. and BROWN, S.L. (1987) Experimental evaluation of the effectiveness of group intervention for dementia caregivers. *Gerontologist*, 27, 377–383.

JOHNSON, J.A. and PRING, T.R. (1990) Speech therapy and Parkinson's disease: a review and further data. *British Journal of Disorders of Communication*, 25, 183–194.

JORDAN, F.M., WORRALL, L.E., HICKSON, L.M.H. and DODD, B.J. (1993) The evaluation of intervention programmes for communicatively impaired elderly people. *European Journal of Disorders of Communication*, 28, 63–85.

KNIGHT, H.G. (1992) *The Neuropsychology of Degenerative Brain Disease.* Hillsdale, NJ: Lawrence Erlbaum.

LISTER, I. (1994) Face to face with Parkinson's. *Therapy Weekly*, 20, 9.

MUTCH, W.J., STRUDWICK, A., SISAR, R.K. and DOWNIE, A.W. (1986) Parkinson's disease: disability, review and management. *British Medical Journal*, 293, 675–677.

OXTOBY, M. (1982) *Parkinson's Disease Patients and Their Social Needs.* London: Parkinson's Disease Society.

PENTLAND, B., GRAY, J.M., RIDDLE, W.J.R. and PITCAIRN, T.K. (1988) The effects of reduced non-verbal communication in Parkinson's disease. *British Journal of Disorders of Communication*, 23, 31–34.

ROBERTSON, S. and THOMSON, F. (1984) Speech therapy in Parkinson's disease: a study of the efficacy and long term effects of intensive treatment. *British Journal of Disorders of Communication*, 19, 213–224.

SCOTT, S. and CAIRD, F. (1981) Speech therapy for patients with Parkinson's disease. *British Medical Journal*, 283, 1088.

SCOTT, S. and CAIRD, F. (1983) Speech therapy for Parkinson's disease. *Journal of Neurology, Neurosurgery and Psychiatry*, 4, 140–144.

ZARIT, S.H., ANTHONY, C.R. and BOUTSELIS, M. (1987) Interventions with caregivers of dementia patients: comparison of two approaches. *Psychology and Ageing*, 2, 225–232.

Chapter 11

Communication in Parkinson's disease with cognitive impairment: a diagnostic and therapeutic medium?

Ruth Lesser and Anne Whitworth

There has been little published research on the communication difficulties experienced by people with Parkinson's disease (PD) who have concomitant cognitive impairment. Cognitive impairment in conjunction with PD is not uncommon, particularly in those who are elderly. Indeed, the impairment may be so severe in up to one in five PD patients as to be classed as dementia (Brown and Marsden, 1984). The impact of cognitive impairment on people with PD and their families can be profound, especially with respect to difficulties in communication on the quality of life. One of the motivations for the present research was to explore these communication difficulties, and in particular to find out how relatives and other carers cope with them.

The immediate spur to the research was the recent development of techniques, on the one hand, of examining language processing by applying psycholinguistic theory and, on the other hand, of analysing everyday communication through 'conversation analysis'. These two methods are becoming widely used in the assessment of people with aphasia, the acquired language disorder which can follow brain damage (Lesser and Milroy, 1993). They have so far not been applied to any extent in the study of dementia, although a few studies of dementia of the Alzheimer type (DAT) have used information from conversations to monitor interaction and change, as well as the influence of different conversational partners on communication (Ripich *et al.*, 1991; Hamilton, 1994; Ramanathan, 1997).

A second motivation for the present study was the potential of conversation analysis for therapeutic intervention. Education of carers (both family members and professional personnel) on how to take an active part in enhancing interaction is central to the management of communication difficulties in people with cognitive impairment. Facilitating communication has usually involved strategies for the carer to integrate into daily situations, to avoid or manage difficulties in communication. Comprehensive lists of strategies can be found in the literature (e.g. Bayles and Tomoeda, 1993). The advice given on strategies that carers may use is both of a non-linguistic nature as well as linguistically specific and related to modifying the conversational partner's language input. An example of the non-linguistic advice offered would be: 'Reduce conflicting stimuli, such as television and radio noise, when talking, in order to maximize concentration and minimize hearing difficulties'. An example of the linguistic advice would be: 'Use questions where only *yes* or *no* is the required answer, in order to reduce the need for your partner to formulate sentences, thereby increasing the likelihood of a response'. Such strategies have generally been instigated by the clinician and not driven by the individual client or carer, with the result that they are of a general nature rather than being necessarily appropriate to each individual.

Such teaching of general strategies can be problematic, therefore, if therapeutic intervention does not take into account the knowledge and skill that the conversational partner has already developed. Research has shown that spouses do accommodate spontaneously to the conversational needs of their impaired partners, a factor which is important for therapists to take into consideration. Kemper *et al.* (1994) demonstrated that spouses adopted a facilitating 'specialized speech register' and modified their way of speaking when communicating with people with DAT. In contrast, Penn (1985) found that some carers of people with aphasia had strategies which were rated as inappropriate, suggesting that it may be equally important to assist carers in 'undoing' strategies. Such findings highlight the importance of undertaking a detailed assessment in order to identify spontaneously developed strategies. Furthermore, Perkins (1995) has shown that aphasic people and their conversational partners develop different strategies to deal with the same communication difficulties, which reinforces the importance of engaging the carer in planning any intervention.

One of the core features of dementia of the Lewy body type (DLB) is the incidence of spontaneous motor features of Parkinsonism, which is indicative of subcortical involvement (in addition to features of DLB which could relate to cortical influences). With the common underlying pathology of PD and DLB, a closer relationship between these disease entities has been suggested (Perry *et al.*, 1995). This places DLB on a subcortical–cortical disease continuum with PD, with both sharing common pathogenic mechanisms where dementia subsequently develops. The existence of different subtypes of dementia in people with PD suggests a heterogeneous group of symptoms that will require different medical management as well as focused counselling and education of carers. The fluctuating cognition in DLB is anecdotally reflected in interruptions during conversation, where the individual fails to finish a sentence, and may or may not resume the topic after a short interval. It was therefore considered that a detailed examination of conversations might be of some assistance in helping to support a diagnosis of probable DLB (rather than DAT) in PD patients who have dementia.

Participants

The approach applied in this research was to undertake a comprehensive, in-depth study of a few people, rather than examine a large number superficially. The analysis was therefore predominantly qualitative rather than quantitative. Six people, who met the criterion of having frequent contact with a cooperative relative, were referred to the study with idiopathic PD with 'subcortical dementia' without symptoms of DLB (PD+SC), using the criteria for subcortical impairment set out by Cummings (1986). All patients reported memory deficits and slowness in thinking which significantly interfered with daily living, and performed below the normal level on tests of verbal fluency (naming items within a category, such as 'animals'). All were men. They ranged in age from 63 to 84 years (mean 72), with a range of scores on the Mini-Mental State Examination (MMSE) (Folstein *et al.*, 1975) from 25 to 30 (mean 27.5).

A second group with cooperative relatives comprised six people with idiopathic PD and a putative diagnosis of mild–moderate DLB (PD +DLB) using the criteria of McKeith *et al.* (1996). Three were men, three women. Their ages ranged from 59 to 79 years (mean 68), and their MMSE scores ranged from 20 to 27 (mean 23.8).

Relatives of both groups (10 spouses, one son and one daughter) formed the control group for formal psycholinguistic and phonetic tests, as well as being the conversational partners. Comparative data were also available from a concurrent study (Perkins *et al.*, 1996) on a further eight patients without PD (four with putative DLB, four with putative DAT). All these were women, with mean ages of 81 and 86 years and mean MMSE scores of 23 and 20, respectively.

Method

In order to characterize the communicative abilities of the two groups of people with PD, an investigation of their language, speech and memory abilities was undertaken using a battery of assessments of two kinds: formal ones, which measured psycholinguistic and phonetic processing; and informal (although structured) ones, which examined everyday communication.

The first were drawn from standard measures used in the study of aphasia and dementia, and assessed the ability to understand and produce single words and sentences, remember stories and recall a sequence of spoken nouns and verbs through pointing to pictures which represented them. Specifically, the ability to process, in comprehension and in production, semantic information (i.e. the meaning of words and sentences) and syntax (i.e. grammar) was examined through tests from Kay *et al.* (1992), Howard and Patterson (1992), Whitworth (1996) and Bishop (1982). The ability to recall stories, with and without a delay, was assessed through a test from Bayles and Tomoeda (1993). Phonetic processing was examined through use of the *'Shortened list of intelligibility'* (modified from Kent *et al.*, 1989), and by asking the patients to read aloud a passage of dialogue and produce sentences with contrasting stress and intonation.

For the second, informal kind of assessments, measures of everyday communication were devised by the researchers. These consisted of a 41-item questionnaire for the relatives about their conversations with the PD patients (including changes in their communicative situations following onset of the cognitive difficulties) and the analysis of a 10-minute conversation between them. This was tape-recorded in their own homes without the researchers present. This procedure, entitled Conversation Analysis Profile for People with Cognitive Impairment (CAPPCI) (Perkins *et al.*, 1997), selected three key areas of conversational management for analysis: turn-taking skills; the ability to repair disruptions brought about by communication difficulties; and the management of topics of conversation. These categories were also used in the analysis of the tape-recordings. This enabled a comparison to be made between the relatives' reports on how these aspects of conversation were handled and observation of them in the actual sample taken.

In addition to recording the frequency with which lapses in the PD person's conversational management occurred, the questionnaire also explored what the relatives' responses were to them, what happened following these responses, and the extent to which the relatives felt that these lapses constituted a problem for them. There were also questions, using the same format, which concerned: memory and attention; language difficulties such as word-finding delays and comprehension problems; articulation and prosody; and daily and weekly cognitive fluctuations in the patient. The questionnaire also elicited information on what had changed in respect of communication since the onset of PD. These questions related to personal style of communication, restrictions on interactions in respect of people, situations and topics, non-verbal communication and hearing.

In summary, the CAPPCI aimed:

- to establish the relatives' perceptions of the conversational abilities of their PD partners;
- to capture the relationship between these perceptions and what actually occurred in a sample of conversation;
- to determine what strategies were being employed and their success;
- to ascertain the extent to which the relative considered the reported behaviours constituted a problem;
- to assess changes from premorbid styles and opportunities for interaction.

Results

Psycholinguistic and phonetic

Semantic abilities at the single-word level were intact for both PD groups and did not distinguish between them. Sentence-processing abilities (both production and comprehension), however, did discriminate between the two: abilities were significantly more impaired in PD+DLB participants than in those with PD+SC. The greater complexity of the task may have made it harder for the PD+DLB group, whose MMSE scores were lower. There was also some evidence to suggest that a mild semantic impairment in the latter group may have contributed to difficulties in sentence processing. Episodic memory, as tested through story retelling, was impaired in some participants from both groups, with performance being significantly more impaired on delayed retelling in PD+DLB. Delayed recall may become more impaired when cortical involvement is present, as in the latter group. Short-term memory, as tested through ability to match heard pseudo-sentences (noun–verb sequences) to picture arrays, discriminated between the two PD groups: abilities were impaired in PD+DLB participants but not in the PD+SC group. This may be one explanation for the sentence-processing impairments of some of the participants. It was also noted that visual perceptual difficulties occurred more frequently in the PD+DLB group than in the PD+SC group.

Comparisons with the non-PD groups in the parallel Perkins *et al.* study (matched for MMSE scores to the PD+DLB group, although older) indicated a difference between the non-PD DLB and the PD+DLB participants. The PD+DLB group had less semantic involvement and less visual perceptual impairment. This result is confounded, however, by the greater age of the non-PD groups. All of the participants with non-PD DAT had a semantic impairment and two had a visual processing impairment, suggesting a similar pattern of performance to the non-PD DLB group.

Auditory analyses of a range of phonetic parameters confirmed that all the PD speakers showed to a greater or lesser extent the characteristics which are known to be typical of such speakers (e.g. flat intonation and monotonous rhythm). All had good levels of intelligibility, however, and no speech parameters discriminated between the two PD groups.

CAPPCI and conversations

The conversational profiles on the CAPPCI of all the PD participants revealed compromised communicative and interactional abilities, with each showing a unique pattern of preserved and impaired conversational abilities. Impairments which are not usually associated with PD were reported and observed. These occurred in the initiation of conversation, in taking turns to speak and in 'managing' topics (i.e. in initiating topics, maintaining them and making clear what or who words like 'he' and 'they' refer to). There were delays and failures in responding, and reliance on minimal acknowledgements such as 'u-huh', 'hmn', 'yes'. Difficulties in repairing trouble spots during conversation were less of a problem overall, but were still present in certain individuals.

The degree to which carers perceived areas of difficulty in conversation to be problematic was lower than would be expected from the severity of the impairments examined. Interestingly, and unexpectedly, it was the conversational features which were perceived to be the most problematic to carers, more so than factors that are more apparently related to speech, language or memory deficits, as reported in the other sections of the interview in the CAPPCI.

There was high agreement (67.5%) between the patterns reported by the carers in both groups and the analyses of conversational data from the tape-recorded samples, suggesting that the carers were often highly accurate in reporting conversational abilities. Carers were also shown to develop spontaneously a large number of strategies in order to manage the communication changes. These could be divided into five broad categories: facilitatory (59.2%), confrontational (12.6%), acceptance (22.0%), avoidance (5.2%) and emotive responses (1.0%). The fact that the majority were facilitatory highlights the sensitivity of carers to modifying both input and output during conversation, a factor that has implications for working with carers. A complex relationship was present, however, between the strategies employed by the carers, the individuals' deficits and the carers' perceptions of these deficits as problematic. Moreover, the degree to which interactional styles and social opportunities were reported as changed since the onset of cognitive difficulties showed wide variability, with some individuals experiencing major changes in the style and context of their interactions. All these findings confirm the need for a highly individualized approach in intervention, in preference to clinicians recommending a more general set of strategies.

Conclusions

The study has shown the value of applying psycholinguistic and conversation analyses to people with PD and cognitive impairment, both in confirming diagnostic categories and in drawing implications for intervention. The psycholinguistic results showed different patterns in the PD+SC group and the PD+DLB group, with performance in three areas discriminating between the two groups. Some caution, however, needs to be exercised in the interpretation of these results, because of both methodological factors and the little known nature of DLB. The greater impairment of the PD+DLB group on selective measures (sentence processing, delayed recall and short-term memory) may have been associated with their lower scores on the MMSE test of general cognitive abilities. It may be that these measures taxed general cognitive abilities to a greater extent than the psycholinguistic and other measures which did not differentiate between the groups. The small number of subjects in the present study also restricts the generalizations which can be made about the use of psycholinguistic measures in the differentiation of the two groups. The results were further confounded by the use of a number of tests which used pictures, and the observation of visual difficulties in picture processing which may have accounted for the lower scores of the PD+DLB group. It was not possible from the data to associate this with the visual hallucinations reported by the carers in some of the PD+DLB participants. Furthermore, the design of the study, without repeated measures, did not enable the fluctuations considered to be typical of DLB to be quantified objectively. The CAPPCI reports, however, showed that daily fluctuations occurred in both groups (PD+SC as well as PD+DLB). No transitory fluctuations were observed in the short tape-recorded samples of conversations,

With the above considerations in mind, however, the finding of differences between the groups is valuable in that it:

- highlights the heterogeneity of cognitive deficits in people with PD (an issue which is relatively unexplored);
- characterizes the patterns within each of the two groups studied, drawing attention to areas of future research from which generalizations could be drawn;

- allows close examination of the interaction between language and other cognitive processes;
- identifies key assessments that may be clinically useful in assisting diagnosis of cognitive impairment.

While the conversation analysis did not reveal any important differences between the two groups, this methodology is highly informative in characterizing both what is happening with the carer and in conversational patterns generally. The analysis showed that carers were using a wide range of strategies in conversation, and that there was a high degree of agreement between the carers' own reports and the researchers' analyses of the samples. This confirms the value of interviewing carers using a highly structured format to elicit information in the specific areas identified by the CAPPCI.

The detailed examination brought into focus the high degree of individual variability in the way that conversational partners manage interactional difficulties in communication when one partner has PD with cognitive impairment. The difficulties which were noted were not in speech production (all participants were intelligible) but in the *management* of the structures of conversation, in particular turn-taking and initiation and maintenance of topics. Furthermore, different patterns were seen in the frequency of occurrence of difficulties, how these were rated as problematic and coping strategies which had been adopted spontaneously. In these two groups of patients it seemed to be these features of conversational interaction which caused most concern to the carers, rather than the disorders of memory, language processing and speech articulation which feature more prominently in the literature on communication difficulties in PD.

The development within the study of the CAPPCI has provided speech and language therapists with a valuable potential resource for their work with people with PD and their carers (as well as for other patient groups). The documentation of the spontaneous use of strategies by carers and the way in which their effectiveness is interrelated with many individual variables has significant implications therapeutically. The speech and language therapist cannot presume that a carer has not already begun to manage the situation, nor assume that every carer will have approached his or her unique position in the same way. Carers will have their own strategies in place to manage the change confronting them. Some may be successful, others ineffective or even detrimental; some may be aware of what they are doing while others may not. By looking closely at the individual communication difficulties experienced by the person with PD and the subsequent ways in which these have been managed, intervention can be guided by:

- providing carers with a better understanding of what is happening in interaction and how they respond to their spouse's difficulties;
- reinforcing existing successful strategies;
- identifying unsuccessful strategies and reducing them;
- developing additional strategies motivated by the analysis;
- providing carers with evidence of the impact of strategies through samples of their own conversations;
- identifying those behaviours which cause most disruption to interaction and which may be suitable for specific therapies focused on the deficits of the person with PD and cognitive impairment.

The CAPPCI therefore enables information to be collected for individualized intervention, using accurate information on the conversational strengths and weaknesses of the person with PD associated with cognitive impairment, on the carer's knowledge and perception of these, and on the strategies already being used to facilitate communication. The therapist can build on this knowledge, in partnership with the carer, to develop and maintain the everyday communication skills of the person with PD.

Acknowledgements

Co-workers on this project were Professor Ian McKeith and Dr Gerry Docherty, of the University of Newcastle upon Tyne.

References

BAYLES, K. and TOMOEDA, C. (1993) *Arizona Battery of Communication Disorders in Dementia (ABCD)*. Phoenix: Canyonlands Publishing.

BISHOP, D.V.M. (1982) *Test for the Reception of Grammar (TROG)*. Oxford: MRC and Thomas Leach.

BROWN, R. and MARSDEN, C.D. (1984) How common is dementia in Parkinson's disease? *Lancet, ii*, 1262–1265.

CUMMINGS, J.L. (1986) Subcortical dementia: neuropsychology, neuropsychiatry, and pathophysiology. *British Journal of Psychiatry, 149*, 682–697.

FOLSTEIN, M.F., FOLSTEIN, E.S. and McHUGH, P.R. (1975) Mini-mental state: a practical method for grading the cognitive status of patients for the clinician. *Journal of Psychiatric Research, 12*, 189–198.

HAMILTON, I.H.E. (1994) *Conversations with an Alzheimer's Patient*. Cambridge: Cambridge University Press.

HOWARD, D. and PATTERSON, K. (1992) *The Pyramids and Palm Trees Test (PPT)*. Bury St Edmunds: TVTC.

KAY, J., LESSER, R. and COLTHEART, M. (1992) *Psycholinguistic Assessments of Language Processing in Aphasia (PALPA)*. Hove: LEA.

KEMPER, S., ANAGNOPOULOS, C., LYONS, K. and HEBERLEIN, W. (1994) Speech accommodations to dementia. *Journal of Gerontology, 49*, 223–229.

KENT, R.D., WEISMER, G., KENT, J.F. and ROSENBEK, J.C. (1989) Toward phonetic intelligibility testing in dysarthria. *Journal of Speech and Hearing Disorders, 54*, 482–499.

LESSER, R. and MILROY, L. (1993) *Linguistics and Aphasia: Psycholinguistic and Pragmatic Aspects of Intervention.* London: Longman.

McKEITH, I.G., GALASKO, D., KOSAKA, K., PERRY, E.K., DICKSON, D.W., HANSEN, L.A., *et al.* (1996) Consensus guidelines for the clinical and pathologic diagnosis of dementia with Lewy bodies (DLB): report of the consortium on DLB international workshop. *Neurology, 47*, 1113–1124.

PENN, C. (1985) Compensatory strategies in aphasia: behavioural and neurological correlates. In K.W.Grieve and R.D. Griesel (Eds) *Neuropsychology III.* Pretoria: Monicol.

PERKINS, L. (1995) Applying conversation analysis to aphasia: clinical implications and analytic issues. *European Journal of Disorders of Communication, 30*, 372–383.

PERKINS, L., LESSER, R. and McKEITH, I. (1996) *Language as a Possible Diagnostic Medium for Senile Dementia of the Lewy Body Type.* Project grant final report. London: Nuffield Foundation.

PERKINS, L., WHITWORTH, A. and LESSER. R. (1997) *Conversation Analysis Profile for People with Cognitive Impairments (CAPPCI).* London: Whurr.

PERKINS, L., WHITWORTH, A. and LESSER, R. (1998) Conversing in dementia: a conversation analytic approach. *Journal of Neurolinguistics, 11*, 33–53.

PERRY, R.H., IRVING, D., BLESSED, G., *et al.* (1995) Senile dementia of Lewy body type: a clinically and neuropathologically distinct type of Lewy body dementia in the elderly. *Journal of Neurological Science, 95*, 119–139.

RAMANATHAN, V. (1997) *Alzheimer's Discourse: Some Sociolinguistic Dimensions.* London: Lawrence Erlbaum.

RIDDOCH, J. and HUMPHREYS, O. (1987) Visual object processing in a case of optic aphasia (semantic access agnosia). *Cognitive Neuropsychology, 4*, 131–186.

RIPICH, D.N., VERTES, D., WHITEHOUSE, P., FULTON, S. and EKELMAN, B. (1991) Turn taking and speech act patterns in the discourse of senile dementia of the Alzheimer's type patients. *Brain and Language, 40*, 330–343.

WHITWORTH, A. B. (1996) *Thematic Roles in Production (TRIP): An Assessment of Word Retrieval at the Sentence Level.* London: Whurr.

Chapter 12

Referral criteria for speech and language therapy assessment of swallowing problems caused by idiopathic Parkinson's disease

Carl E. Clarke, Elaine Gullaksen, Sandra Macdonald and Felicity Lowe

Background

Swallowing problems (i.e. dysphagia) have been demonstrated (using videofluoroscopy) in 75–100% of patients with idiopathic Parkinson's disease (PD) (Logemann *et al.*, 1975; Bushmann *et al.*, 1989; Stroudley and Walsh, 1991; Bird *et al.*, 1994; Wintzen *et al.*, 1994). However, only 20–41% of patients complain of dysphagia when questioned (Logemann *et al.*, 1975; Bushmann *et al.*, 1989; Hartelius and Svensson, 1994). It has also been suggested that patients with severe swallowing difficulties may allow food to enter their lungs, so-called 'silent aspiration' (Robbins *et al.*, 1986; Bushmann *et al.*, 1989). The clinician is therefore faced with a dilemma: asking patients whether they have swallowing difficulties may underestimate the problem, but performing videofluoroscopy on all patients is impractical because of the shortage of facilities in the United Kingdom and because in many cases it would entail unnecessary exposure to X-rays.

It is important to resolve this issue, as pneumonia is a common cause of death in PD patients (Hoehn and Yahr, 1967) and, if due to aspiration, can be prevented, although 'mild' aspiration may not be life-threatening (Wintzen *et al.*, 1994). Mild to moderate swallowing problems are amenable to dietary changes, such as thickening liquids. More severe problems can be treated with dietary changes and voluntary airway protection techniques, or direct feeding into the stomach via a percutaneous gastrostomy.

One approach to determining which PD patients require such interventions is to select patients to refer to a speech and language therapist, who will assess the patients clinically and only occasionally with videofluoroscopy. The disadvantage is that clinical assessment is fallible compared with videofluoroscopy in diagnosing aspiration (Splaingard *et al.*, 1988). This method has the additional drawback that there are no criteria available to select patients from the clinic to refer on to the therapist.

The present study was designed to examine the size of the dysphagia problem in a PD clinic population and to investigate whether simple questions regarding dysphagia and a simple timed swallowing test are suitable screening methods to select patients for referral to a speech and language therapist for formal swallowing assessment.

Methods

Over four months, a consecutive series of 64 patients with PD attending the Movement Disorders Clinic in Hull gave written informed consent to take part in the study. The Hull and East Yorkshire Medical Ethics Committee had previously approved the work. Patients were interviewed by a research nurse, who recorded demographic data, duration of PD, score on the Hoehn and Yahr (1967) clinical rating scale (see Chapter 1), information on swallowing difficulties and recent chest infections. The relatives of patients were used as control subjects provided they had no history of gastrointestinal or neurological disorder.

An objective swallowing test developed by Wiles and colleagues was administered in the clinic (Nicklin *et al.*, 1990; Nathadwarawala *et al.*, 1992). The patient was asked to swallow 150 ml of cold water quickly, but as safely as possible, or a smaller volume if the examiner felt dysphagia or tremor precluded the full amount. If any sign of aspiration developed, the test was terminated. Any residual volume was measured. The time taken to swallow all the water was noted, from which the swallowing speed was calculated. The number of swallows was also noted so that the bolus volume could be calculated. Any suggestion of a wet voice or cough after the test was noted. In this pragmatic design, tests in the clinic were to be performed with patients 'on' or 'off', depending on their clinical state at the time, but in practice all were in the 'on' phase.

Each patient underwent a formal speech and language therapy assessment in the 'off' state by asking them to withhold all anti-Parkinsonian medication overnight. The 'off' state was felt appropriate since most patients take their medication around meal times when they are 'off' and this is accepted as a more robust baseline condition for assessment. The timed swallowing test was repeated at this stage to provide a uniform value in the 'off' state.

A standard therapy assessment was performed using various consistencies of liquids and foods and then rated according to the scale developed by Kennedy *et al.* (1993) by adaptation of the Rehabilitation Institute of Chicago's Clinical Evaluation of Dysphagia Scale (Cherney *et al.*, 1986). In this, ten variables were rated each on a 1–5-point scale by observing the patient while swallowing. Also used was a novel global rating scale, based on the therapist's overall clinical evaluation of swallowing: 0 – no swallowing problem; 1 – mild dysphagia, not requiring dietary change at present; 2 – moderate dysphagia, requiring dietary advice or which has already prompted dietary changes; 3 – severe dysphagia leading to aspiration, managed with dietary advice only; 4 – severe dysphagia, gastrostomy/tracheostomy performed. Videofluoroscopy was available if the therapist felt this necessary to evaluate a patient's dysphagia but in practice this was not required.

Results

Sixty-four patients (39 men, 25 women) entered the study. Their mean age was 66.7 years (range 50–83) and the median duration of PD was nine years (range 1–43). The median Hoehn and Yahr score was 3 (range 1.5–5). Ninety-two per cent of patients were receiving standard and/or controlled-release levodopa preparations, 16% an oral dopamine agonist, 33% selegiline and 17% an anticholinergic.

Eighty controls (36 men, 44 women) were recruited. Their mean age was 67.1 years (range 50–86). The mean age of both the male controls and patients was 65.9 years; the mean age of the female controls was 68.1 years compared with 67.9 years in the patient group.

The responses to questions regarding dysphagia are shown in Table 12.1. Where subjects responded affirmatively to the question concerning

Table 12.1. *Swallowing history of patients compared with controls: numbers (%) answering 'yes'*

	Controls		Patients	
Do you have any difficulty swallowing food?	3	(4%)	19***	(30%)
Do you have any difficulty swallowing liquids?	1	(1%)	10**	(16%)
Do you have any difficulty swallowing tablets?	6	(8%)	14*	(22%)
How many chest infections requiring antibiotics have you had in the last 12 months?	12	(15%)	8	(13%)
Have you lost any weight in the last 12 months, excluding deliberate dieting?	14	(18%)	20	(31%)
Do you cough after meals or drinks?	4	(5%)	16***	(25%)
Total	80	(100%)	64	(100%)

*$p < 0.05$, **$p < 0.01$, ***$p < 0.001$ using chi-squared test.

weight loss in the last 12 months, the mean amount lost was 4.3 kg in the 14 controls and 4.4 kg in the 20 patients.

The mean swallowing speed was highly significantly slower in the patients when 'on' in clinic (8.3 ml/s) than in the controls (16.8 ml/s). The mean bolus volume was also highly significantly smaller in the patients (22.3 ml) than in the controls (14.6 ml). Forty-six patients (72%) had a swallowing speed less than 10 ml/s compared with 18 controls (23%), and 23 patients (36%) a speed less than 5 ml/s compared with three controls (4%). Swallowing speed in patients significantly declined with age, as did bolus volume. No correlation existed between either speed or volume and duration of disease. Swallowing speed and bolus volume did significantly decline with deteriorating Hoehn and Yahr rating. Eight patients (13%) had a cough after the test compared with three controls (4%) (a significant difference) and ten patients (16%) a wet voice compared with six controls (8%) (not significant).

All 64 patients were assessed by the therapist but six failed to omit their medication on the morning of the test. The mean swallowing speed in the 'off' state was 6.7 ml/s for those who omitted their medication overnight compared with 7.8 ml/s for those who did not, raising the possibility that swallowing speed is affected by treatment. Therefore, these six will be omitted from further data analysis.

There was a highly significant mean fall in swallowing speed between the 'on' and the 'off' state, of 1.5 ml/s. However, bolus volume was not affected by medication. Of the 58 patients who were 'off' when assessed, 48 (83%) had a swallowing speed less than 10 ml/s, compared with 46 patients (72%) in the 'on' phase, and 31 (53%) had a speed of less than 5 ml/s compared with 23 patients (36%) in the 'on' phase. Six patients (10%) had a cough after the test when 'off', which was not significantly different from the eight (14%) when 'on'. Three patients (5%) had a wet voice after the test when 'off', which was significantly less than the ten patients (17%) when 'on'.

Of those patients who were 'off', none had a speech therapist's global rating of 3 or 4, six patients (10%) had a score of 2, 17 (29%) a score of 1 and 35 (60%) a score of 0. The total score on the Chicago scale was significantly correlated with global rating scale. However, only four of the individual items of the Chicago scale showed a robust decline with global rating. Significant correlations were found between the global rating scale and Hoehn and Yahr rating, duration of disease, swallowing speed both 'on' and 'off' and bolus volume both 'on' and 'off'. The global rating scale was also correlated with the complaint of dysphagia for food but not dysphagia for liquids or tablets. No patients required videofluoroscopy to assess their dysphagia and only one required follow-up for their dysphagia after the study assessment.

Table 12.2. *Predictive statistics for nominal data*

Category	Sensi-tivity (%)	Speci-ficity (%)	False positives (%)	False negatives (%)	Positive predict-ive value	Negative predict-ive value
Dysphagia for food	100	75	25	0	0.32	1.0
Dysphagia for liquids	50	85	15	50	0.27	0.94
Dysphagia for tablets	17	75	25	83	0.07	0.89
Chest infection(s)	0	85	15	100	0	0.88
Weight loss	50	71	29	50	0.17	0.93
Cough after food	50	79	21	50	0.21	0.93
Cough after clinic swallowing test	33	88	12	67	0.25	0.92
Wet voice after clinic swallowing test	33	85	15	67	0.20	0.92

Notes: Standard
(global rating of 2 or more)

		Yes	No
Test (response	Yes	a	b
to question)	No	c	d

Sensitivity = a/(a+c)
Specificity = d/(b+d)
False positive = b/(b+d)
False negative = c/(a+c)
Positive predictive value = a/(a+b)
Negative predictive value = d/(c+d)

Since the critical time for a patient to be referred to a speech therapist for dysphagia evaluation is when positive intervention is required, this point has been taken as when dietary advice is necessary or dietary change has already been made. This corresponds to a score of 2 or more on the therapist's global rating scale. The prevalence of this finding in the group was low, at six patients (10%). The predictive statistics for nominal variables are shown in Table 12.2. Discriminant analysis using various combinations of variables showed that it was impossible to improve on the discrimination of the global rating scale provided by the patients' complaint of dysphagia for food, with a sensitivity of 100% but a false-positive rate of 25%.

Discussion

The size of the dysphagia problem

The complaints of dysphagia for food, liquids and tablets were significantly increased in patients with PD compared with age-matched controls (Table 12.1). The prevalence of dysphagia for food of 30% in this study compares favourably with the 20–41% reported by others (Logemann *et al.*, 1975; Bushmann *et al.*, 1989; Hartelius and Svensson, 1994). Swallowing is abnormal in the oral, pharyngeal and oesophageal phases in PD (Logemann, 1988; Edwards *et al.*, 1992). It is not known whether this results from the underlying pathological process affecting the myenteric plexus, as has been shown in the colon (Singaram *et al.*, 1995), the autonomic nerve supply, such as the dorsal motor nucleus of the vagus (Jackson *et al.*, 1995), bulbar structures or their descending control. In spite of this level of dysphagia, the frequency of chest infections requiring antibiotics and weight loss was no greater in patients than in controls (Table 12.1). Therefore, it seems unlikely that this degree of dysphagia leads to clinically significant aspiration in most patients.

Swallowing test

The swallowing test developed and validated by Wiles and colleagues (Nicklin *et al.*, 1990; Nathadwarawala *et al.*, 1992, 1994) was found to be quick and easy to perform in the outpatient setting. Swallowing speed and bolus volume were significantly lower in patients compared with controls. The decline in swallowing speed with age in patients paralleled that seen in controls. The significant decline in swallowing speed and bolus volume with increasing Hoehn and Yahr score mirrors the findings of Edwards *et al.* (1992) of increasing dysphagia as ratings of PD deteriorated. The lack of any correlation between disease duration and the swallowing test emphasizes that the development of dysphagia is dependent upon the severity of the disease, not its duration. The finding of a significant increase in cough after the test compared with controls correlates well with the patients' complaints of cough after meals, which was also significant compared with controls (Table 12.1). In comparison, a wet voice after this liquid swallowing test was not significant in patients compared with controls, although this does not exclude such a problem in the patients after food.

The significant fall in swallowing speed which occurred when the patients withdrew medication overnight justifies the decision to omit from the final data analysis the six patients who had not omitted medication. Interestingly, the bolus volume was not reduced in the 'off' state. Using videofluoroscopy, it has been shown that levodopa can improve abnormal swallowing in some patients, as in the present study, although some patients also deteriorated (Bushmann *et al.*, 1989). Improvement was shown in vallecular residue, coating of the pharynx and in transit times for thick boluses. A dose–response relationship between levodopa and swallowing could not be demonstrated reliably and improvements in dysphagia did not correlate with improvements in scores on general Parkinsonian rating scales (Bushmann *et al.*, 1989). However, in another videofluoroscopy study, swallowing did not improve in PD patients in response to levodopa or apomorphine, in spite of unequivocal motor responses (Hunter *et al.*, 1994).

Dysphagia assessment by a speech and language therapist

The global dysphagia rating scale developed for the present study proved to be a practical instrument to categorize patients according to what treatment was required. Global ratings were significantly correlated with Hoehn and Yahr scores, duration of disease, swallowing speed and bolus volume 'on' and 'off' and also the complaint of dysphagia for food. Global ratings also correlated with the total score on the Chicago rating scale and many of the individual items on the scale. The largest falls on the Chicago scale were seen in posterior propulsion of the food bolus by the tongue and the complaint of food sticking in the throat or upper oesophagus. In Kennedy *et al.*'s (1993) work with eight patients with PD and one with post-encephalitic Parkinsonism, more marked deficits were found in all ten facets of the Chicago scale. This can probably be attributed to their smaller population being selected for the presence of swallowing or speech disturbance. The authors also concluded that measures of dysphagia and dysarthria in their Parkinsonian patients were not correlated and they therefore questioned the need to include motor speech acts in the evaluation of dysphagia.

According to the global rating scale, none of the study patients had severe dysphagia (grades 3 or 4) and only 10% had moderate dysphagia (grade 2). Extrapolating this to the whole population of patients with PD attending neurology clinics, only 10% require advice from a speech and language therapist regarding their swallowing. While this is likely to be greater than the number who are referred at present, it does not approach the 30% of patients in this study who complained of dysphagia for food and the 75–100% of patients found to have swallowing problems in previous studies using videofluoroscopy (Logemann *et al.*, 1975; Bushmann *et al.*, 1989; Stroudley and Walsh, 1991; Wintzen *et al.*, 1994; Bird *et al.*, 1994). It seems clear from these statistics and the present results that abnormalities on videofluoroscopy in PD do not imply that the patient is at risk of life-threatening aspiration. Furthermore, the complaint of dysphagia for food does not imply that the patient is at risk of life-threatening aspiration. Regarding the 10% of patients in this study with a global rating of 2 and the need for dietary intervention, it seems unlikely that they were all at risk of aspiration. In a smaller prospective study of 22 PD patients with videofluoroscopy, including tests for chest infection, Wintzen *et al.* (1994) showed that 'subjective and objective oropharyngeal dysfunction is frequent in ambulant Parkinsonian patients, but apparently does not produce demonstrable pulmonary infection'. It is well established that videofluoroscopy is superior to bedside assessment by a speech and language therapist at disclosing laryngeal penetration (Linden and Siebens, 1983; Splaingard *et al.*, 1988). However, the patient population examined in these studies is rarely detailed and the conclusions may refer mainly to stroke patients. Such work is also rarely adequately controlled. It is suggested that, in PD at least, the poor availability, expense and radiation dose involved in videofluoroscopy, along with its overestimation of clinically significant aspiration, makes it inferior to the clinical judgement of an experienced speech and language therapist. The therapist has the additional advantage of being able to begin treatment immediately.

Predictive tests

One of the primary aims of the present work was to assess which criteria should be used in the outpatient clinic to select PD patients to refer to a therapist for assessment of dysphagia. Since the first time for positive intervention is when dietary changes are required, this point corresponds to a rating of 2 or more on the global dysphagia rating scale. The predictive statistics for this and nominal data (i.e. responses to 'yes/no' questions) show that the patient's complaint of dysphagia for food was the best predictor, with a high sensitivity and specificity (Table 12.2). However, the low prevalence of clinically significant dysphagia according to the global rating scale (i.e. 10%) leads to a low positive predictive value for the complaint of dysphagia for food (i.e. 32%). Thus, a patient's prior probability of clinically significant dysphagia of 10% only rises to a chance of 32% if they suffer dysphagia for food.

Combining a series of variables can improve the ability to select a given outcome. This is achieved with discriminant analysis. In this statistical technique, the results of each variable are weighted according to their contribution to the final prediction. This has been applied to the present study to attempt to find the best method of predicting a global swallowing rating of 2 or more. It was found that various combinations of selection criteria were no better than using the simple question 'Do you have any difficulty in swallowing food?' The highest sensitivity achieved was 100% but with a specificity of 75%. Used in clinical practice, this would mean that all of the 10% of clinic patients with a global rating of 2 or more would be identified and referred to a therapist, but an additional 20% with a rating of less than 2 would be unnecessarily referred to a therapist. Adding other factors such as the

Hoehn and Yahr rating or the swallowing test to the question will not improve discrimination. In the Hull clinic, referral of all 30% of patients with dysphagia for food would result in an estimated 76 patients per annum being referred to a therapist. Assuming none of these patients are referred at present and that three patients can be assessed per session, this amounts to around 25 extra sessions annually, at a cost of £1,100 per annum. On a national basis, this would prove very costly, considering that two-thirds of patients will not have a significant swallowing problem. However, some of these 'unnecessary' referrals may have speech pathology which would benefit from therapy. The alternative of referring all of these patients for videofluoroscopy would be even more expensive and many, if not all, would be found to have significant abnormalities and some aspiration, but this would be of uncertain clinical significance. The cost of the therapist would not be saved in the latter scenario, as videofluoroscopy is best performed with a therapist present to assess the effects of using different consistencies of food, postural changes and airway protection techniques.

In conclusion, this work suggests that all patients with PD should be regularly asked whether they have difficulty swallowing food. The frequency of the question cannot be recommended with any certainty from the present work or the literature but at least an annual assessment would seem appropriate. Patients answering in the affirmative should be referred to a speech and language therapist with experience of assessing such cases. Dietary advice and airway protection techniques can be taught to those requiring them and the rest referred back to the clinic or kept under review if more severe. For more difficult cases, videofluoroscopy may be necessary. Such a scheme should be tested prospectively and the opportunity taken to compare the results of the therapist's assessment with that of videofluoroscopy.

References

BIRD, M., WOODWARD, M., GIBSON, E.M., PHYLAND, D. and FONDA, D. (1994) Asymptomatic swallowing disorders in elderly patients with Parkinson's disease: a description of findings on clinical examination and videofluoroscopy in 16 patients. *Age and Ageing*, 23, 251–254.

BUSHMANN, M., DOBMEYER, S.M., LEEKER, L. and PERLMUTTER, J.S. (1989) Swallowing abnormalities and their response to treatment in Parkinson's disease. *Neurology*; 39, 1309–1314.

CHERNEY, L.R., CANTIERI, C.A. and PANNELL, J.J. (1986) *RIC Clinical Evaluation of Dysphagia*. Maryland: Aspen Systems Corporation.

EDWARDS, L.L., QUIGLEY, E.M.M. and PFEIFFER, R.F. (1992) Gastrointestinal dysfunction in Parkinson's disease. *Neurology*, 42, 726–732.

HARTELIUS, L. and SVENSSON, P. (1994) Speech and swallowing symptoms associated with Parkinson's disease and multiple sclerosis. *Folia Phoniatrica er Logopedica*, 46, 9–17.

HOEHN, M.M. and YAHR, M.D. (1967) Parkinsonism: onset, progression, and mortality. *Neurology, 17*, 427–442.

HUNTER, P.C., CRAMERI, J., AUSTIN, S., WOODWARD, M. and HUGHES, A.J. (1994) The response of parkinsonian swallowing dysfunction to dopaminergic stimulation. *Movement Disorders*, 9 (suppl. 1), 84.

JACKSON, M., LENNOX, G., BALSITIS, M. and LOWE J. (1995) Lewy body dysphagia. *Journal of Neurology, Neurosurgery and Psychiatry*, 58, 756–758.

KENNEDY, G., PRING, T. and FAWCUS, R. (1993) No place for motor speech acts in the assessment of dysphagia? Intelligibility and swallowing difficulties in stroke and Parkinson's disease patients. *European Journal of Disorders of Communication, 28*, 213–226.

LINDEN, P. and SIEBENS, A.A. (1983) Dysphagia: predicting laryngeal penetration. *Archives of Physical and Medical Rehabilitation, 64*, 281–284.

LOGEMANN, J.A. (1988) Dysphagia in movement disorders. *Advances in Neurology, 49*, 307–316.

LOGEMANN, J.A., BLONSKY, E.R. and BOSHES, B. (1975) Dysphagia in parkinsonism. *Journal of the American Medical Association, 231*, 69–71.

NATHADWARAWALA, K.M., NICKLIN, J. and WILES, C.M. (1992) A timed test of swallowing capacity for neurological patients. *Journal of Neurology, Neurosurgery and Psychiatry, 55*, 822–825.

NATHADWARAWALA, K.M., McGROARY, A. and WILES, C.M. (1994) Swallowing in neurological outpatients: use of a timed test. *Dysphagia, 9*, 120–129.

NICKLIN, J., KARNI, Y. and WILES, C.M. (1990) Measurement of swallowing time – a proposed method. *Clinical Rehabilitation, 4*, 335–336.

ROBBINS, J.A., LOGEMANN, J.A. and KIRSHNER, H.S. (1986) Swallowing and speech production in Parkinson's disease. *Annals of Neurology, 19*, 283–287.

SINGARAM, C., ASHRAF, W., GAUMNITZ, E.A., TORBEY, C., SENGUPTA, A., PFEIFFER, R. and QUIGLEY, E.M.M. (1995) Dopaminergic defect of the enteric nervous system in Parkinson's disease patients with chronic constipation. *Lancet, 346*, 861–864.

SPLAINGARD, M.L., HUTCHINS, B., SULTON, L.D. and CHAUDHURI, G. (1988) Aspiration in rehabilitation patients: videofluoroscopy vs bedside clinical assessment. *Archives of Physical and Medical Rehabilitation, 69*, 637–640.

STROUDLEY, J. and WALSH, M. (1991) Radiological assessment of dysphagia in Parkinson's disease. *British Journal of Radiology, 64*, 890–893.

WINTZEN, A., BADRISING, U., ROOS, R., VIELVOYE, J., LIAUW, L. and PAUWELS, E. (1994) Dysphagia in ambulant patients with Parkinson's disease: common, not dangerous. *Canadian Journal of Neurological Sciences, 21*, 53–56.

Chapter 13

A targeted physiotherapy service for people with Parkinson's disease from diagnosis to end stage: a pilot study

Colin Chandler and Rowena Plant

Background

Parkinson's disease is a chronic, progressive neurological condition typified by a triad of symptoms – tremor, rigidity and slowness of movement ('bradykinesis'), along with a general disturbance of posture (see Chapter 1; and Rothwell, 1995). Pathologically, it is characterized by a progressive degeneration of dopaminergic neurones in the substantia nigra. Pharmacological approaches (see Chapter 1) have been the mainstay of therapy since the 1960s. However, while they resolve some of the primary symptoms, they fall short of completely relieving the problems of postural stability, resting tremor and impaired motor planning (Gauthier and Gauthier, 1983; Cutson *et al.*, 1995). Pharmacological therapy has its own problems in terms of secondary complications, response fluctuations, dyskinesias and psychiatric disturbances, which may affect up to 75% of patients after five years of levodopa therapy (Fahn, 1996). Indeed, now the validity of the model is being questioned, with a call to review it in the light of recent evidence (Parent and Cicchetti, 1998).

Within the context of this movement disorder and its primary line of treatment, it is somewhat surprising that physiotherapy has not featured more prominently. Referral rates to physiotherapy are low, with studies reporting 7% (Mutch *et al.*, 1986), 17% (Oxtoby, 1982) and 38% (Chesson *et al.*, 1995) of patients ever having contact with a physiotherapist. There is a recognition that referral, if made at all, comes late in the course of the disease, when drug therapy is seen to be failing and the opportunity for preventive strategies is lost (Jones and Godwin-Austin, 1998).

Current thinking would suggest that referral to physiotherapy made early after diagnosis and subject to regular review within the context of a multidisciplinary team would provide the optimum approach (Turnbull, 1992). The role of the physiotherapist would not replace the first-line pharmacological approach, but augment it by addressing problems such as mobility, secondary complications with gait and posture, and functional difficulties. Such an approach is in line with the concept of empowerment of people with Parkinson's disease, facilitating their participation in life within their capabilities (Rodwell, 1996).

To date, physiotherapy has been hampered by a lack of rigorous and systematic research into its effectiveness (Jones, 1998). This has led to low referral rates (Hildick-Smith, 1987) and may threaten the purchasing of such services (Baker, 1994).

While many physiotherapists intuitively know their intervention may be of benefit, this is insufficient evidence to influence purchasers and convince sceptics. In this study, the role of physiotherapy in the management of all stages of Parkinson's disease was explored within the context of a client-centred, holistic approach.

Aims

The study had three principal aims:

1 to set up a pilot physiotherapy service targeted at people with Parkinson's disease;
2 to establish the role of physiotherapy in the management of all stages of Parkinson's disease;
3 to evaluate (i) focused physiotherapy management of people with Parkinson's disease, and (ii) rates of referral to, and networking with, other statutory and voluntary agencies.

The study population

Ethical permission was obtained from Newcastle and North Tyneside Joint Ethics Committee to recruit and study subjects from a regional movement disorders clinic and an outpatient clinic served by a consultant neurologist with an interest in Parkinson's disease. The inclusion criteria for subjects were:

1 a diagnosis of idiopathic Parkinson's disease;
2 not receiving physiotherapy treatment;
3 no access (including self-referral) to a physiotherapy review system.

Table 13.1. *Numbers of subjects in each stage allocated (completing) to control and intervention groups*

	Stage 1 (< 2 years)		Stage 2 (2–4 years)		Stage 3 (5–9 years)		Stage 4 (< 10 years)		Totals	
Control	10	(9)	5	(2)	8	(7)	12	(8)	35	(26)
Intervention	11	(10)	6	(5)	6	(5)	9	(6)	32	(26)
Totals	21	(19)	11	(7)	14	(12)	21	(14)	67	(52)

Sixty-seven subjects were recruited. Their stage of disease was categorized according to Langton-Hewer's (1994) system: stage 1 – less than two years since the onset of the disease; stage 2 – at least two years but less than five since onset; stage 3 – at least five years but less than ten since onset; stage 4 – ten or more years since onset. After they had given their informed consent for assessment, subjects were randomized into control and intervention groups and further consent was sought from subjects in the intervention group for physiotherapy treatment.

Table 13.1 shows the numbers starting and completing the study. In all, 15 subjects did not complete the study. Three died during the 12-month study period and the remainder withdrew for a variety of reasons (e.g. moved away from the area, serious illness not related to Parkinson's disease in the subject or a close relative).

The staging of subjects by time since onset of the disease was used as a means to ensure that recruitment covered the full time scale of the disease from the time of diagnosis to end stage. This stratification method allowed a simple and relatively unambiguous means of achieving this end. Other strategies could have been employed, such as Hoehn and Yahr's (1967) scale, but these would have required assessment before recruitment and are themselves prone to difficulty (Wade, 1992). A retrospective comparison was made of the study population stratification with Hoehn and Yahr staging (Table 13.2). While the data are incomplete, as only 47 of the 67 subjects had Hoehn and Yahr staging recorded in their medical notes, broad agreement is seen between the two methods of staging the disease, although there is also a wide range within each of the groups.

A senior physiotherapist with community and neurological experience was employed to undertake assessment for both the control and intervention groups. The assessments were undertaken at three-monthly intervals by the physiotherapist and at six-monthly intervals by the researcher. Physiotherapy was offered throughout the 12-month study period to the intervention group. Detailed physiotherapy notes were kept of all contacts, including both assessment and treatment.

Table 13.2. *Comparison of subjects in each stage with Hoehn and Yahr*
staging derived from the subjects' notes

Hoehn and Yahr stage	Stage 1 (< 2 years)	Stage 2 (2–4 years)	Stage 3 (5–9 years)	Stage 4 (< 10 years)	Totals
I	9	1	2	1	13
II	1	1	–	2	4
III	4	6	4	6	20
IV	–	–	2	8	10
Totals	14	8	8	17	47

Data available for only 47 of the 67 subjects.

For subjects completing the study, no significant differences were found in age of the overall control and intervention groups (mean age 65.5, s.d. 8.8 years, range 49–83) or within the stages. Likewise, the age at diagnosis was not significantly different between control and intervention groups (mean age 60, s.d. 9.6 years, range 39 – 83). However, subjects in stage 4 were significantly younger (9–10 years younger) at diagnosis than those in stages 1 and 2. Within each stage, there were no significant differences between the control and intervention groups with respect to time since diagnosis.

Thirty-one of the subjects completing the study were men and twenty-one women. Forty-two of the subjects were married, and the majority (44) were retired, with only two individuals in paid employment. Thirty-two lived in a house, 11 in bungalows and the remainder in flats. No significant differences between the control and intervention groups were found in any of these respects.

The subjects recruited to the study came from a wide geographical area across the counties of Tyne and Wear, Northumberland and Durham. This reflects the populations served by the movement disorders and outpatient neurology clinics. In consequence, the therapist was involved in considerable travelling to service this population. She also had little opportunity to explore the use of group work with the subjects.

Assessments and record keeping

Initial assessments were conducted by the physiotherapist and involved the recording of the subjects' medical and social histories and their current drug regimen. This was accompanied by a detailed physical assessment built around standard physiotherapy guidelines and incorporating a battery of standardized tests (Table 13.3). The assessment

Table 13.3. *Assessments undertaken throughout the research period*

Nature of timing of assessment	Tests undertaken
Physiotherapy assessment	
Initial	Detailed physiotherapy assessment
3 months	Functional Independence Measure (FIM) (Granger *et al.*, 1986)
6 months	Nottingham Extended Activities of Daily Living (ADL) Index (Nouri and Lincoln, 1987)
9 months	Motor section of the Unified Parkinson's Disease Rating Scale (UPDRS) (Fahn and Elton, 1987)
12 months	Timed walk (Wade, 1992) Nine-hole peg test of hand dexterity (Mathiowetz *et al.*, 1985)
Researcher assessment	
Initial	Semistructured interview to investigate current service access, utilization and satisfaction
6 months	Short Form 36 Health Survey Questionnaire (Ware and Sherbourne, 1992)
12 months	Parkinson's Disease Questionnaire (Peto, 1995)

was completed by the researcher, who undertook a semistructured interview and recorded the subjects' self-assessment.

Systematic records of physiotherapy contacts were kept on each subject in the intervention group. The physiotherapy standard SOAP format (subjective, objective, analysis and plan) was used to facilitate communication between health professionals. This also provided a standard format for analysis of the data.

Results were collected in the form of an enhanced set of physiotherapy notes, which included records of all contacts made with the subjects, whether assessment or treatment, throughout the research period.

Physiotherapy intervention

The physiotherapy intervention focused on the individual subjects and their particular problems. This client-focused approach was based on a holistic stance, in which the bio-psychosocial context of the subject and carer is considered. This approach was at variance with many reported intervention studies which adopt a treatment approach. It provided a meaningful model of intervention in Parkinson's disease and potentially other long-term neurodegenerative disorders. Subjects were encouraged to participate in their own care, identifying problems (current and potential) to direct intervention in a participative, proactive and problem-oriented way. Strategies that the subjects already used to address problems were identified, encouraged and developed. An added advantage of the use of personal strategies was the possibility of passing them on and benefiting other subjects. Secondary complications of Parkinson's disease and its treatment were identified and anticipated. Actions to reduce their effects were adopted to minimize their effect on lifestyle. In the intervention group, subjects were free to contact the physiotherapist throughout the 12-month period for further consultation or treatment in addition to the three-monthly assessments.

Intervention was based upon the sound training and experience of the physiotherapist, who responded to the subject with advice, education and, where appropriate, specific treatment. These specific treatments included: neurophysiological techniques of movement re-education, sequencing and cueing movement; and biomechanical techniques to increase flexibility, balance and posture, often by encouraging exercise. Pain-relieving techniques were also used where indicated (e.g. transcutaneous electrical nerve stimulation (TENS), acupuncture). Thus, a personalized rather than prescriptive approach to physiotherapy was adopted.

In summary, the intervention was built on an empowerment model (Rodwell, 1996), in which the subjects were encouraged to take back or retain the locus of control over their own lives.

Subjects in the control group received no physiotherapy intervention from the research physiotherapist.

Outcomes

Themes were identified through the preliminary analysis of data by focusing on problems experienced by the subjects. The following main themes emerged through qualitative analysis:

- mobility – including gait, posture and transfers;

- activity – including hand dexterity, personal care, leisure and hobbies, housework and do-it-yourself, emotion, cognition and communication (in this context the effects of emotional change, cognitive change and communication ability are also considered);

- pain.

These themes reflected a descending order of magnitude with respect to physiotherapeutic intervention. Mobility formed the major theme which influenced activity and was interlinked with pain. These themes also formed the core domains of physiotherapy treatment in this condition.

The data illustrated the trajectory of the disease, with an overall clear progression from the time of diagnosis. Individually, this progression was not so clear, with some showing remarkably advanced problems early and others few problems at a late stage. Outcomes (observations and evidence of the effectiveness of the physiotherapy intervention) are considered under the above themes in relation to progression, from the early group – stage 1 ($n = 19$), less than two years since diagnosis – through the middle group – stages 2 and 3 ($n = 19$), two to ten years since diagnosis – to the late group – stage 4 ($n = 14$), more than ten years since diagnosis.

Mobility

Assessment of gait and posture

In the early group, a spectrum of problems were seen. These ranged from a very slight change in posture, slight dragging of a foot, reduced step height and reduced arm swing, to a stooped posture with balance problems, hesitancy in gait, shuffling and freezing problems, particularly marked in crowded environments or where obstacles or distractions were evident.

In the middle group, the problems overlapped with the early group but extended further, with increased postural disturbances and an increase in the incidence of trips and falls. Some subjects demonstrated an increasingly stooped posture with marked curvature of the spine (thoracic kyphosis) and flexion of the hip and knee. Added to these were problems of propulsion and a reduced awareness of surroundings. Poor balance, reduced head and trunk movement, festinating gait and reduced range of axial and limb movement with decreased arm swing were all seen. Problems with initiation of gait were identified. Overall, there was an increase in the bilateral nature of signs and problems. Four subjects in this group were able to go outside the house only with the aid of a wheelchair.

The late group again overlapped with the earlier groups, but extended the range of problems further still. An increase in stooped posture and more difficulty in doorways, narrow places or crowds due to freezing was observed. An increased incidence of the use of walking aids and wheelchairs was seen. Three subjects in this group achieved mobility by crawling around the house.

Outcome of intervention for gait and posture problems

The physiotherapy approaches adopted with this group were focused on the presenting problems. They included advice, balance and gait re-education, the use of cueing, adoption and reinforcement of strategies, education in the use of walking aids, risk assessment and referral to other health professionals.

In the early group, advice and discussion resulted in information sharing. Often this led on to the development of strategies to overcome specific problems, which were tried out with the physiotherapist. For example, strategies were tried to overcome freezing, and to adjust posture. In many cases, the need to think through the activity as it was being undertaken was introduced. The use of cueing – verbal, by counting out steps, or visual, using tape on the floor to get round a difficult corner – was tried with some subjects. Advice on lifestyle and environment was frequently recorded, for example organizing activities within the day to avoid shops when they are likely to be crowded and avoiding distractions while walking.

A gait re-education approach was used with some. This involved discussion to increase the subject's understanding of the pattern of walking and its different elements. For example, heel strike, arm swing, posture, step length, step height and fluency of movement were all explained and demonstrated. Practice in appropriate elements was used to improve walking. Often, general exercises were used to increase mobility and flexibility; these were normally incorporated into the subject's everyday routine.

Following such interventions, some of the problems which had been identified were reduced or ceased to be a problem. In two cases, strategies introduced to facilitate making turns (walking wide and counting) were recorded as successful. In two other situations gait re-education and increased conscious effort afforded a marked improvement in walking.

In the middle group, a similar approach was used but there was increased need to address the problems of balance and gait re-education. In one subject who frequently tripped while walking, specific work was undertaken to increase step height by practising stepping up and down the bottom step of the stairs. Concurrently, discussion of hazards, known difficult pavements and uneven ground enabled the identification of safer routes to reduce the risk of tripping. 'Retropulsion' (a tendency to walk backwards characteristic of Parkinson's disease) also featured as a problem in some subjects. Again, postural and gait re-education techniques were employed, as was the use of a mirror or other visual cues to check posture. In one subject, an ex-soldier, marching to encourage rhythm and pace was used. For some subjects for whom walking aids had been supplied, often the instruction had been either forgotten or inadequate. In these situations, the physiotherapist was able to instruct the subjects in safe use of the aids.

Individuals in this group reported an increase in confidence in their walking and a reduced tendency to stumble and trip.

In the late group, similar approaches were used. Gait and posture re-education methods were extended and strategies to cope with the problems of motor fluctuations developed. Discussions concerning the reorganizing of the subject's environment to facilitate movement and reduce hazards were recorded. Exercises were introduced in several cases to reduce stiffness, increase flexibility, improve muscle tone and increase trunk rotation. Two subjects commented on the short-term benefits of the exercises. Risk assessment was undertaken with this group and advice given on safety. In many cases, it was clear that the subjects had developed their own strategies to overcome problems. Where this was so, the work was mainly to improve and encourage these existing strategies rather than to introduce new strategies.

No significant differences were found between the control and intervention groups in the UPDRS motor section, the FIM motor section, the Nottingham Extended ADL mobility section or the timed walk. Similar problems were seen at all stages in both control and intervention groups.

Assessment of transfers

These activities included lying to sitting, sitting to standing and standing to sitting, from both a bed and a chair; getting in and out of the bath; getting on and off the toilet; and getting into and out of a car. Again, a wide range of ability was seen for these activities.

In the early group, a third of the subjects had no problems with these activities at all. Others had some problems initiating movement or with balance once the standing position was reached and would fall forward or back (propulsion and retropulsion, respectively). In some, difficulty was experienced when attempting to turn in bed. When bathing several used grab-rails or bathroom furniture for support. Five of the subjects needed supervision or assistance to get into or out of the bath. Some made use of grab-rails, bathroom furniture and fittings to get on and off the toilet.

In the middle group, a similar range of problems was seen, although there was an increased need for assistance and aids.

The late group again covered a similar range but extended it further. For example, one subject required the assistance of two carers and a hoist to get into and out of the bath.

Outcome of intervention for transfer problems

Physiotherapy intervention with respect to transfers covered a wide range of modalities. Discussion and identification of problems with the development of strategies and their rehearsal were undertaken. Sequencing to break down movements and balance re-education to reduce the problems of propulsion and retropulsion were also tried. Cueing and mental rehearsal of activities coupled with advice were used. Safety and risk assessment were particularly important. Referral to social services for the provision of aids and appliances was also made.

The outcomes of intervention were evident by reports of less propulsive/retropulsive tendencies, easier and safer access to the bath, and provision of further aids from social services. The general observation made after physiotherapy intervention was that life was easier and in particular the stress and burden on carers were reduced with the increase of safe and independent transfers.

Assessment of general mobility

Mobility around the house, up and down stairs and in public places formed the core of this theme. In the early group, the range extended from those with no problems, to those with difficulty due to fatigue and hence limited endurance, and those for whom hesitancy and freezing made cluttered environments and crowds a problem. Lack of confidence was also a problem. In the middle group, a similar range was observed though it was extended particularly by greater fatigue and lack of confidence. Safety especially on stairs became an issue. Some subjects adopted the strategy of crawling up and down stairs to avoid the risk of falling. One subject moved from a house to a bungalow during the course of the study. In the late group, the problems were further extended, and more difficulty with fatigue and self-confidence was recorded. Worse problems with freezing in confined and cluttered spaces were seen.

Outcome of interventions for general mobility problems

Interventions again focused on discussion to identify the problems that individuals were facing and the strategies that they were using. Increased use of handrails on the stairs was encouraged. The strategy of crawling up and down stairs was again encouraged as a safe approach in some. Others used the stairs as part of an exercise regimen. Advice on reducing obstacles and rearranging the environment to facilitate everyday living was given. Planning of lifestyle to undertake activities during 'good' periods of the day was often discussed. Likewise, planning trips out of the house in a way that accounted for endurance with sensible use of rest stops, public transport and other facilities was considered. Strategies and cueing were used to overcome some of the hesitancy, freezing and gait initiation problems.

Activity

Assessment of activity

In the early group, little effect was seen on activity in household and personal care tasks besides some slowing due to a reduction in hand dexterity. There was a reduction in some subjects of their ability to undertake more strenuous activities, such as gardening or carrying shopping or heavy loads of washing. Five subjects in this group were keen walkers and had had to limit this activity; likewise, two had played golf regularly but had reduced or stopped playing. A slight reduction in independence was seen across the group. Some subjects experienced difficulty with their speech and some with writing. A few showed problems with short-term memory.

In the middle group, there is a further reduction in hand dexterity, leading to a further slowing of everyday activities. Reduction or cessation of some hobbies requiring dexterity was evident. More problems with communication were seen, with greater difficulties in speech and facial expression making social conversation harder. Bouts of depression and mood swings were seen. Impaired memory was also evident in some subjects.

In the later group, more help and support were needed in many areas of personal care. Everyday activities were sometimes taking excessive times to complete, and so required assistance or supervision from a carer. Communication difficulties were increasingly evident, with a consequent withdrawal from social situations. In some subjects there were signs of dementia, with impaired memory, reduced ability to concentrate and confusion.

In all groups, some problems with sleep were identified, with many reports of night-time disturbance. In some cases, stress and anxiety were causing problems, while in others vivid dreams and nightmares disturbed sleep.

Outcome of interventions for activity problems

Interventions in this area were again focused on problem identification and the identification of strategies that were being employed. Advice then followed to enhance existing strategies, introduce new strategies or find alternative ways of accomplishing the task. Several subjects in the early and middle groups benefited from hand exercises to reduce stiffness; one subject played the piano regularly in the mornings as exercise. Subsequent improved hand dexterity facilitated a range of self-care activities and writing ability. In one subject with impaired short-term memory, the use of a daily diary as a memory prompt was introduced successfully. Consideration of the pattern of daily activities was made in many cases. Discussion centred on how best to plan the day to make the most of the subject's abilities. Leisure pursuits and social contacts were encouraged after strategies had been adopted to facilitate these. For example, one subject who had lost contact with her social network was encouraged to use public transport and taxis. This resulted in increased self-confidence, a re-establishment of these contacts and consequently a more fulfilling social life. The two golfers were encouraged to resume the sport but to lower their expectations (e.g. undertake half a round rather than a full round).

In the later group, many of the existing strategies were reinforced by the physiotherapist. For example, the use of more leisure clothing to avoid problems with buttons, zips and other fastenings. The use of labour-saving appliances was encouraged (e.g. an electric razor).

Relaxation techniques (e.g. audio-tapes and aromatherapy) were successfully used with some subjects to improve their sleep patterns.

Pain

The theme of pain clearly provided a context for mobility and activity, which often limited participation in these areas. In essence, pain was seen in all the groups and mainly originated from muscles and joints, although some non-specific pain was reported. In many subjects, musculoskeletal pain was attributed to a secondary arthritic condition. However, given the picture of increasingly stooped posture in combination with hip and knee flexion and muscular fatigue, many of these musculoskeletal problems were not at all surprising. Specific intervention for pain relief was incorporated into the overall treatment strategy. It included such techniques as postural awareness, exercise, TENS and acupuncture.

Conclusions

Physiotherapy intervention throughout the stages of Parkinson's disease was based on a holistic approach in which empowerment of the subject and carers was a strong element. While the major theme which emerged from the data was that of mobility, it was clear that the focus of therapeutic intervention was that of enhancing the performance of activities. Pain provided a context in which mobility and activity were set. A clear partnership was developed between the physiotherapist and the subject. This enabled the identification of problems. Steps were then taken to explore, enhance and enable strategies to overcome them. In some cases, these were reactive to the situation; often, though, they were proactive. The relevance of physiotherapy was clearly shown throughout the whole time scale of the disorder. With subjects in the early or middle stages of the disease, more opportunity existed to introduce new and different strategies to enhance life, while in the late group only small changes were possible to existing strategies to encourage or improve their use.

While scant reference has been made to the standardized scales in this report, they were shown to be of limited use and sensitivity when applied to an individualized approach to therapy where the subject's problems and needs drive the direction of intervention.

Acknowledgements

Our thanks go to the individuals with Parkinson's disease and their carers who gave up much time to this project; Dr David Burn who granted access to his patients; Sheila Harrison, Samantha Maher and Marion Ellison for their input into the project; and our colleagues for their support. Funding from the Parkinson's Disease Society, Newcastle and NorthTyneside Health purchasing authority and the Northern and Yorkshire Regional Health Authority is gratefully acknowledged.

References

BAKER, M. (1994) Presidential address. Presented at the European Parkinson's Disease Association Annual Conference, Glasgow.

CHESSON, R., COCKHEAD, D. and MAEHLE, V. (1995) *Availability of Therapy Services to People with Parkinson's Disease Living in the Community.* Aberdeen: Robert Gordon University.

CUTSON, T., LAUB, K. and SCHENKMAN, M. (1995) Pharmacological and non-pharmacological intervention in the treatment of Parkinson's disease. *Physical Therapy,* 75, 363–373.

FAHN, S. (1996) Controversies in the therapy of Parkinson's disease. In L. Battista, G. Scarlato, T. Caraceni and S. Ruggieri (Eds) *Parkinson's Disease.* Philadelphia: Lippincott-Raven.

FAHN, S. and ELTON, E. (1987) The Unified Parkinson's Disease Rating Scale. In Fahn, C. Marsden, M. Goldstein and D. Calne (Eds) *Recent Developments in Parkinson's Disease.* New Jersey: Macmillan Healthcare Information.

GAUTHIER, L. and GAUTHIER, S.(1983) Functional rehabilitation of patients with Parkinson's disease. *Physiotherapy Canada, 35*, 220–222.

GRANGER, C., HAMILTON, B.B. and SHERWIN, F.S. (1986) *Guide for the Use of the Uniform Data Set for Medical Rehabilitation*. Buffalo, NY: Buffalo General Hospital, UD System for Rehabilitation Project Office.

HILDICK-SMITH, M. (1987) Has rehabilitation a role in the treatment of Parkinson's disease? In F. C. Rose (Ed.) *Parkinson's Disease: Clinical and Experimental Advances*. London: Libbey.

HOEHN, H. and YAHR, M. (1967) Parkinsonism: onset, progression and mortality. *Neurology, 47*, 427–442.

JONES, D. (1998) Research into physiotherapy and Parkinson's. *Parkinson's: The Physiotherapist*. London: Parkinson's Disease Society.

JONES, D. and GODWIN-AUSTIN, R.(1998) Parkinson's disease. In M. Stokes (Ed.) *Neurological Physiotherapy*. London: Mosby.

LANGTON-HEWER, R. (1994) Challenges for the future. Presented at the European Parkinson's Disease Association Annual Conference, Glasgow.

MATHIOWETZ, V., WEBER, K., KASHMAN and VOLLAND, G. (1985) Adult norms for the nine hole peg test of finger dexterity. *Occupational Therapy Journal of Research, 5*, 24–37.

MUTCH, W., STRUDWICK, A., ROY, S.K. and DOWNIE, A.W. (1986) Parkinson's disease: disability, review and management. *British Medical Journal, 293*, 675–677.

NOURI, F. and LINCOLN, N. (1987) An extended activity of daily living scale for stroke patients. *Clinical Rehabilitation, 1*, 301–305.

OXTOBY, M. (1982) *Parkinson's Disease Patients and Their Social Needs*. London: Parkinson's Disease Society.

PARENT, A. and CICCHETTI, F. (1998) The current model of basal ganglia organization under scrutiny. *Movement Disorders, 13*, 199–202.

PETO, V. (1995) The development and validation of a short measure of functioning and wellbeing for individuals with Parkinson's disease. *Quality of Life Research, 4*, 241–248.

RODWELL, C. (1996) An analysis of the concept of empowerment. *Journal of Advanced Nursing, 23*, 305–313.

ROTHWELL, J. (1995) The basal ganglia. In F. Cody (Ed.) *Neural Control of Skilled Human Movement*. London: Portland Press, on behalf of the Physiological Society.

TURNBULL, G. (Ed.) (1992) *Physical Therapy Management of Parkinson's Disease*. New York: Churchill Livingstone.

WADE, D. (1992) *Measurement in Neurological Rehabilitation*. Oxford: Oxford Medical Publications.

WARE, J. and SHERBOURNE, C. (1992) The MOS 36-Item Short Form Health Survey (SF-36): conceptual framework and item selection. *Medical Care, 30*, 473–483.

Chapter 14

The use of video recording in the assessment and management of Parkinson's disease

Yvonne Awenat

Background

The setting for this innovation was a 23-bed elderly care ward in a rehabilitation centre. This ward serves the rehabilitation needs of a teaching hospital some five miles away, taking patients mainly from a deprived inner-city area. The author is a clinical nurse specialist in Parkinson's disease, whose role involves the introduction of innovations and advancement of nursing practice. Work with patients mostly seeks to establish the production of smooth, controlled movement.

The use of a video recorder to film patients was introduced after a pilot study carried out by a medical student under the supervision of a medical consultancy with a special interest in Parkinson's disease. This study used the medium of video to assist in the assessment of patients and was mainly carried out within their own homes (Roberts, 1995). The positive findings gave the authors confidence to devise a way of developing this idea, with a particular focus on inpatients.

Aims

We wished to improve interprofessional, multidisciplinary communication, patient–professional communication and pharmacological treatment regimens, as well as patient management in general.

We were also interested in the acceptability of using this mode of patient assessment to both patients and professionals.

Development of the project

Application for ethical approval was made and received from the local ethical committee.

The idea of using video was discussed with the ward staff, all of whom were enthusiastic. Because one staff nurse expressed a particular interest in being involved, it was decided to use this as a developmental opportunity for her and we arranged for her to attend a research methods course. A camcorder video was purchased and the project began. The staff nurse soon became familiar with the correct operation of the video and she took opportunities to practise before starting to film patients.

All patients and carers where appropriate received full explanations of the project and gave their permission before being filmed. Before filming started, I sat in on the weekly multidisciplinary meeting and conducted process recording of events. This allowed for first-hand witnessing of the communication difficulties encountered when various staff endeavoured to relate their assessment of a patient's abilities and progress to other team members.

It is acknowledged that drug treatment is the mainstay of treatment in Parkinson's disease and this places a heavy responsibility on the medical consultant, who is strongly reliant on staff to communicate the patient's situation. Accurate information is therefore needed in order to modify drug therapy so that disease progression can be optimally controlled, and the patient can be assisted with any distressing symptoms.

Opportunity to observe this can be severely limited in the traditional weekly ward round, where the consultant will usually only spend a few minutes with each patient.

A format was developed that involved patients being filmed as they were receiving therapy. Additionally, when patients were taken on a home visit (i.e. accompanied home by one or two members of staff so that realistic assessments of their ability to cope at home could be made) the opportunity was used to film proceedings. On a few occasions the camcorder was lent to a patient and carer so that they could record the extremes of the 'on' and 'off' periods.

The recordings were edited and then used as a basis for staff discussion at the weekly multidisciplinary meetings.

Benefits

A definite improvement in communication between team members was noticeable and commented on by them. The viewing of the video recordings gave everyone the same information and allowed specific disciplines to determine how they could best operate for the patient's benefit. In particular, the recording of a patient's 'on' and 'off' periods gave the medical consultant better information from which modifications to drug therapy could be made. The alternative of the entire team watching a patient walking or dressing, for example, could prove rather intimidating and it is known that anxiety or nervousness will worsen symptoms, thereby providing an inaccurate picture.

The recordings provided a permanent record of a patient's progress, or otherwise, over time, which helped staff to make comparisons and so to determine the best treatment.

Staff were able to see how a patient had managed on a home visit and saw the patient's home environment and the particular difficulties faced. Also, such videos can highlight the need for certain aids or adaptations. If, for example, the patient is filmed negotiating movement through a narrow doorway, then advice can be given by the physiotherapist on how best to accomplish this. Video recording of the home visit can also provide valuable information on how the patient's carer normally copes, and advice can be given if necessary.

Video recordings can also be used as a form of staff education. For example, the physiotherapist can be filmed handling the patient, assisting with transfers and so on, and these specialized measures designed specially for an individual patient can then be viewed and learnt by other groups of staff who will have to handle the patient. This particularly lends itself for use by night staff and nurses who are unfamiliar with a new patient.

The films can also be used (with patient permission) for more formal professional education, for example for teaching use with student nurses, therapists and medical students.

The videos can be shown to patients themselves for their education and may also be useful at boosting morale during times of discouragement.

Limitations

The main restriction to widespread use is the cost of the video recorder. However, to put things in perspective, the cost (in our case about £800) is much less than half that of an intravenous infusion pump.

Proficiency in using the video is required but, in practice, we did not find this to be a problem.

Acceptability to patients was one of our concerns. However, they were usually keen to participate in something which they saw as leading to an improvement in the care they would receive. In particular, they wanted their doctor to know more about the particular challenges which they faced when at home.

Discussion

The use of video proved to be very successful. In particular, it enhanced interprofessional communication. This led to higher-quality care being delivered by all groups of staff and proved of especial value in helping the medical consultant to make decisions about drug therapy. It also provided a valuable developmental opportunity for the staff nurse: not only did she become more interested in Parkinson's disease but she also became motivated to learn more about the research process.

Video is now regularly used to enhance both patient assessment and the evaluation of response to care and therapy.

The project also raised everyone's awareness of the features and problems of Parkinson's disease.

Conclusions

Study of this innovation has convinced us that it was well worth doing and we have now developed an accepted and valued adjunct to patient assessment and evaluation.

There is no reason to believe that it would not be equally successful if used for other groups, such as stroke patients, and this is something which we would like to explore in the future.

This project concentrated on inpatients. However, if resources permitted, it would be very useful to lend patients or carers a video in order to film their home situation so that the consultant could view the video when they attended an outpatient clinic.

For the future, it is possible that we may see more technological innovations. Hubble *et al.* (1993) have described the use of interactive video conferencing with patients who have Parkinson's disease. This has major resourcing implications and is unlikely to become standard practice in the near future in the UK.

References

HUBBLE, J.P., PAHWA, R. and MICHALEK, K. (1993) Interactive video conferencing – a means of providing care for Parkinson's disease patients. *Movement Disorders*, 8, 380–382.

ROBERTS, P. (1995) *The Use of Home Video Recording in the Assessment of Parkinson's Disease.* Unpublished thesis, University of Manchester.

Chapter 15

Driving and Parkinson's disease

Nadina B. Lincoln and Kate A. Radford

Driving is an important activity of daily living for many people. However, Parkinson's disease (PD) may affect people's ability to drive a car safely. As the disease progresses, there comes a point at which individuals need to discontinue driving, in the interests of both their own safety and that of others. It is, however, difficult to decide the point at which someone ceases to be a safe driver and becomes an unsafe one.

Driving habits

In surveys, people have been asked about their driving habits and previous accidents, in order to determine whether people with PD differ from people without disabilities. Dubinsky *et al.* (1991) interviewed 150 people with PD and compared them with 100 controls. Patients with PD had no more lifetime accidents and committed fewer driving offences than other drivers. However, they had more accidents per mile driven. Some (21%) of the PD drivers had stopped driving because of concerns over their safety. Those with more advanced disease had significantly more accidents per mile than those in earlier stages. However, the correspondence between disease severity and accident rates was not so close that the disease severity alone could be used to indicate whether people with PD were safe to drive. Those with cognitive impairment had higher accident rates than the non-cognitively impaired, irrespective of the disease severity.

There are problems with asking people about their driving accidents, in that some individuals may not report errors in driving or may be unaware of them. Although Dubinsky *et al.* (1991) obtained supporting evidence from families, people's recall of accidents may not have been accurate. This is particularly likely to be a problem in those with cognitive impairment affecting their memory or attention. An alternative is to test people in a driving simulator. Madeley *et al.* (1990) examined the effects of PD on driving ability using a computerized driving simulator. They compared ten patients with PD with ten healthy controls and found that both simulated reaction time and accuracy of steering were impaired in the PD group. They also found that the impairment on measures of driving (reaction time and accuracy) was related to the severity of PD assessed on Webster's rating scale (Webster, 1968). They suggested that Webster's rating scale might be used as a guide to fitness to drive.

Lings and Dupont (1992) conducted a similar study but failed to support the recommendation that Webster's rating scale is a useful predictor. They tested 28 patients with PD and 109 healthy controls in a mock car and showed that PD patients committed more serious errors, in particular directional errors, and sometimes completely failed to react to stimuli. However, they found these errors were not related to the score on Webster's rating scale and suggested the Unified Parkinson's Disease Rating Scale (UPDRS) (Lang and Fahn, 1989) as an alternative to Webster's rating scale. The discrepancies between the two studies serve to emphasize the need for further research.

Driving licence policy

The policy of the Driving Vehicle Licensing Authority (DVLA) is that anyone who has a disability lasting more than three months, which affects or may in future affect their ability as a driver, should notify the DVLA of their condition. The DVLA sends the patient a questionnaire to complete. If a patient with PD reports no problems, he or she is sent a letter advising that the licence may be kept, but that any change in the condition should be notified. A letter is also sent to the general practitioner (GP) explaining what has been done. This gives the GP opportunity to notify the DVLA if there has been a mistake or if the patient does not understand the disorder.

If the answers to the questionnaire are unfavourable, then further details are sought from the GP about manifestations of PD which may affect the person's safety as a driver. This method of self-declaration has been found to be acceptable for people with PD, and cross-checking of a sample of 2,000 patients showed a very small proportion of mistakes (Rowse, personal communication). The GP may also consult the neurologist. These doctors use as a guide *Medical Aspects of Fitness to Drive* (Taylor, 1995). This states that people with chronic neurological disorders (such as PD), provided medical assessment confirms that driving is not impaired, may retain their licence until the age of 70 years. The licence may be restricted to driving with controls to suit the disability. If the condition is likely to deteriorate rapidly or if the diagnosis is recent, a short licence of one, two or three years may be issued. The guide recommends that the licence is withdrawn if the condition is progressive or disabling. If the condition is stable and driving would not be impaired, people may be issued with a licence, which is reviewed annually. The periodic review restrictions placed on driving licences, together with fluctuations in the condition, means the question of driving safety arises regularly.

Some patients may be referred to specialist driving assessment centres, known as regional mobility centres. These offer independent advice that is tailored to the individual's needs. The staff are qualified to assess and advise on fitness to drive. These centres will give a medical assessment of the physical abilities needed for driving, such as visual acuity, visual fields, grip strength and foot control. People are assessed on a static rig to check whether they can depress car pedals and turn a steering wheel. These static rigs usually include measures of reaction time for both hand responses and foot responses. The client is then taken for a test drive by a Department of Transport approved driving instructor (ADI) specializing in the assessment of disabled drivers. This is carried out in a dual-control car with adaptations, if necessary, to compensate for physical problems. Clients start on a test track, where they are asked to show that they have control of the vehicle. The assessment then progresses to public roads, if performance is satisfactory, to ensure they can cope with traffic and driving at speed. The ADI makes a recommendation about their safety on the road. The precise procedures used vary from one centre to another. They do not have fixed criteria for their recommendations but rely on the clinical experience of the assessors.

However, the locations of driving assessment centres, long waiting lists and assessment costs may deter some patients from seeking specialists' advice. Instead, they look to families and health professionals for advice about their fitness to drive. Many patients with PD discontinue driving without specific recommendation from licensing authorities. Campbell *et al.* (1993) conducted a survey of community-dwelling elderly people and found that 17% of those who had previously driven had given up, most of these voluntarily. PD was one of the six main conditions associated with cessation of driving.

The proportion of people with PD seeking professional advice is low. Ritter and Steinberg (1979) reported that only 23% of patients with PD had been told about their suitability to drive by their doctor. A survey (McLay, 1989) of 15 members of branches of the Parkinson's Disease Society found that, although most of the individuals had given up driving a car, only a third of the group had notified the DVLA of their disorder. When professional advice is sought, in the UK most people with PD are allowed to drive. Of the 3,850 people with PD who notified the DVLA in 1996/7, only a small proportion had their licences refused (0.01%) or revoked (0.02%) (Rowse, personal communication). Police notifications to the DVLA are also rare (Anonymous, 1990), indicating that few people are found to be hazardous on the road. However, there may be variations in other countries since in Australia, for example, Peterson *et al.* (1988) found that 32% of PD patients had lost their licence because of the disease.

Although simulators have been used in research, they are often little more than measures of reaction time. The introduction of more sophisticated simulators may provide better means of assessing people with PD. However, at present, the most accurate assessment of driving ability is thought to be a road test given by an experienced driving examiner (Anonymous, 1990; Pentland *et al.*, 1992). This is usually available only through the specialist driving assessment centres.

Barnes and Hoyle (1995) conducted a survey of 11,000 people in Newcastle upon Tyne to identify those who were disabled. They then sent the 611 who had a locomotor disability and were aged 16–80 years old a questionnaire about their driving status. They found that the assessment of driving ability was rarely included in the rehabilitation programme. A significant proportion of those who were driving felt they would have benefited from advice on their fitness to drive. They assessed 23 people who were driving and found that 17 could have benefited from further advice in relation to car and control adaptations. In addition, there were some who were not driving who were considered probably able to control a car safely. On the basis of this survey, they recommended an improvement in the provision of specialist driving assessment centres.

Most of the time, the DVLA's process of inquiry and existing methods of assessment are probably sufficient. On the whole, people with PD are considered to be conscientious (Ritter and Steinberg, 1979). They are more likely to relinquish a licence before their own safety or that of other road users is compromised, rather than to continue driving. However, concern exists about the few individuals who lose insight into their own ability to drive safely, either directly as a result of cognitive changes or because of a combination of physical and cognitive limitations. The decision regarding fitness to drive is subjective. This means there are inconsistencies, in that some unsafe drivers continue to drive, while others who may be safe are refused a licence. There is consensus that at present we do not have an objective, reliable criterion against which to make a decision about stopping driving (Madeley *et al.*, 1990; Hansotia, 1993).

Physical aspects of driving

There are several common physical problems experienced by PD sufferers that may affect driving safety. Unpredictable, sudden 'on–off' episodes, freezing attacks or involuntary movements caused by the long-term use of preparations containing levodopa will affect vehicle control. Slowness of movement affects reaction times.

Rigidity, especially in the neck and shoulders, may inhibit the ability to turn and look behind. This will cause problems when reversing or parking and when merging with streams of traffic. Tremor may affect pedal control or pressure and smooth handling of the car. Sensory or proprioceptive loss may affect control and speed of movement on the pedals, and the ability to steer and to position the car in the road.

Many physical symptoms of disabling conditions can now be compensated for by adapting the vehicle.It may be that conversion to a car with automatic transmission can adequately overcome the loss of fine motor coordination required for smooth gear changes in a manual transmission vehicle. Powered steering can reduce the force required to turn the steering wheel. Where it is not standard issue, most cars can now be converted (Barnes, 1997). More sophisticated adaptations may assist other physical deficits, such as modified seating (such as swivel and side-sliding seats), seat belt extensions, steering wheel grips (such as knobs that allow steering with one hand) or conversion of brake and accelerator function to hand control. There are many devices that are commercially available to suit most vehicle types. However, the need for adaptation can sometimes be avoided or facilitated by the choice of vehicle. Seeking advice about the most suitable type of car and the dimensions required for an adaptation can save time and money. New devices in cars that are designed to assist drivers making judgements, such as computerized route planners and systems to inform the driver of speed and distance, may help compensate for some physical problems. However, for drivers who have impairments of cognitive function they may impede rather than assist.

For advice about what is available and what is suitable, individuals should consult one of the regional mobility centres. People have an opportunity to try out car adaptations and some centres can design one-off solutions for specific problems. There is sometimes a charge for the service. For more information on services offered, centres may be contacted directly.

Cognitive aspects of driving

It is more often the cognitive and intellectual difficulties that preclude driving, rather than physical problems (Barnes, 1997). Cognitive changes include impairments in memory, information processing speed, concentration, attention, depth perception and spatial awareness. All of these skills are thought to be essential for driving. Drivers must respond to complex stimuli, make simultaneous decisions and perform manoeuvres in a limited time period. For example, driving through an unfamiliar town centre, drivers may be reading and following road signs and road markings. They may be required to change lanes and merge with other traffic streams. They need to make judgements about the speed at which they are travelling and the distance between themselves and other road users. They must be conscious of the proximity of vehicles behind, in front and to either side of them. They must at all times be aware of the intentions of other road users, including pedestrians and cyclists. They may also be listening to the radio or responding to weather conditions and traffic signals. They must remember to signal, slow down and possibly change gear before making a manoeuvre. At all times they must concentrate and attend to visual and auditory information. They must be able to process incoming information at speed, so that they can react appropriately. Failing to do any one of these might result in a road accident.

Cognitive factors are an important component of PD (Bloxham *et al.*, 1987; Bradley *et al.*,. 1989; Cooper *et al.*, 1993; Jones and Donaldson, 1995) and may affect driving safety. Many people with PD, however, exhibit no such changes and remain mentally alert throughout their illness, restricted only by physical limitations. For some people any cognitive changes are indistinguishable from those that occur as part of the normal ageing process. Given that PD is itself a disease more typically associated with older age, these changes may go unnoticed. They may become apparent only on formal neuropsychological tests. They can, however, occur in younger PD sufferers and have a greater impact on the individual's life.

Whether occurring in younger or older PD sufferers, whether related to the disease itself or simply part of the ageing process, these cognitive changes are important determinants of fitness to drive a car. Not all specialist driving assessment centres have facilities for assessing cognitive deficits. Despite the importance of cognitive abilities in driving, research has shown only a weak relationship between cognitive abilities, as assessed by formal testing, and the patient's performance on the road.

There has been only one study of the relation between cognitive abilities in PD and performance on the road. Heikkila *et al.* (1998) assessed 20 people with PD and 20 healthy age-matched controls. Each person was assessed by a neurologist, completed a battery of cognitive tests with the psychologist and was observed driving by a driving instructor. Patients were also asked to rate their own driving ability. Neither the neurologist's nor the patient's ratings corresponded with the rating of driving ability on the road. There was, however, good agreement between the psychologist's rating and that of the driving instructor. This indicated that performance on cognitive tests, which assessed visual memory, choice reaction time and speed of information processing, were related to driving ability and could be used in the assessment of fitness to drive in people with PD. The PD patients had particular difficulty in heavy traffic in an unfamiliar city. It may be that the driving task used was more demanding than the type of driving that most people with PD would attempt. We do not know how much of driving is automatic. Cognitively impaired people may appear to be safe in most driving situations. It may be only when new or different road situations present themselves that problems arise. This would explain why people with PD who were driving at the time they were recruited for the study – and reported no problems – performed worse than might be expected. However, driving situations do change and it is therefore appropriate to check people's safety in a new or different driving environment.

Screening for fitness to drive

Two types of cognitive assessment procedure are needed in relation to driving ability. Cognitive abilities need to be assessed as part of the comprehensive evaluation carried out at driving assessment centres. However, the number of people with potential cognitive impairment and the shortage of driving assessment facilities mean that a screening procedure administered before referral to a specialist driving assessment centre is also needed. The purpose of this would be to identify those who were severely cognitively impaired, such that they would not be safe to drive. It would also need to detect those with no impairments, who could be allowed to drive. There would be a middle group in whom there was uncertainty about their fitness to drive, who would need to be assessed at a driving assessment centre. This would mean valuable resources would be concentrated on those most in need of them. Resources at driving assessment centres are scarce and the number of potential people to be assessed is very large. Specialist resources may then be used for those for whom there is doubt about their road safety.

The aim of our research was to develop a short screening procedure which could be used by health care professionals to screen patients before assessment at a specialist driving centre. The research was based on previous work on stroke patients (Nouri and Lincoln, 1992) and other neurological conditions, mainly traumatic brain injury and multiple sclerosis (Lincoln and Radford, 1998; Radford and Lincoln 1999). The overall design of the study was to assess patients with PD on a series of physical and cognitive assessments and to assess them on the road. The tests were then examined to determine which would predict safety on the road.

Patients with PD were recruited from those referred to Derby Regional Mobility Centre (DRMC) for advice about fitness to drive.

Patients attending a movement disorders clinic were contacted by letter and also invited to take part in the study. Local branches of special interest groups for occupational therapists and physiotherapists, neurologists and general practitioners were invited to refer patients. In addition, people were invited to take part through the local branch of the Parkinson's Disease Society. People were included if they had PD, were driving at the time of referral and gave their consent. In addition, they had to live within 50 miles of Nottingham so that the same assessors could see all the patients.

Patients were asked to undergo a series of physical and cognitive tests that were thought to be potential screening procedures. The assessments included measures of both physical and cognitive abilities and were selected on the basis of previous research on assessing fitness to drive. The physical assessments included the Webster's rating scale (Webster, 1968) and the UPDRS (Lang and Fahn, 1989) (see above). The tapping task was included as a measure of motor speed and coordination, as it has been used as a measure of motor ability in drug studies. Cognitive abilities were assessed on the Stroke Drivers Screening Assessment (SDSA) (Nouri and Lincoln, 1994). This test had been found to be predictive of the driving performance on the road of stroke patients (Nouri and Lincoln, 1992, 1993) and principally measures attention and reasoning skills (Hawkins *et al.*, in press). In addition, the Adult Memory and Information Processing Battery (Coughlan and Hollows, 1985) was used to assess memory. The Stroop colour word test (Trennery *et al.*, 1991) was included to assess reasoning skills. The Paced Auditory Serial Addition Task (Gronwall, 1977) was used to measure attention.

The PD patients were also assessed on the road by an ADI, experienced in the assessment of people with physical disabilities. They were taken for a test drive along a route which included quiet roads, dual carriageways and busy town roads. The assessment was carried out in their own car or, if they had not driven recently or were unsure about their ability, in a dual-control car with either manual or automatic gears. Modifications were available to compensate for physical disabilities. The ADI was asked to grade them as definitely unsafe, probably unsafe, probably safe or definitely safe. Neither the ADI nor the occupational therapist completing the cognitive tests knew each other's results, as this might bias their opinions.

Eleven patients were recruited at the movement disorders clinic, 20 were referred by neurologists, two people referred themselves and seven people were recruited through DRMC. After recruitment, two people withdrew from the study. Of the 38 patients assessed, only three were found to be unsafe driving on the road. These three were significantly older than those who were found safe to drive – with mean ages of 75 and 64 years, respectively. Examination of their individual scores showed that these three patients were slow on the colour-naming task of the Stroop test, made a large proportion of errors on the dot cancellation task of the SDSA and had moderate disability as assessed on Webster's rating scale. These suggest that both attention problems and level of physical disability may be important determinants of driving safety in people with PD.

Further analyses will be carried out when more patients have been assessed. From the results obtained so far, it seems that the majority of PD patients are safe to drive. There may, however, be some selection of drivers for the study that has affected the results. People with PD who have doubts about their driving capabilities are unlikely to volunteer for a research project examining their driving skills. This may have accounted for the high proportion of safe drivers. However, if patients had been recruited exclusively from DRMC, then an abnormally high proportion of unsafe drivers might have been seen. This is because patients are likely to be referred for assessment only if there are doubts about their safety as a driver. These selection biases can affect the proportions of safe and unsafe drivers obtained. Nonetheless, the factors that differentiate between the safe and unsafe drivers should not be affected by these selection biases, provided a sufficient number of patients is recruited in each group.

This study should help to identify factors that need to be considered when assessing people with PD for their fitness to drive. The aim is to provide a short screening procedure, which could be carried out in a neurology clinic or GP surgery, to identify those who need to be assessed on the road.

Conclusions

More research is needed into the driving safety of people with PD. Research has yet to identify the unique combination and level of physical and cognitive abilities required to operate a motor vehicle. Where cognitive skills are impaired, it is not yet known at what point the ability to drive safely is compromised and at what point driving should cease. Since cognitive problems are present in people with PD, they are an important consideration in decisions concerning driving safety. Cognitive difficulties are more likely to preclude driving than physical problems, yet these are often overlooked by specialist centres offering advice and assessment to disabled and elderly motorists.

Surprisingly few PD sufferers seek advice from specialist driving assessment centres such as regional mobility centres. It is possible that those who do are overcautious. At the other end of the spectrum, people who attend may have lost insight and have been persuaded to attend by a relative or GP. The cost of assessment, distance from the centre and long waiting lists may deter people from seeking specialist advice, together with the fear that they may lose their driver's licence.

Limited resources at regional mobility centres, the prevalence of the driving safety question and the fact that cognitive factors may be overlooked in existing methods of assessment indicate the need for a cognitive screening device. A device is needed that can identify those with severe cognitive impairment and those with no or little cognitive impairment. This could be used to differentiate between unsafe and safe drivers and direct those about whom there was uncertainty for more specialized assessment.

Acknowledgements

We would like to thank Dr Graham Lennox, Dr Christian Murray-Leslie and Ms Karen Anderton for their help with this research and the Parkinson's Disease Society for its financial support.

References

ANONYMOUS (1990) Editorial. Driving and Parkinson's disease. *Lancet, 336,* 781.
BARNES, M.P. (1997) Driving for disabled people. *Critical Reviews in Physical and Rehabilitation Medicine, 9,* 75–92.
BARNES, M.P. and HOYLE, E.A. (1995) Driving assessment – a case of need. *Clinical Rehabilitation, 9,* 115–120.
BLOXHAM, C.A., DICK, D.J. and MOORE, M. (1987) Reaction times and attention in Parkinson's disease. *Journal of Neurology, Neurosurgery and Psychiatry, 50,* 1178–1183.
BRADLEY, V.A., WELCH, J.L. and DICK, D J. (1989) Visuospatial working memory in Parkinson's disease. *Journal of Neurology, Neurosurgery and Psychiatry, 52,* 1228–12235.
CAMPBELL, M.K., BUSH, T.L. and HALE, W.E. (1993) Medical conditions associated with driving cessation in community-dwelling ambulatory elders. *Journal of Gerontology, 45,* S230–S234.
COOPER, J.A., SAGAR, H.J. and SULLIVAN, E.V. (1993) Short term memory and temporal ordering in early Parkinson's disease: effects of disease chronicity and medication. *Neuropsychologia, 31,* 933–949.
COUGHLAN, A. and HOLLOWS, S.E. (1985) *Adult Memory and Information Processing Battery.* St James' University Hospital, Leeds (unpublished).
DUBINSKY, R.M., GRAY, C., HUSTED, D., BUSENBARK, K., VETERE-OVERFIELD, B., WILTFONG, D., PARRISH, D. and KOLLER, W.C. (1991) Driving in Parkinson's disease. *Neurology, 41,* 517–520.
GRONWALL, D. (1977) Paced Auditory Serial Addition Task: a measure of recovery from concussion. *Perceptual and Motor Skills, 44,* 367–373.
HANSOTIA, P. (1993) Seizure disorders, diabetes mellitus and cerebrovascular disease: considerations for older drivers. *Clinics in Geriatric Medicine, 9,* 323–339.

HAWKINS, K.S., RADFORD, K.A., LINCOLN, N.B., MURRAY-LESLIE, C., MELLY, S., LILLEY, S.A. and GORMAN, W.P. (in press) Validation of the Stroke Drivers Screening Assessment (abstract). *Clinical Rehabilitation.*

HEIKKILA, V.M., TURKKA, J., KORPELAINEN, J., KALLANRANTA, T. and SUMMALA, H. (1998) Decreased driving ability in people with Parkinson's disease. *Journal of Neurology, Neurosurgery and Psychiatry, 64*, 325–330.

JONES, R.D. and DONALDSON, I.M. (1995) Fractionation of visuoperceptual dysfunction in Parkinson's disease. *Journal of Neurological Sciences, 131*, 43–50.

LANG, A.E.T. and FAHN, S. (1989) Assessment of Parkinson's disease. In T.L. Munsat (Ed.) *Quantification of Neurologic Deficit.* Stoneham, MA: Butterworth.

LINCOLN, N.B. and RADFORD, K.A. (1998) *Assessing Fitness to Drive in Neurological Patients.* Behavioural Research in Road Safety VIII, Road Transport Research Laboratory Report PA 3371/98. Crowthorne, Berks: Transport Research Laboratory.

LINGS, S. and DUPONT, E. (1992) Driving with Parkinson's disease: a controlled laboratory investigation. *Acta Neurologica Scandanavica, 86*, 33–39.

MADELEY, P., HULLEY, J.L., WILDGUST, H. and MINDHAM, R.H.S. (1990) Parkinson's disease and driving ability. *Journal of Neurology, Neurosurgery and Psychiatry, 53*, 580–582.

McLAY, P. (1989) The Parkinsonian and driving. *International Disability Studies, 11*, 50–51.

NOURI, F.M. and LINCOLN, N.B. (1992) Validation of a cognitive assessment predicting driving performance after stroke. *Clinical Rehabilitation, 6*, 275–281.

NOURI, F.M. and LINCOLN, N.B. (1993) Predicting driving performance after stroke. *British Medical Journal, 307*, 482–483.

NOURI, F.M. and LINCOLN, N.B. (1994) The Stroke Drivers Screening Assessment. Nottingham: Nottingham Rehab.

PENTLAND, B., BARNES, M.P., FINDLEY, L.J., OXTOBY, M., PEARCE, V.R., QUINN, N.P. and SCOTT, S. (1992) Parkinson's disease: the spectrum of disabilities. *Journal of Neurology, Neurosurgery and Psychiatry, 55* (suppl.), 32–35.

PETERSON, G.M., NOLAN, B.W. and MILLENGEN, K.S. (1988) Survey of ability that is associated with Parkinson's disease. *Medical Journal of Australia, 149*, 66–70.

RADFORD, K.A. and LINCOLN, N.B. (1999) Validation of the Stroke Drivers Screening Assessment in neurological patients (abstract). *Clinical Rehabilitation, 13*, 81–82.

RITTER, G. and STEINBERG, H.J. (1979) Parkinsonismus und Fahrtauglichkeit. *Munchener Medizinische Wochensschrift, 121*, 1329–1330.

TAYLOR, J.F. (Ed.) (1995) *Medical Aspects of Fitness to Drive.* London: Medical Commission on Accident Prevention.

TRENNERY, M.R., CROSSON, B., DE HOE, J. and LEBER, W.R. (1991) *Stroop Neuropsychological Screening Test.* Windsor: NFER-Nelson.

WEBSTER, D.D. (1968) Critical analyses of the disability in Parkinson's disease. *Modern Treatment, 5*, 257–282.

Chapter 16

The Romford Project:
action research in a time of rapid change

Marie Oxtoby

The story of the Romford Project began in 1983 and has several chapters or phases, all of which offer some insights into the nature of action research. As the project has been written up in several other places, this chapter offers only brief summaries of the findings and concentrates instead on some of the strategic and methodological issues raised by the project.

Genesis

The project grew organically out of the early activity and research of the Parkinson's Disease Society (PDS). The 1979 survey of people with Parkinson's disease in touch with the PDS (Oxtoby, 1982) had shown that they had many unmet needs for information and support, that they were very rarely informed about the PDS by doctors or hospital workers, that hardly any had had access to the physical therapies and that they often suffered from other health problems as well as diverse and pervasive Parkinsonian symptoms. These conclusions were reinforced by the daily experiences of PDS staff and volunteers, by the findings of other early PDS welfare research projects (Kelson, 198; Nanton, 1985) and by the growing number of patient accounts of misdiagnoses and unsatisfactory management. It was clear that there was no planned strategy of care to help people through an often long and complex life with Parkinson's disease. Meanwhile, in the wider world outside, there was a growing awareness of the limitations of levodopa drug therapy, a reawakened interest in the possible contributions of the physical therapies and a movement among people with health problems and disabilities to have more of a say in their lives and in the groups working for them.

On the pragmatic ground that it is usually more effective to demonstrate a better way rather than to tell people what they are doing wrong,
a strategy for management and support from the point of diagnosis was
devised. Almost two years were spent in planning and negotiations with
dozens of people so that all those involved would understand what was
being proposed and have a chance to express their hopes, reservations
or fears. The fact that the funding of a pilot stage was to come from the
PDS itself allowed us this freedom. I believe that the relative absence of
intergroup problems in the project owed a great deal to this patient
spadework and that nowadays there is often insufficient time to do this
kind of preparation.

The project design

The original application to the Welfare Advisory Panel of the PDS summarized the design as follows:

The aim is to devise a model for the management of Parkinson's disease and put it into practice within an NHS neurology department. The
essential features of the model are:

1 a multidisciplinary approach,
2 special attention to telling and to the provision of further information and support at this time,
3 special attention to the social and emotional aspects of chronic illness in patients and their carers,
4 the involvement of patients and carers in monitoring and decision
making.

Accounts of how these principles were put into action can be found
in the end-of-pilot report (Oxtoby *et al.*, 1988) and in three short articles,
'Starting from the beginning' (Oxtoby, 1989), in the *Parkinson*. By the
end of the pilot, 36 patients had been identified, of whom all but three
had been involved with all aspects of the strategy. These three were
encouraged to use what they could and to come back if they chose (two
did return and in the other case some support was offered to the carer).
The pilot therefore showed that an unselected group of new patients
could make use of the information and counselling offered by this approach to care. It also showed that more than a half had other serious
conditions at the point of diagnosis and that a sizeable minority (about
25%) already had more severe Parkinson's symptoms. Although there
remains a perception among some doctors and health planners that
newly diagnosed people with Parkinson's disease have no need for intervention from counsellors or therapists, this is directly contrary to the

project evidence that two-thirds of the first 36 patients required extra input from three or more team members.

The pilot results also highlighted the enormous variability in the needs of newly diagnosed people for information about the condition and so contributed to the production of a revised introductory leaflet and a change in the PDS policy of sending large amounts of information to first enquirers.

The pilot report also suggested that, even when offered information about the local branch, most newly diagnosed people did not choose to make contact immediately. This finding supported our contention that the only reliable way to provide information and support to all new patients is as an integral part of the diagnostic process. (The 1998 survey of PDS members – see Chapter 4 and Yarrow (1998) – found that there was an average gap of 4.5 years between people being diagnosed and making contact with the PDS.)

At the strategic level, the team approach pioneered in this project not only survived for the lifetime of the pilot with almost 100% retention rates but continues to survive (as part of the Romford Neurocare Team) in 1998, still with very high retention rates. Its feasibility and its acceptability to patients are therefore proven. Staff working in this way also find it satisfying and supportive.

The application for funds also outlined the three ways in which the project would be evaluated:

1 continuous assessment of the strategy itself by members of the team,
2 careful recording of the responses and comments of patients and carers,
3 a small-scale comparison at 12 months after diagnosis of the project group and another group of patients diagnosed by another consultant over the same period.

The continuous evaluation by team members yielded early dividends (e.g. an adjustment in the amount of self-assessment requested of newly diagnosed people and the withdrawal of a speech self-assessment schedule which proved to be inappropriate for most people at an early stage of the disease).

Team members kept their own professional records, which facilitated their direct work with patients and also allowed them to evaluate the amount of input required in each case. They also contributed a short formal report of routine assessments to the central file so that all team members could have access to up-do-date information.

The project did not have any outcome measures related to what users wanted from the intervention but even with hindsight it is not easy to see how this could have been achieved. Most people do not have clearly formulated expectations about unplanned events like a medical diagnosis and questioning them about this just after the event is inconceivable. Also we tried to minimize the 'Hawthorn effect' (by which merely the presence of the researchers and their interest in the patients lead to improvements in their condition) by keeping a low profile and just explaining that this team approach was the way things were done in Romford. This was important to make the comparative study as fair as possible. Having recently been involved in an attempt to get more advanced patients and carers with recognized problems to formulate their outcome hopes, I realize just how difficult this exercise can be.

The small-scale comparative study had to overcome some difficult problems and it may be instructive to consider some of these.

1 In identifying patients who meet certain strict criteria, the researchers have no control over numbers (and my experience suggests that doctors almost always overestimate the likely numbers). The numbers achieved over two years were insufficient to allow many statistically significant findings.

2 Finding a truly comparable group is almost impossible. A neurologist working in a similar socio-economic area agreed to identify new patients with Parkinson's disease over the same two-year period. However, in the event, the comparison group members were somewhat older than those in the project group and also had more additional medical conditions. There are special problems in Parkinson's disease in this respect because of the shortage of neurologists and the average age at diagnosis. New patients are therefore distributed in variable proportions between neurologists, geriatricians, general physicians and general practitioners.

3 The independent interviewers also discovered that (contrary to the original instructions) some of the comparison group had received their new diagnoses in the course of a domiciliary visit rather than in the outpatient clinic. This clearly undermined the validity of comparing responses to the giving of the diagnosis. It raises the whole issue of how to motivate and monitor the person who agrees to provide a comparison group in this type of longitudinal study. There is, after all, not much in it for them.

4 The changing environment also added to our problems. The neurologist providing the comparison group decided, half way through the project period, to start a Parkinson's disease clinic while, on the home front, there were ethical and methodological dilemmas about whether and/or how to involve project patients in trials of new drugs.

5 Last but not least, there was the problem of the effect of the project's activities on its participants' response to interviews and questionnaires. The project had encouraged patients to feel that they had a

role in the management of their own conditions and had allowed, even encouraged, the expression of anger, hurt or disagreement. The independent interviewers discovered that, in general, members of the project group were more talkative than those in the comparison group. They tended to give longer answers or multiple answers rather than just one. Given that the interviewers were asking for their views on the giving of the diagnosis and subsequent management, there is a real possibility that members of the project group approached these topics with higher expectations and more confidence to be critical if they saw fit.

It was some consolation to find that, in spite of all these difficulties, the results of the comparison study showed a trend towards more satisfaction in the project group on most issues and statistically significant differences on adequacy of explanations about drug treatment and on knowledge of the existence of the PDS. The results were reported at the Society for Research in Rehabilitation's summer meeting in 1990 and appear in the record of that meeting and as Appendix 5 of the *Final Report* of the Romford Neurocare Project (1993). It was less consoling to have a fuller account of the comparison study rejected by the *British Medical Journal* partly because of these methodological difficulties.

Development

The idea that the patient-centred approach to diagnosis and management pioneered at Romford might be applicable to a wider range of neurological conditions was present from the beginning. Indeed, it seemed likely that it would be more acceptable and economically viable if it could be shown to work for a range of conditions. Several other voluntary organizations – the Motor Neurone Disease Association, the Friedreich's Ataxia Group (now Ataxia), the Dystonia Society, Action for Research in Multiple Sclerosis and the local branch of the Multiple Sclerosis Society – were able to identify strongly with the principles and procedures of the project and agreed to participate in a second pilot.

Negotiations for this stage began well before the end of the first pilot, in January 1988, and continued, with many deviations and setbacks, until the Romford Neurocare Project was launched in January 1990. Throughout these two years, a basic service to patients with Parkinson's disease was maintained because of the commitment of team members and hospital staff, the continued support of the PDS, some very welcome financial support from the Motor Neurone Disease Association and the persistence of the project director. There may be some messages in this for attempts to ensure that good projects do not disappear as soon as the original funding comes to an end. During this hiatus, we negotiated, with great difficulty, a new arrangement for providing therapy services to the project. Originally, therapists had been recruited on a sessional basis and had been paid directly by the PDS. This arrangement gave us great flexibility but, for the therapists themselves, it often meant isolation from their professional colleagues and no security of tenure. The eventual, hard-fought solution of a quarter-time share of an established post within the relevant departments resolved both these problems and had the further advantages of access to locums and opportunities to share knowledge and expertise.

It did not, however, resolve the longer-term problem of a national shortage of therapists. Although the funding was in place (half joint finance and the other half shared between the participating charities), we began to have problems recruiting therapists early in the Neurocare Project (Oxtoby, 1999) and those problems have continued to the present. They are exacerbated by the difficulty of obtaining the funding necessary to expand staff hours for all team members as the demands increase. Staff resources were severely stretched in March 1993, when there were 151 patients in contact with the Neurocare team. No additional resources had been allocated by December 1996, when the number of patients in touch with the team had increased to 327. Clearly, the standard of service has been affected, although the original principles remain in place. A chapter on the team aspects of the Neurocare Project (Oxtoby, 1999) has the following section headings:

- a team for outpatients;
- a team to bridge the hospital–community divide;
- a team for everyone with a relevant diagnosis;
- a coordinated team (i.e. with a designated coordinator);
- a team with therapists and dietician;
- a team with nursing input;
- a less hierarchical team;
- a team involving the patient and family;
- a team which recognizes the role of the general practitioner.

The chapter also discusses the advantages and disadvantages of this approach to care.

The final phase of the Romford Project – its absorption into statutory mainstream care – coincided with the introduction of community care in April 1993. When we first read the papers about community care, we felt excited by references to working together, seamless care, a greater voice for patient and family and, above all, multidisciplinary needs-based assessment. All this seemed to chime with many of the project's objectives and made us hopeful about the continuation of the service. In the end, the project was offered funding within the BHB Community Health Care Trust for one year and in fact continues (in 1998) to be located within this Trust. However, the negotiations were drawn out and conducted in an atmosphere of great uncertainty and constant changes of roles and personnel within the statutory sector. As already mentioned, no new resources have been put into the project and seamless care, here as elsewhere, does not seem to be facilitated by the division between hospital and community trusts.

Spin-offs

Sometimes expensive and esoteric research programmes (e.g. space re-search) are justified by their spin-offs. The Romford Project was neither esoteric nor expensive (the Parkinson's pilot and interregnum cost £37,000 between 1985 and 1989 and the Neurocare Project cost £125,000 between 1990 to 1993), but it did have many spin-offs. These included not only other neurocare services, as at Chelmsford and Jersey, but courses for newly diagnosed patients, drop-in centres and information points. Between 1990 and 1993, over 80 educational and promotional activities were undertaken by project workers and overall awareness of the needs of people with neurological conditions was increased. The close resemblance between the Romford principles and the Parkinson's Charter, launched on the first-ever World Parkinson's Day in 1997, is surely not a coincidence.

Conclusions

I hope this chapter has drawn attention to some of the difficulties of conducting action research at any time, but particularly at times when so much in the environment is changing. However, much was achieved, too, not least being the patient-centred support and care delivered to hundreds of patients and families from the point of diagnosis. The *Final Report* of the Romford Neurocare Project (1993) also lists the following outcomes:

- A model of good practice for people with Parkinson's disease has been devised and put into practice.
- Contributions have been made to two new pamphlets for people with Parkinson's disease, motor neurone disease, multiple sclerosis, dystonia and ataxia have been designed and used.
- Large numbers of people in both the statutory and voluntary sectors have been educated about the needs of people with progressive or long-term neurological conditions.

- Other initiatives to improve the quality of life of people with progressive neurological conditions have been encouraged by the Romford example and helped by the project's willingness to share its ideas and experience.
- A group of voluntary organisations have shown that they can work together for the benefit of their members.
- Good relationships have been built between the project team and the statutory services, the local hospice and local voluntary organisations.
- The project has monitored its own activities and so provided a basis for continuous evaluation of the service. The audits have also provided evidence of the levels of need in these groups of people with neurological conditions.

References

KELSON, N. (1985) *The Short Term Care Project.* London: Parkinson's Disease Society.

NANTON, V. (1985) *The Regional Welfare Project.* London: Parkinson's Disease Society.

OXTOBY, M. (1982) *Parkinson's Disease Patients and Their Social Needs.* London: Parkinson's Disease Society.

OXTOBY, M., *et al.* (1988) A strategy for the management of Parkinson's disease and for the long-term support of patients and their carers . London: Parkinson's Disease Society.

OXTOBY, M. (1989) Starting from the beginning: a new approach to the management of PD. *The Parkinsonian*, March, May and September.

OXTOBY, M. (1999). A team approach to neurological disease. In A. Williams (Ed.) *Patient Care in Neurology.* Oxford: Oxford University Press.

ROMFORD NEUROCARE PROJECT (1993) *Final Report.* London: Parkinson's Disease Society.

YARROW, S. (1998) *Survey of Members of the Parkinson's Disease Society.* London: Policy Studies Institute.

Chapter 17

Implications of welfare research for the Parkinson's Disease Society and its members

Ray Percival and Peter Hobson

Most of the research funding allocated by the Council of the Parkinson's Disease Society is used by the Medical Advisory Panel, with the hope that this may eventually lead to a cure or better drugs and procedures to alleviate the condition.

The aim of the Welfare Research Committee is mainly that the results of their funded research can be incorporated into the day-to-day work of the Society. After discussion of completed projects, comments are passed to the Welfare Advisory Panel, which may result in action.

This book represents a sample of these researches. Jones's study, much of which is expressed in comparisons with results from the researches by Oxtoby and Mutch, was carried out by a team of nurses and researchers covering a wide area and, although some of the figures are not strictly comparable with the other studies, the snapshots from the four different studies of distinct populations at different times succeeds in giving an overall impression. This impression, together with the introductory chapter by Dr Pentland and the rest of Part I, sketches the scene in respect of Parkinson's disease.

Research projects often have side-effects not expected when they are planned. One of the results of Jones's and Oxtoby's researches was that both of these authors became members of the Welfare Advisory Panel, and the knowledge they had gained can be seen in the way in which aspects of the Society's work developed.

Chapter 2 should be of interest to all service providers, to central and local government, and all those who attempt to put in motion ideas that culminate in legislation. It tells a similar story that has been told in respect of other types of illness, that is, that although medical and social care have probably improved over the years prior to the Community Care Act 1990, the seamless service between medicine and other disciplines has not developed at the same rate and the systems often remain self-contained.

Chesson's two projects (Chapter 5) lay emphasis on the 'quality of life' and the nature of the disease which can gradually erode first physical and later mental capacities. She is presently working on a third project with a similar theme. An unexpected finding from Chesson's work came as a result of her attempts to use the Parkinson's Disease Society's list of members on which (with strict safeguards) to base her questionnaires. It soon became apparent that the lists did not differentiate between sufferers, carers and others and was obviously in need of revision.

The research by Grimshaw – Chapter 6 – was carried out through the auspices of the National Children's Bureau at a time when a number of younger members, who had been diagnosed as having Parkinson's disease, were forming a group later described as YAPP&Rs (Young Alert Parkinsonians, Partners and Relatives), and it is appropriate to include this study which emphasizes that Parkinson's disease is not exclusively a disease of old age. Dr Pentland, in his introduction, considers that one in ten of those diagnosed are likely to be under 50 years of age. Anyone working with children will recognize the value of the final notes in this report.

Much of the strength of the Parkinson's Disease Society, particularly at branch level, lies in the hands of those who care for the sufferers from the disease, and both Chapters 7 and 8 explore and comment on the changes which occur in the relationship of sufferer and carer over a period of time. This is dramatically illustrated in Chapter 7, where in one first interview much was made of the strong spiritual and religious aspects of caring and the support that a religious background gave. Local Parkinson's Disease Society groups were criticized for not recognizing this. At the second interview, when there had been marked deterioration in the physical condition of the sufferer, thoughts of this nature had apparently totally vanished.

One of the values of Chapter 7 is the way the study was organized to obtain firm evidence of the time spent by carers in looking after their charges. The high attrition rate between the two interviews is also noteworthy. The picture that is most often painted is that of the same one-to-one relationship persisting to the end. The figures quoted imply a change of carer in many instances and this in itself is likely to produce further difficulties.

All the studies in Chapters 7–9 conclude that the need exists for psychological intervention and advice. If the booklet promised by the Salford team (Chapter 8) becomes reality it will be invaluable for either direct work or as a teaching aid and would be welcomed by the Parkinson's Disease Society.

It has long been recognized that speech and language therapy is important in helping those with Parkinson's disease who have particular speech and language problems, some of which are mentioned in Chapter 1. Chapter 10 gives a fairly straightforward account of the present-day approach of such therapists. Chapters 10 and 11 indicate how far research has progressed in this field, both being of a technical nature. Chapter 12 discusses the diagnosis of the presence of Lewy bodies in conjunction with Parkinson's disease. These later studies indicate the difficulty at times in deciding whether some requests for research funding should be referred to the Medical Advisory Panel or the Welfare Research Committee.

On looking through the studies available for this book, a lack of those involving physiotherapy was noticeable. Whether this was the result of there being fewer research studies in this subject funded by the Welfare Research Committee, or whether they were just not available, was hard to ascertain. The new rotating programme of the Welfare Research Committee will see that all the formal therapies are given a fairer chance to compete for an allocation of funding.

Chapter 13, a pilot project by Chandler and Plant to assess the value of physiotherapy shows the difficulties encountered in such research. Fortunately, elsewhere within the Parkinson's Disease Society is the beginnings of a large-scale physiotherapy research project which will no doubt take into account this pilot project.

Chapters 14 and 15 refer to the interesting studies on video recording and fitness to drive motor vehicles. Video recording obviously has much to offer in diagnosis and treatment, not only of Parkinson's disease, and the attempt to find a cognitive test of fitness to drive has much wider application when the overall problem of road safety is considered. This would cut the expense of travel and of waiting time of those forced to attend the present driving assessment centres.

Despite the way in which welfare research funding has been allocated until recently, a certain balanced pattern emerged. Background studies, in-depth studies, suggestions in the field of major therapies, and papers urging the use of psychological techniques, are all included. An attempt is made to examine and report on the results of legislation. Chapter 16 is by Dr Oxtoby, who uses the Romford Project as a basis to outline the problems she knows exist in attempting research with sufferers from Parkinson's disease, and will be invaluable to future researchers.

In concluding, the editors would like to thank the researchers for readily agreeing to provide papers about their work. Thanks are also due to the J. K. Brunner Settlement, who provided money to produce this book. The GMT, as a result of one of their programmes on disability sent a large donation to the Parkinson's Disease Society and a small part of this has been used to keep this book at an affordable level. As mentioned in the Preface, thanks are also due to the British Psychological Society for agreeing to publish it and thereby drawing it to a much wider potential readership than otherwise would have been the case. Above all, thanks are due to the sufferers with Parkinson's disease and their carers who took the time, trouble and effort to fill in questionnaires and talk with researchers.

Glossary

Agonist – dopamine agonists are often used to help control the symptoms usually related to motor fluctuations of advanced Parkinson's disease in chronically levodopa-treated patients. Apomorphine, pergolide and lisuride for example are all agonists used in the treatment of Parkinson's disease.

Alzheimer's disease – is a progressive brain disorder with a strong association with age. It is expressed clinically by disorders of cognitive impairment and behavioural functioning.

Anticholinergic – this class of drugs is used in Parkinson's disease to reduce the symptoms of Parkinsonism, especially bladder symptoms. It can, however, cause confusion, especially in elderly patients.

Autonomic nervous system – the part of the nervous system that regulates vital functioning. It comprises two sections: the sympathetic nervous system and the parasympathetic nervous system.

Basal ganglia – large body of grey matter located in the midbrain and the cerebral hemispheres. Basal ganglia degeneration can disrupt motor function in Parkinson's disease.

Bradykinesia – or akinesia, is a poverty of all voluntary movements and speech.

Cerebellum – this part of the brain is concerned with coordination of voluntary movements.

Dementia – global impairment of memory, intellect and personality.

Dementia of the Lewy body type – this dementia is controversial in that some view it as a variant of Alzheimer's disease, while others view it as a distinct entity. Clinically it presents with Parkinsonism, progressive dementia, fluctuating mental state, hallucinations, paranoia and sensitivity to neuroleptic medications.

Dopamine – a chemical neurotransmitter produced in the substantia nigra. Degeneration of the production of dopamine in the substantia nigra is associated with Parkinson's disease.

Dysarthria – impaired articulated speech.

Dysphagia – difficulties in swallowing.

Dystonia – characterized by abnormal involuntary movements often as a result of the effects of anti-Parkinsonian medication in patients with advanced Parkinson's disease.

Extrapyramidal system – the part of the nervous system that includes the basal ganglia, substantia nigra, subthalamic nucleus, a portion of the midbrain and the motor neurones of the spine.

Festinating gait – the stride in many Parkinson's disease patients, characterized by short, quick steps where patients appear to be chasing their centre of gravity.

Gastrostomy – surgical procedure to create an artificial opening into the stomach through the abdominal wall so that a patient can be fed.

Hypokinesia – an abnormal condition of diminished motor activity.

Levodopa – a precursor of dopamine and a highly effective treatment for Parkinson's disease.

Lewy body – a structure (or 'inclusion') found in the brains of people with Parkinson's disease, Alzheimer's disease, motor neurone disease and also in people without these diseases.

Mean, mode, median, standard deviation – mathematical terms used to describe data. Mean (average), mode (most frequently occurring value), median (mid-point that divides a distribution into two parts), standard deviation (variance of scores from the mean).

Micographia – refers to the handwriting impairments that are often a presentation in Parkinson's disease.

Neurone – basic cells of the nervous system, which transmit and receive nerve impulses.

Neurotransmitter – these are chemicals in the brain such as acetylcholine that transmit impulses across nerve endings.

Osteoarthrosis – chronic arthritis, usually without inflammation.

Parkinson's disease – slowly progressive neurological disorder.

Parkinsonism – conditions that have the signs and symptoms of Parkinson's disease, often as a result of vascular lesions, toxic exposure or side-effects of antipsychotic medication.

Proprioceptive – the patients' awareness of their posture and their ability to orientate themselves without spatial cues.

Prostatectomy – surgical procedure that involves the removal of the prostrate gland in males.

Pyramidal system – or pyramidal tract, a pathway of nerve fibres and cells which regulate voluntary and reflex activities of muscles.

QALY – or quality-adjusted life years, is a measurement tool employed by health economists to determine the cost of clinical interventions in terms of the number of quality life years gained for the patient.

Qualitative research approach – is research that is not amenable to traditional statistical methods.

Quantitative research approach – is research that employs statistical methods to analyse data.

Regimen – refers to therapeutic programmes such as exercise or diet plans.

Retropulsion – is falling backwards.

Rigidity – often described as cogwheel rigidity, is an increase of tone in the range of motions in the patient's joints.

Selegiline – is a monoamine oxidase inhibitor (MAOI), a drug used in the treatment of Parkinson's disease in its early and late stages. However, this drug has been associated in one study with higher rates of mortality and it remains controversial whether it offers neuroprotection.

Semistructured interview – is an interview technique that has a formal fixed item format which also allows the interviewer ask open questions in order to probe certain aspects that are not easily quantifiable.

Sign – refers to clinical signs of symptoms of a disease such as bradykinesia, rigidity, resting tremor balance and gait impairments found in Parkinson's disease.

Subcortical – refers to dementias in Parkinson's disease; however, cortical dementia signs may also be present.

Thalamotomy – is a surgical procedure in which lesions, if properly placed in the thalamus, help to reduce rigidity and tremor.

Transfers – refers to the patient's ability for example to rise from a chair unaided.

Tremor – involuntary resting tremors are one of the cardinal features of Parkinson's disease.

Videoflurosocopy – technique in radiology used to examine bodily functions and organs visually.

Index